Designing Social Science Research

Oddbjørn Bukve

Designing Social Science Research

Oddbjørn Bukve
Western Norway University of Applied Sciences
Sogndal, Norway

Translated by Bjørg Hellum

This translation has been published with the financial support of NORLA.

ISBN 978-3-030-03978-3   ISBN 978-3-030-03979-0 (eBook)
https://doi.org/10.1007/978-3-030-03979-0

Library of Congress Control Number: 2018964561

© The Editor(s) (if applicable) and The Author(s), under exclusive licence to Springer Nature Switzerland AG 2019
This work is subject to copyright. All rights are solely and exclusively licensed by the Publisher, whether the whole or part of the material is concerned, specifically the rights of translation, reprinting, reuse of illustrations, recitation, broadcasting, reproduction on microfilms or in any other physical way, and transmission or information storage and retrieval, electronic adaptation, computer software, or by similar or dissimilar methodology now known or hereafter developed.
The use of general descriptive names, registered names, trademarks, service marks, etc. in this publication does not imply, even in the absence of a specific statement, that such names are exempt from the relevant protective laws and regulations and therefore free for general use.
The publisher, the authors and the editors are safe to assume that the advice and information in this book are believed to be true and accurate at the date of publication. Neither the publisher nor the authors or the editors give a warranty, express or implied, with respect to the material contained herein or for any errors or omissions that may have been made. The publisher remains neutral with regard to jurisdictional claims in published maps and institutional affiliations.

Cover illustration: Chris Parsons / Getty Images

This Palgrave Macmillan imprint is published by the registered company Springer Nature Switzerland AG
The registered company address is: Gewerbestrasse 11, 6330 Cham, Switzerland

PREFACE

Starting a research project is a challenging task whether you are a student or a novice researcher. I have had the opportunity to observe this through many years as a supervisor of master's degree and PhD theses, as head of research at a number of institutions, and as a teacher at seminars for research strategies and method. I believe that the knowledge of how research projects can be designed in a good way is sadly underestimated as compared with the knowledge of methods and general theory of science.

A great number of books on research methods exist. The teaching within the social sciences that prepares students for research activities usually takes these books as its starting point, often in combination with textbooks on theory of science. What I have been missing in my capacity as a facilitator is a book that in a clear way bridges the gap between perspectives from the theory of science and the practical use of method. In other words, what I missed was a book on how to justify and deal with the basic choices in a research project—the design of the project. This book is not a substitution for the method book; on the contrary it deals with the choices one has to make before deciding on the method.

Although little has been written about research design compared with the literature on method, it is a rapidly developing academic field. The international literature discusses the consequences of the development in recent theory of science on our understanding of what social science is and of how social scientists should work. An example of this is the discussion of the role and status of models in the research process, and also the discussion on how to study and uncover social mechanisms. Another example

v

vi   PREFACE

is the literature on case studies where recent contributions strongly emphasise design. Also, some statisticians point out that design trumps method, to quote one of them. They doubt that the majority of social scientists actually use quantitative methods in a reflective way.

Consequently, there is an abundance of academically relevant issues to discuss for those who wish to write about design. My goal was to write an up-to-date scientific book critically discussing the various understandings of design in social science research. Another goal was to write the book in a way that can be useful for those who are new researchers, perhaps just starting their first project. My hope is that master's degree and PhD students will use the book when designing their projects and, additionally, that more experienced researchers will also find something that can motivate to reflection on their design choices, thus resulting in better research.

The motivation and inspiration to write such a book arose out of my many years as a teacher and facilitator of research strategies and method. Those who have contributed with their opinions all deserve a big thank you for having listened and given feedback to, and tried out in practice, all the variants of the thinking that has now materialised as a book.

The original edition of the book was published in Norwegian by the Norwegian University Press in 2016. For the English edition, minor changes have been made in a number of chapters. Notably, Chap. 8 has been revised and updated in order to keep pace with the most recent developments in the design field.

The Norwegian Literature Agency Abroad (NORLA) and Western Norway University of Applied Sciences (HVL) have supported the translation of the book into English. HVL is also acknowledged for providing generous work conditions during the preparation of the book.

I owe thanks to my colleagues in the research group for collaboration, innovation, and governance at HVL, who read and commented on chapter drafts on several occasions. Special thanks to Erik Fossåskaret and Gigliola Mathisen Nyhagen for thorough and useful comments to the first version of the book, and to Harald Torstensen, who read through and made several insightful comments to Chap. 8. Palgrave Macmillan's reviewer made a number of most appreciated suggestions for the English version.

Thanks to Erik Juel at the Norwegian University Press and Jemima Warren at Palgrave Macmillan who guided me through all stages of the publication process. Last, but not least, thanks to Bjørg Hellum, who translated the book into English.

Sogndal, Norway
September 2018

Oddbjørn Bukve

CONTENTS

1	**Introduction**	1
	Hypotheses from Heaven	3
	Into the Fog Without a Compass	3
	The Cart Before the Horse	4
	Picking Only the Sweet Fruits	5
	Unresearchable Problem Statements	5
	The Rule of Action	6
	Organisation of This Book	7
	References	9
2	**Scientific Knowledge and Practice**	11
	The Characteristics of Scientific Knowledge and Practice	11
	Scientific Statements	15
	Empirical Statements, Norms, and Practice	16
	More on Testing of Scientific Statements	17
	Our Social Construction of the World	19
	Science and Knowledge Development	22
	The Contested Truth	24
	From an Understanding of Knowledge to Social Science Practice	26
	References	26

x CONTENTS

3 Social Science as Reconstruction of Social Phenomena — 29
The Study of Social Facts and Phenomena — 29
Explanations in Social Science — 32
Social Science as Reconstruction of Social Patterns and Processes — 35
The Elements of Reconstruction — 38
Backgrounds — 39
Concepts — 39
Theories and Hypotheses — 43
Models — 44
Data Construction — 49
From the Building Stones of Reconstruction to the Logic of Reconstruction — 49
References — 50

4 The Logic and Methodological Rules of Reconstruction — 53
Hypothetical-Deductive Research Logic: Explaining by Laws — 54
Abductive Research Logic: Uncovering Social Mechanisms — 57
Hermeneutic Research Logic: Interpretative Understanding of Social Phenomena — 59
Critical Theory — 63
Discourse Analytical Research Logic: Hegemonic and Alternative Frameworks of Understanding — 64
A Comparison of the Research Logics — 68
References — 70

5 Design of Research Projects — 73
Research Purposes, Data Construction, and the Phases of the Design Process — 74
Research Designs and Purposes — 76
Theory- and Hypothesis-Testing Purposes — 80
Concept- and Theory-Developing Purposes and Questions — 80
Theoretically Interpretative Purposes — 81
Intervention-Oriented Purposes — 82
Mere Description? — 83
Purpose and Design of an Analytic Frame — 84
Research Design and Data Construction — 85
Variable-Centred Strategies — 87
Case-Oriented Strategies — 88

CONTENTS xi

Combination Strategies 89
Requirements of a Good Research Design 91
From Design as Concept to Design Variants 94
References 95

6 Variable-Centred Designs 97
What Is a Variable-Centred Design? 97
Construction Validity and Knowledge Development 99
Theory Testing in Variable-Centred Designs 101
Theory Development in Variable-Centred Designs 106
Variants of Variable-Centred Designs 107
Experimental Designs 109
Cross-sectional and Longitudinal Designs 111
References 112

7 Case Designs 115
What Is a Case Study? 115
What Is the Case in a Case Study? 117
Case Studies and Knowledge Development 118
Case, Context, Embeddedness 120
Theory Testing in Case Designs 121
Interpretative Reconstruction and Theory Development in Case Designs 123
Variants of Case Designs 125
Critical Cases as Design for Theory Testing 126
Congruence Design: Case Analysis with Structured Frames 128
Process Tracing 130
Two Exemplifying Cases 133
Theoretical Interpretative Reconstruction 135
References 138

8 Integrated Designs 141
Triangulation 143
Mixed Method Designs 146
Nested Design 149
Designs for Multimethod Research 152
Summing Up 158
References 159

xii CONTENTS

9 Comparative Designs — 161
What Is a Comparative Study? — 161
Typologies and Typological Theories in Comparative Designs — 164
The Use of Typologies — 168
Variable-Centred Comparisons — 171
References — 176

10 Intervention-Oriented Designs — 179
What Is an Evaluation Design? — 179
Goal Evaluation — 182
Effect Evaluation — 184
Process Evaluation and Action Theory Evaluation — 185
Comprehensive Programme Evaluation — 186
Action Research — 187
References — 190

11 The Design Process — 193
The Design Process: An Overview — 193
Choice and Justification of a Topic — 196
Literature Review and Knowledge Status — 198
Purpose Description — 201
Theory and Analytical Framework — 203
The Research Questions — 205
Data Construction and Choice of Method — 207
Selection of Data and Requirements for Representativeness — 208
Various Types of Data — 210
Structure of a Project Draft — 211
References — 214

Index — 215

LIST OF FIGURES

Fig. 2.1	A representation—of what?	19
Fig. 3.1	Social science as reconstruction of social phenomena	38
Fig. 3.2	Ogden's semiotic triangle	40
Fig. 3.3	The relationship between a theory, the models of the theory, and a system in the world. According to Clarke and Primo (2012)	45
Fig. 4.1	Hypothetical-deductive research logic	56
Fig. 4.2	Abductive research logic	59
Fig. 4.3	The hermeneutic circle	62
Fig. 4.4	The discourse analytical logic	67
Fig. 5.1	Different strategies for data construction	91
Fig. 6.1	A concept model for the relationship between the teacher's academic competence, teaching methods, and the pupils' learning	102
Fig. 6.2	Combined concept model and empirical model for the connection between the teacher's academic competence, teaching methods, and the pupils' learning	103
Fig. 6.3	Concept model to study effects of an independent variable	103
Fig. 6.4	Concept model to explain the causes of a phenomenon	104
Fig. 6.5	Model for theory development	106
Fig. 7.1	Analytical model of an embedded case	120
Fig. 7.2	Policy windows and policy entrepreneurs as connectors. (Adapted from Zahariadis, 2007)	134
Fig. 8.1	The research triad: causal mechanism, cross-case inference, and within-case causal inference. (Adapted from Goertz, 2017)	153
Fig. 9.1	Cases and design	162

xiii

xiv   LIST OF FIGURES

Fig. 9.2	Implementation of public policy—a typology. (Adapted from Matland, 1995)	167
Fig. 9.3	Example of empirical typology with selected cases for analysis	169
Fig. 9.4	Example of theoretical typology with the placing of cases through congruence analysis	170
Fig. 11.1	The first phase of the design process	195
Fig. 11.2	Choice of strategy and methods for data construction	196

LIST OF TABLES

Table 4.1	Comparison of research logics	69
Table 5.1	Ideal-typical approaches to data construction	87
Table 6.1	The data matrix of variable-centred designs	98
Table 6.2	Variants of variable-centred designs	108
Table 7.1	Variants of case designs	126
Table 8.1	Case study selection: X-Y configurations	154
Table 8.2	Variants of integrated designs	158
Table 9.1	Variants of comparative designs	165
Table 9.2	Most similar system designs and most different system designs	174
Table 9.3	Hypothetic truth table with three causes of strike success	175
Table 10.1	Variants of evaluation designs	183
Table 11.1	Strategies for data selection	209
Table 11.2	Types of data	210

CHAPTER 1

Introduction

A research design is a plan or an approach for carrying out a research project. The plan renders visible the logical structure of the project, the goals of the project, and the strategy to reach these goals. Thus, composing a research design includes two central elements: (1) defining the knowledge goals or purpose of the project and (2) deciding how to proceed to reach the goals. The distinguishing mark of a specific research design is the combination of knowledge goals and strategies to produce data. The knowledge goal has to do with what we want to find in the project, what we want to know. The strategy for data production must be planned in such a way that we will find data that are good and relevant enough to reach the knowledge goals of the project.

This book presents a number of research designs and shows how they are based on certain combinations of knowledge goals and strategies for data construction. It further presents the process of making a research design, step by step. The goal is to render the readers capable to make an expedient design for their project. I regard a clear and goal-oriented design to be the key to carrying out a successful project.

The starting point of the design is to identify and delimit the main knowledge goal of the project. To do so, we need to place the project goals in a theoretical context, at the same time clarifying the current status of our knowledge of the phenomenon we wish to research. In order to create a good knowledge goal, we need to identify a knowledge gap the project intends to fill or a problem that needs to be solved. The goals of a

© The Author(s) 2019

O. Bukve, *Designing Social Science Research*,

https://doi.org/10.1007/978-3-030-03979-0_1

1

project can be formulated in a number of ways and vary from project to project. There can, however, be different types of purposes, which is how I wish to discuss knowledge goals in this book. Testing an established theory can be one goal; another is to precisely define and develop a theory about the phenomena and connections we are studying. Other goals can be to use established theory to understand and explain the phenomenon under investigation, or using it as a tool to find whether and why social interventions succeed or fail. The introductory question in a project should be related to one or more of these purposes, and a good design requires the project to be placed in the field of knowledge goals.

The other important element in a research design is how we construct data. The main division is between a case-centred and a variable-centred strategy for data construction. From a case-centred perspective we see the object for study as a whole or a system in which the parts are mutually dependent on each other and have to be studied in relation to each other. From a variable-centred perspective we decompose the object of study to its individual elements or variables, thus being able to isolate and study the effect of each element.

Creating a research design comprises more than choosing a method. The choice of method is primarily a question of technique, that is, of what techniques should be used to select, collect, and analyse data on the research phenomenon. If you take your starting point in the technical questions when planning your project, the tool will take control of the researcher rather than vice versa. The choice of method should therefore be part of a total design for the project. The method should not steer the knowledge goals but rather be a tool to achieve those goals. This book will show how different methods can be beneficial in different designs. Still, I do not treat the question of method in any detail. That is a task for the many books discussing research method.

Before going into this in more detail, I choose a somewhat different approach. I aim to show what difficulties we may get into if we do not sufficiently understand the role that design plays in the successful implementation of a research project. Through my experience as a thesis adviser I have found that there are some typical pitfalls that tend to make the realisation of research projects more challenging than necessary. These pitfalls will be described here before I go on to show how a research design may be developed. I believe that knowing the most common pitfalls is useful in order to avoid falling into them. For that reason, I will start with a review of some beginners' problems often observed.

Hypotheses from Heaven

The first pitfall is the one I will call "hypotheses from heaven". A number of books on research methods tell students to make precise hypotheses that can be tested through data collection. This makes some students start the planning of their project with only a rough presentation of the topic, then continuing by presenting a long "shopping list" containing various hypotheses. A hypothesis is an assertion of a possible or expected connection between two phenomena. Problems with such lists are that students often do not explain how they have arrived at the hypotheses and how they justify their choice and design of those hypotheses. Such an approach will soon lead you into trouble.

That said, there is nothing wrong with formulating precise hypotheses. They are necessary in many projects, although not in all. Still, hypotheses in a research project have to be either anchored in former research findings pointing towards such a hypothesis or one that deducts them from established theoretical perspectives. Before formulating hypotheses, you need to study the results of earlier research as well as what expectations can be derived from central theoretical perspectives in that particular field of research. With such a starting point, testing the hypotheses can support established knowledge or show that it will have to be revised. Thus, your research project will also be relevant to others. For this reason, the hypothesis formulation should not be made before you have proceeded some distance into the creation of a research design. In other words, wait with the hypotheses until you can anchor them and justify them in earlier research, and until you see that you really need them; maybe your project is of such a kind that you can use a more open approach.

Into the Fog Without a Compass

Just as common is the pitfall we can call "out into the fog without a compass". Not all books on research method advise you to develop hypotheses and precise questions in advance. Some approaches to research tell you to proceed with an open and unbiased mind into the collection of data and only during the analysis link your findings to scientific concepts and theories. This piece of advice is not always wrong. Many interesting projects, development of new concepts, and new ways of understanding a phenomenon have been conducted in such a way. However, it is not a coincidence that these projects were usually developed by experienced researchers.

This is a challenging approach that does not always give particularly interesting results. The approach should best be used when researching new and scarcely researched topics.

For master's degree students or inexperienced researchers, confusing their own lack of knowledge in a research field with the belief that there is no other knowledge available is easily done. The danger then exists of repeating what has already been done. Another dilemma is that if we do not clarify what theoretical framework and concepts we find relevant to our project, we become blind to our own point of view. It is not easy to convincingly persuade others that we have seen something they have not seen if we do not understand where we are standing in relation to other researchers. There is also a practical side about clarifying our own point of departure before collecting data: the remaining research process will be much simpler. Making sense of a set of data collected without the compass of earlier research and established theories can create a lot of frustration and as a worst-case scenario result in a non-completed project.

The Cart Before the Horse

Pitfall number three may occur when at an early point in the process students decide that they want to use either a qualitative or a quantitative method in their project. The reason is often that they are more comfortable with the one or the other method. So far, it is not a problem. A potential problem arises when the student later starts working with the research topic and formulates research questions, and it becomes evident that the questions are not compatible with the chosen method. The research questions could, for instance, be meant to describe and understand a phenomenon in depth; but the student wants to use a quantitative method, which has its strength in explaining the relationship between various phenomena. Or the other way around: the student wishes to test hypotheses concerning a topic for which a quantitative method would be best suited, but has already decided to use a qualitative method.

In a well-constructed research project, the choice of method should ideally be adapted to and follow up the goals and questions the researcher has set for the project. The method is meant as a tool to find good answers to the problems the researcher wants to solve; it is not an ideal in itself. Choosing the method first can be compared to putting the cart before the horse (Gobo, 2008).

Picking Only the Sweet Fruits

Sometimes a student has a great interest in a particular theory. Mostly this is a general and wide theory with the zealous ambition of understanding and explaining a number of different phenomena, for instance, theories on organisational learning, institutional organisation theory, and theories on change management. The student wishes to use this particular theory to analyse a research topic. What is almost bound to happen is that the student will give a comprehensive and enthusiastic presentation of the theory, at the same time not being quite clear about what data will be useful to support the theory and what findings will weaken it. This makes the theory not suited to govern the data collection. The student will possibly choose and emphasise such data that support the theory while ignoring the data that do not. This means that the theory will not be subjected to critical testing.

The same could, of course, happen the other way around: The researcher is very sceptical to a particular theory, so much so that he or she is only open to data that can serve to weaken the theory. In both cases the researcher is only picking the fruits that are perceived as sweet, letting the others hang (Hancké, 2009). The best remedy is to be clear about what data may support or weaken the theory and then design the investigation in such a way that the chances of catching each type of data are equally good.

Unresearchable Problem Statements

Finally, you may run into problems in the course of the process because the way the problem statement is formulated makes it difficult to design a project that can give good answers to the research questions asked. A typical problem is a too wide and imprecise problem statement. It is not possible to include everything in a research project subject to limited time and resources. Good problem statements therefore need to be delimited to a degree that makes it possible to find answers to them. A later chapter discusses how such delimitations can be made.

The last pitfall mentioned here has to do with the problem statement being formulated in such a way that we cannot give an answer to it by use of scientific methods. Typically, the problem statement is formulated as a normative question, that is, a "should question". To make an example, "What should teachers do to make the pupils interested in their subject?" This question is normative; it asks what should be.

It is easy to understand why such questions are made, since we all have an interest in research contributing to solving practical problems by giving us recipes to follow. But a scientific approach does not take such normative questions as the starting point for research. Science has to do with giving answers to questions about what is actually the case. A problem statement suitable for research will then be "What do those teachers do who make pupils interested in their subject?" This is a question about what exists, called an empirical question. Using such a question as a starting point, we can collect data on what various teachers do and to what degree their pupils have an interest in their subject. We can then search for patterns: Are there common characteristics to be found for those teachers who make pupils interested, or is it possible to identify different approaches? Only when we have studied empirically formulated questions in this way and found an answer to them can we say something basic about what teachers should do to create an interest in their subject. The practical and normative advice we may give as researchers must be anchored in empirical findings. For that reason, normative questions should not make up the leading problem statement in a social science project. Obviously, they may have been decisive for what we chose to study; however, during the research work itself we have to place the normative on the back burner and wait with the answers until we have solid data to support them. The normative question belongs at the end of the list of research questions, where we could pose it like this: "Based on our findings, what advice can we give to teachers on how to make their pupils interested in their subject?"

The Rule of Action

If from what has been said above we are to deduce a basic rule of action for how to create a project design, it will have to be the following: The purpose of the project must be in keeping with the chosen strategy for data production. The design of the research project must be a consequence of what we wish to acquire knowledge about, in other words, of the questions we ask and what knowledge goals we have for the project. The mentioned pitfalls are all examples of the rule not having been followed. The problems arise because we make choices of design without having made clear the goals and premises, or because the goals have not been delimited and formulated in a reliable way. Neither the particular research questions nor the overall project goals originate in vacuum; we also have to relate to the context that the project is part of in order to ensure that the project goals are relevant. The context partly has to do with what knowledge is already available, partly with how we place ourselves in a theoretical and academic context. The rest of this book deals with how to proceed in order to formulate goals and questions that are researchable, and how to create plans for the investigation that are relevant for answering the questions.

ORGANISATION OF THIS BOOK

This book has three main parts. In the first part, Chaps. 2, 3, and 4, I clarify the conditions for the production of scientific knowledge about society and social facts; this part consequently discusses questions within the theory of science. Part two—Chaps. 5, 6, 7, 8, 9, and 10—presents and discusses the core of a research design. In five chapters I present the main variants of research design, concluding with the practical process of creating a concrete design for a research project. Within this framework the individual chapters have the following content:

Chapter 2 looks more closely into the main characteristics of scientific knowledge and scientific practice in general—and into the science of society in particular. The most important characteristic of scientific knowledge is that its form makes it possible to test it. Scientific practice means testing and developing knowledge through collection and analysis of data in a systematic and methodologically guided way. The difference between observation statements and general statements is constitutive of scientific practice. Still, this division is not carved in stone; observations always depend on the cognitive frames and perceptions of the observer. Thus, knowledge is socially constructed. Social constructivism concerns the way we achieve knowledge; it is not a contention that reality is an arbitrary construction.

The next chapter discusses social science as a form of systematic reconstruction of social facts and phenomena. We have a convincing reconstruction when there is a correlation between the ideas and analytical frameworks in our minds when studying some particular social patterns or processes, and the data collected and analysed through systematic use of scientific approaches. The building blocks of the reproduction are on the one hand scientific concepts, theories, and models, and on the other hand data. The last part of the chapter deals with the role these building blocks play in the research process.

Chapter 4 deals with another side of the reconstruction, namely the kind of logic and rules we apply to link observations and data with theoretical ideas. I discuss various forms of research logics: hypothetical-deductive research logic; abduction; hermeneutics; critical theory; and discourse analysis. These strategies build on different premises and imply different research methods. In my view, we should not be too puritanic in the use of these research logics, as they are complementary rather than mutually exclusive.

Chapter 5 discusses the main elements of a research design. A research design is defined as a plan for how to organise the project in order to get from questions to answer. Two elements are essential in such a plan: First, the purpose of the project has to be clarified as well as—connected to it—the research questions. As main categories of purposes I regard theory testing, theory development, theoretically informed interpretation, and intervention. The other element has to do with how to produce data to answer the questions. In this I distinguish between case-oriented and variable-centred approaches to data production.

Chapters 6, 7, 8, 9, and 10 discuss common designs in social science research. Chapters 6 and 7 present variable-centred designs and case designs, showing how these designs can be used in accordance with the various purposes of a research project. Chapters 8, 9, and 10 present various combination forms, where case-oriented and variable-centred approaches to data production are combined in the same project. Chapter 8 presents integrated designs, where the researcher intends to do both theory testing and theory development through a combination of case-oriented and variable-oriented strategies in the same project. The subject of Chap. 9 is comparative designs, where the main research purpose is to study variation between cases. To do that, one needs research strategies to analyse the individual cases from within as well as to compare between cases. Chapter 10 looks more closely at intervention-oriented designs where research strategies are combined in order to study intervention processes and effects of an intervention. The defining characteristic of such designs is their practical purpose.

The final chapter, Chap. 11, deals with the design process. I describe the design process as a process in which the task is to develop and stitch together the different elements or work tasks of the design. In practice these work tasks do not follow sequentially; more often than not we can talk about a pendulum process. Moreover, the purpose will decide how rigid a framework it is convenient to outline in an early stage of the project. In this chapter I therefore distinguish between design processes with a structured framework and those with multiple, flexible, or open frameworks.

The presentation of the design process makes up the conclusion of this book. From this point on, books on research methods and methodological rules will have to be consulted to ensure a sound implementation of the entire research project. That said, the following aphorism applies as much to research projects as to most other things: A good beginning is half the battle!

REFERENCES

Gobo, G. (2008). *Doing ethnography*. Los Angeles, CA: Sage.

Hancké, B. (2009). *Intelligent research design: A guide for beginning researchers in the social sciences*. Oxford, UK: Oxford University Press.

CHAPTER 2

Scientific Knowledge and Practice

This chapter looks at some of the basic questions concerning the development of scientific knowledge. These are fundamental questions if we wish to carry out a research project. We need to inform ourselves of rules and standards concerning the field of practice that we enter into. The disciplinary field that discusses the conditions of scientific knowledge and the rules of scientific practice is the theory of science. Before talking more about design, I will therefore make a short excursion into some basic questions of the theory of science: What are the characteristics of scientific knowledge? Does this knowledge have a different status than our everyday common knowledge? What is the role of cognitive frames in the development of scientific knowledge, and what is the role of theories and scientific concepts? Are theories to be understood as products of data and observations, or do our theoretical lenses shape the way we see the world? Is there such a thing as objective knowledge about society and the world?

The Characteristics of Scientific Knowledge and Practice

Carrying out a research project means entering the scientific field of practice. The scientific field, like the other fields of society, has its norms and rules for what counts as good and acceptable approaches and practices. In the field of science, these rules and requirements are about how to proceed to develop new or support existing knowledge. To perform quality

© The Author(s) 2019

O. Bukve, *Designing Social Science Research*,

https://doi.org/10.1007/978-3-030-03979-0_2

11

research that adds relevant knowledge, we have to acquire knowledge in a way that is acceptable in the community of researchers.

What is the hallmark of scientific knowledge? Most experts today agree that the division between scientific knowledge and other knowledge is less fundamental than we are apt to think. There are many types of knowledge and ways of possessing it. For one thing, we can have *skills knowledge*, for instance being able to ski or cycle. It can be difficult to explain what exactly it is that we do to maintain balance and make a forward thrust when we perform such activities. However, we do know when we succeed in doing the required procedure. Another word for skills knowledge is *procedural knowledge*.

Another type of knowledge is the knowledge of our own experience, like when we hurt ourselves or are tired. Such bodily knowledge is in a sense subjective. We experience it ourselves, in a direct way. Others cannot have a direct access to our knowledge in the same way as we do. Still, we sense this knowledge as true. We do not doubt that we have pain or feel tired. There are also other forms of experience-based or *acquaintance knowledge*. What we have learnt about other people's way of reacting—for instance pupils in a classroom context, clients in a conversation, or patients in a care situation—can lead to an experience-based knowledge that enables us to reflect on and deal with the situation. Everyday knowledge of the kind mentioned here is something we perceive as relatively trustworthy, because we have seen proof of its validity in various situations. We do not usually doubt what we experience, or what we see is working in practice. That does not mean that we have no room for doubt. Sometimes, we can doubt our senses or experiences. However, doubt in itself entails that we accept the existence of a division between true perceptions and those that are not true.

Consequently, it is not so that only scientific knowledge is objective and reliable, while other kinds of knowledge are subjective and unreliable. However, there is another requirement to *scientific knowledge*: It must be testable. The form of a scientific statement must be such that it claims something is the case or not. We can test a statement with such a form, in order to find out whether we can disprove it. "At noon the sun is in the south" is an example of such an assumption. "Wipe your shoes before entering" is a statement of another kind. It is an imperative in the form of an order or a norm for what you should do or are required to do. For a researcher it is important to understand the difference between these two types of statements.

We can test the first assertion through observations. It is possible to make many observations that apparently verify that the sun is always in the south at midday. Every day, provided it is not too cloudy, observations from my sitting room window are in accordance with the statement. Many other persons can also make similar observations. Still, it is possible to make the opposite observation, at least if we move to the southern hemisphere. South of the equator the sun is not in the south at noon; it is in the north. Thus, we can make observations that disprove or falsify the assumption.

This little example illustrates an essential quality of scientific assertions: Their form must be such that we can *test* them. Differently said: It must be possible to *falsify* or disprove them through new observations and data (Popper, 1992/1959).

> **Three Types of Knowledge**
> *The theory of science usually employs three main forms of knowledge: Acquaintance knowledge (or familiarity), procedural knowledge, and propositional knowledge (Truncellito, 2007). Propositional knowledge is the form of knowledge that states that something is the case or not. It is a proposition describing a fact or a state. The common view is that scientific knowledge is of this kind. Procedural knowledge has to do with competence or skills, such as being able to drive a car or stitch together a wound on a patient. Familiarity or acquaintance knowledge has to do with recognition based on experience, such as recognising a person in the street or knowing Paris.*

An important aspect of research and science is to organise observation and data collection in a way that puts established assumptions and ideas to the test. Together, and through critical discussion, scientists have developed systematic methods directed at making the knowledge and insight we arrive at as reliable as possible. Research is a systematic activity in the sense that it applies systematic and recognised methods and approaches. That is why we need to learn about research design and the choice of method. Scientific method is about concretising the requirement that scientific knowledge must be testable.

Research takes place in academic communities. When doing research, we relate to peers who know how to discuss, evaluate, and criticise what we do. Criticism is an important part of academic knowledge building, and a way to bring knowledge development forwards. We perform this activity in small groups in every research context, as well as in broader research communities both nationally and internationally. Researchers within the same discipline or topic exchange knowledge and experiences across national borders. Institutionalisation of these scholarly communities takes place through conferences where researchers from different environments attend and through journals where researchers in a particular discipline or field publish their scientific articles. Before a scientific journal publishes an article, it is peer reviewed and found acceptable for publication. Thus, peer reviews constitute an authorisation of scientific work, and publication gives a scientific finding or argument status as valid knowledge.

Knut Erik Tranøy summarised these points in a precise way with his definition of scientific activity (Tranøy, 1986), stating that it is

> systematic and socially organised search for, acquisition and production of, as well as management and communication of knowledge and insight [translator's translation].

Simply formulated we can say that scientific knowledge has a form that makes it testable; it is provided through the use of methods found acceptable by the research community and has not yet been convincingly disproven by new findings or criticism from other researchers.

In this way, it is possible to compare the scientific practice field with other social fields that have their own rules for what the purpose of the activity is and how we ought to perform it. Just as there are rules and norms for playing football or chess, or for entering a programme of professional study, it is the rules of the game that constitute scientific practice. We can perform this practice at different levels. There is a difference between children playing football in the schoolyard and a professional football match in the Champions League. My leisure chess game with a colleague is also at another level than the games played by chess champion Magnus Carlsen. Still, the rules and goals of the activities constitute them as a game of chess, a football match, or a programme of professional study. This is also the case in the scientific field. We cannot all perform research at world elite level and compete for Nobel Prizes. However, as long as we follow the rules that constitute the scientific field, we are doing research, which also pertains to the activity of writing a master's degree or PhD thesis.

SCIENTIFIC STATEMENTS

Let us take a closer look at the two statements cited above. "At noon the sun is in the south" is a statement claiming that something is always the case. "It is now noon and I see the sun in the south" is a less ambitious statement, just mentioning what I see here and now. The difference between these two types of statements is also important in science. The former statement is an example of generalisation, also called a categorical statement. Scientific theories belong to this type. Their form excludes certain experiences, for instance that the sun is in the north at noon. The second statement is an example of an observation statement. We can disprove generalisations by means of observations that contradict the claims of a generalising statement.[1]

The idea that a scientific statement must have a testable form and thus face the possibility for disproval or falsification dates from the theory of science philosopher Karl Popper (1992/1959). He put forward this idea as a reaction to perceptions maintaining that the goal of science is to arrive at absolutely reliable and irrefutable knowledge. According to Popper, all scientific knowledge is in principle uncertain, as we can refute it by new observations. Thus, an observation statement can never completely prove a theory. Further, a wide acceptance of a theory is no final criterion for its validity, as shown by several historical examples. As we know, it was at one time a generally accepted claim that the sun circled around the earth. Astronomical observations led to the development of another theory with wide acceptance today, although it is less straightforward to grasp when assessing it by everyday observations.

Rather than seeing a division between perfectly reliable knowledge and unreliable ideas, Popper's thinking makes us understand scientific knowledge as more or less robust. When a categorical statement has withstood many attempts to refute it, we will consider it as robust knowledge. The great benefit of Popper's approach is that it fosters critical thinking in the researcher community, and that its focus on testing may give us better and more reliable knowledge.

In addition to the division between observation statements and generalisations (categorical statements), there are a couple of other differences

---

[1] A third type of statement is analytical statements. These are logically true, for instance, "all bachelors are unmarried," or "2+2=4." Such statements are the topics of mathematics and logic and not of empirical testing.

16   O. BUKVE

between statements that it is useful to know. One is the difference between definitions and empirical statements. If we turn the categorical statement "All swans are white" into "Swans are white", we arrive at a definition. We must assess definitions by their usability, not by their degree of truthfulness. The definition "The horse is a four-legged animal" is not refuted by the observation of a horse born with three or five legs; instead, we conclude that this particular horse has a flaw, a deformity. It is not how a horse *should* be. We can understand definitions as guidelines telling us something about how things should be. In this sense, definitions are norms; they are not empirical statements. In short, we can say that empirical statements are "be" statements while normative statements are "should" statements.[2] However, as the examples above show, the differences between normative and descriptive statements are not carved in stone; although definitions have a normative side they also contain a statement that something *is* something (swans are white, horses are four-legged animals).

EMPIRICAL STATEMENTS, NORMS, AND PRACTICE

The greater philosophical discussion about the relationship between norms and empirical statements is not a topic here. Most contributors will agree that the difference is relevant, although not entirely clear. They will also usually believe that we may not infer normative conclusions and practical advice from empirical knowledge alone. For normative advice based on scientific activity, we need three components:

1. What is valuable; a difference between good and bad
2. What we have reasons to do
3. What we should do

The point of the three-piece division above is that a statement saying what you should do ("remove your shoes before entering") does not follow directly from an empirical observation ("your father has just mopped the floor"). That father has just mopped the floor can, of course, be understood as a reason to remove one's shoes. However, in order to draw the conclusion about what you should do you also need a norm of the type "you should respect the work of the person who has just mopped the floor", or

---

[2] We also use terms such as "descriptive statements", while normative statements can be termed prescriptive.

component number one in the above list. When scientists take the role of practical advisors in social matters, such advice always has a normative component. That is the case even when this component is only implied.

At the same time, the difference between empirical and normative statements is not entirely clear. All our statements and arguments about the world have a certain element of evaluation. Looking at the empirical statement above, "your father has just mopped the floor", we find an evaluative element in accepting somebody or something as "father" or "floor". For most practical purposes, this is not of great interest. Quite likely the two involved in the dialogue above will not have any problems in agreeing on the empirical content of "father" or "floor". Few people will also have problems with understanding the difference between the statement "Norway is a society with a great deal of equality between people" and the statement "Everybody should have the same wages no matter what work they perform". The former statement is clearly empirical, the latter just as clearly normative. Being able to distinguish between the two is essential to understand what kind of questions we discuss at any time.

Although there is not always a crystal-clear division between science and normative issues and advice, we need to make clear what practice we are involved in at any given time. Science and research play an increasingly important role in society, and politicians, experts, and others often refer to research when justifying an action or a point of view. Science is without doubt an important supplier of conditions for social practice in a number of areas. Yet that does not mean that science is able to tell us the right thing to do in a given situation. Normative assessments and acquaintance knowledge about a given context will also play a role for practical action.

MORE ON TESTING OF SCIENTIFIC STATEMENTS

It is a basic rule in the scientific community that scientific statements must have a form that makes them testable. Yet the procedure of falsification testing does not necessarily solve all problems related to the solidity of scientific knowledge. Firstly, it is always possible to save a categorical statement by introducing additional premises. In the above example of the sun, we could add as a premise that the observer stays on the northern hemisphere: "Seen from an observation post on the northern hemisphere, the sun is in the south at noon." This saves the theory to the extent that there will no longer be observation statements to refute it. Yet the additional premise reduces the scope of the theory, which then becomes less interesting. As we may make other observations on the southern hemisphere, a researcher will be more interested in a general theory that can explain the variation in the sun's position relative to a given point on earth.

Secondly, we can always ask what is more reliable, the theory or the observation. Our measuring instruments, for instance a compass, may have been defective, or our senses have deceived us. If we trust the generalisation "all swans are white", and then observe a black swan, we may for instance think that somebody wants to play a hoax on us and have spray-painted the swan black. Or, in the case with the sun, we may think that a local magnetic field has played havoc with our compass, making us confused about the directions.

A third problem concerning the requirement of testing and falsification as formulated by Popper is that it presumes a clear distinction between observation statements and generalisations. What then if our observation statements are not neutral, but in some way or other dependent on our position?

Consequently, there are a number of different pitfalls and problems when we try to develop and test scientific knowledge. First, we will look more closely at the relationship between observation statements and categorical statements seen from an epistemological perspective. In scientific knowledge, we usually distinguish between data on the one hand and theories, concepts, and models on the other. We produce scientific data, also called empirical data, through some kind of observation of the world. In that sense, we can talk about data production as a way of establishing observation statements.

Scientific method is about how to collect and analyse data in a reliable way. This is an important topic for textbooks on methodology, qualitative as well as quantitative ones. We need to be familiar with research methods in order to collect reliable data and make judgements about what conclusions we can infer from the given data. However, methods of data collection and analysis are not the main topic in this book; there are method books for that. This book introduces what we have to do *before beginning to collect data.*

In what follows, I want to make the reader aware of the relationship between observations and generalisations. How do observation statements and categorical statements, or data and theories, relate to each other? If mutually dependent, how should we understand their relationship? What do we do when drawing conclusions about the world based on theories? What role do our observations play when we formulate, stick to, or change theories?

Our Social Construction of the World

How do we actually acquire knowledge about the world through observations and generalisations? Do the observations come first so that we as a next stage use the observations to create generalising statements? This has long been the prevailing belief in the theory of science. Establishing reliable knowledge was a question of depicting the world as objectively as possible. Said differently, our minds and perceptions were supposed to mirror the world. Then, is this the way we establish knowledge?

Let us look at the image in Fig. 2.1. We will quickly form an opinion of what the image is supposed to represent. However, we do not all see the same thing or form the same notion. Some will see a vase while others will see two faces turned to each other. When we have become aware of the ambiguity of the image, most of us will agree that it may represent one as well as the other of the alternatives.

The point illustrated by this image is that what we see depends on our focus. If our focus is on the centre of the image, we see a vase. If we focus on the sides, we see the profiles.

The other point made evident by this exercise is that we focus and interpret observations through cognitive frames and mechanisms that make us recognise patterns that we are familiar with. Strictly speaking, this image *is* neither a vase nor two profiles. We could also describe it as two coloured fields on a white paper. What happens when we interpret these coloured fields and the space between them as a vase or two faces cannot be understood as a mirroring of the world. It is rather a *re-presentation* or reconstruction where we actively interpret our visual impressions through acquired cognitive patterns and mechanisms. In fact, it is a double repre-

Fig. 2.1 A representation—of what?

sentation. The image represents the vase and the faces while our interpretations and concepts represent the image as either "vase" or "faces".

A theory of knowledge maintaining that our knowledge re-presents the world rather than mirroring it is what we call constructivism (Berger & Luckmann, 1967; Searle, 1995). Constructivism indicates that our observations depend on our pre-understandings. Pre-understanding in its turn is a product of our personal experiences and the time and society in which we live. Today's theory of knowledge, however, sees language as the most important element of pre-understanding. Language gives us tools and frames to understand the world (Rorty, 1967; Wittgenstein, 1953). Concepts like "vase" or "face" are meaningful; they constitute cognitive tools we can use to categorise sense impressions. Our cognitive tools also contribute to understanding and classifying scientific data or observations. Creating meaning and order entails that we place our observations in mental "drawers" or categories. As such, our observations are not neutral; they are "charged" with theories and pre-understanding.

Another way of saying it is that we try to achieve a congruence between what we observe and experience, and the conceptions and cognitive frames we work with. If we cannot establish this congruence, the consequences are often that we disregard or fail to see observations that are not in accordance with our cognitive frames; what we observe depends on what frequencies we tune in to.

We develop cognitive frames and conceptions largely through language. It is through language we name and categorise our experiences. We can also say that we "grasp" the world through linguistic concepts. That language is a decisive element in our pre-understanding has another important consequence: neither is our knowledge an objective mirroring of the world, nor is it completely arbitrary or subjective. There is no such thing as a private language. Language is a meta-individual communication tool that exists prior to the individual language user. We express ourselves through language, thus giving others a basis to understand us. As such, language is intersubjective: it is between subjects. Through language, we establish many common perceptions of what is true or right.

Still, some new issues arise if we accept the view of our knowledge as linguistically and socially constructed. How are we to decide whether a theory or an argument is better than another? How do we develop better knowledge? How can we verify theories by help of observation statements if the observations depend on our pre-understanding or our theoretical constructions? These are some of the big and controversial issues in the theory of science.

One point is that we should always understand the question of congruence between observation statements and categorical statements as a matter of coherence between different types of statements rather than a correspondence between reality "out there" and our theories. Language always stands between the world and ourselves. Thus, what we attempt to achieve in our scientific work is a coherence between statements on different levels.

Another point is that even though our observations are "theoretically charged", that is, dependent on our pre-understanding and our beliefs, they are not necessarily charged with the beliefs and theories that are to be tested in scientific work. Even simple observations depend on an entire system of former beliefs that we cannot test in a research project. There are always things that we take for granted. What we can and should do in scientific work is to clarify our assumptions as much as possible and be explicit about what is to be tested.

I use an example to illustrate the point in the paragraph above, looking again at Fig. 2.1. Even a simple observation like the one we did of the drawing in the figure depends on a set of former impressions that exceed our ability to distinguish between the concepts of vase or face; for instance, that we know what a drawing is and accept the drawing as a way of representing three-dimensional physical objects. We also know what a vase is by knowing something about its normal use, and what a face is by knowing what a human being is. All this is an example of backgrounds and perceptions that we do not question or doubt when judging what the drawing is supposed to represent.

We may also imagine that we do not see the contours in the figure as a drawing, but as a contour behind a curtain with backlight. We may then have imagined that if the black fields would start to move, we must be looking at faces rather than a vase. Let us say we observe for a minute or five before making up our minds about what we have seen. What we have actually done is constructing a testing situation. We do that by specifying what observations would be able to support or disprove one or the other of the two impressions we have. Yet there is a lot we take for granted and do not doubt in this situation, for instance that faces belong to people who can move, while vases cannot move on their own.

This is also the case in scientific work. A team of researchers will always be working with a number of previous beliefs and impressions that are not problematised in a given research project. Theory of science philosophers have given various names to those frames we take for granted in scientific work. They have been called paradigms (Kuhn, 1996), research programmes (Lakatos, 1978), and backgrounds (Searle, 1995), to mention some well-known concepts in the discussion of the role played by pre-understanding in the development of scientific, and for that matter also other knowledge. Their point is that when we produce and interpret data and observations, we do so in the light of such general frames and theories accepted within the frames.

SCIENCE AND KNOWLEDGE DEVELOPMENT

Even though we interpret and develop knowledge in the light of pre-understanding, our frames do not completely imprison us. We can develop our knowledge by specifying expectations of what observations will be in accordance with the frames and what observations will not (Gilje, 1987). Let us imagine a researcher who considers research a creative activity rather than a craft, also believing that there are reasons to think that we perform creative activities better in flat, network-organised research teams than in top-managed hierarchies. Based on this perspective the researcher would claim that network-organised research teams are more creative than hierarchical research organisations. This is a categorical statement, similar to the examples presented earlier in this chapter. For such a statement to be tested, the researcher must collect data on research environments and research activities. In order to direct the data collection according to the research purpose, the researcher must also specify what kind of observations should characterise creative research. Is it the number of published articles, the number of patents, the surrounding world's perceptions of a research environment, the participants' perceptions, or is it the one, history-making discovery that the researcher should take as proof? Only then can she use the observations for an evaluation of the background statement.

It is still too early to discuss the different ways we can design the research. I deal with that in later chapters. Here, I aim to make the reader aware of what may happen if the researcher arrives at a conclusion in conflict with the general beliefs in his or her community of researchers. The problem is, in fact, about how we accept something as valid knowledge. Let us say that the community of researchers believes networks are the most creative, while our researcher believes her findings indicate the opposite. Reactions among the colleagues could then vary. For one thing, they may doubt her findings, criticise her method or the conduction of the research. Secondly, they may say that this is interesting but in no way reliable; we need more investigations in order to conclude. Thirdly, they may claim that we still have no sufficiently good theories about what makes research creative and that this is a field where more work is needed. Finally, it is conceivable that someone will launch a new theory, explaining why research is more innovative when coordinated through a hierarchical organisation. As shown, the discussion in the community of researchers may take different directions. A community of researchers will have to live with the fact that there are conflicting findings in a number of research fields, often also conflicting theories (Kuhn, 1996). Our knowledge is not organised and certain; there are many uncertainties and anomalies (Gilje, 1987).

At the end of the day, testing and development of knowledge has to do with how good our reasons are for the one or the other belief. We cannot defend as true those beliefs that we have no good reasons or arguments to keep. The discussion and argumentation in the community of researchers and in other contexts will deal with the plausibility of an empirical statement or observation statement, what theories or generalisations it is coherent with, and what theories are most in accordance with the observations we believe to be valid.

Epistemological Positions

We can roughly talk about three sets of positions in the science of knowledge. One is the correspondence theory that sees knowledge as a question of correspondence between the world and our representations of it. Early theory of knowledge believed this question of correspondence to be a question of how thoughts and beliefs mirrored what exists in the world around. This simple mirroring theory proved to be unusable through the attempts of the logical positivists to perfect it, as well as the proofs of the language philosophy that we represent the world through language rather than mirroring it. This was the beginning of a coherence theory of knowledge, where knowledge is a matter of coherence between statements at different levels rather than a correspondence between statements and reality. In such a coherence-theoretical context, we can reformulate the question of true knowledge as a question about the relationship between justification and truth. The third position of the theory of knowledge is the pragmatic or practice theory of knowledge, seeing truth as a question of what functions in practice. This position opens up for an understanding of knowledge that goes beyond statement knowledge, and thus for a discussion of the relationship between statement knowledge and the other forms.

According to Gunnar Skirbekk (2004a, 2004b), when we leave the simplified conception of knowledge as a mirroring of the world around us, the question of truth again arises, now as a question of how we justify our statements about the world. What are our reasons to maintain that something is true or not? In principle, we can view every justification or reason as interim and incomplete. It depends on time, place, and person. A justification we see as valid at one point in time may be lost in another time.

What is truth? This is a difficult question. Some science philosophers regard truth as that which can be justified under ideal conditions (Apel, 2003; Habermas, 1999). Others are sceptical to such a view of an ideal truth beyond time and space. The most radical theorists will maintain that we do not even need concepts of truth beyond that which can be justified (Rorty, 1999, 2000). Others again will emphasise the critical element—truth is something we can approach through critical approaches, testing of argument, and development of new and better descriptions of phenomena and connections. Moreover, we cannot delimit the question of truth to the propositional knowledge of science. Action-related knowledge is also a "window to the world" and a point of departure we can use to develop statement knowledge (Skirbekk, 2003, 2004a; Wellmer, 2003). We have a lot of everyday knowledge developed through our own experiences and practices, which we find no reason to doubt.

THE CONTESTED TRUTH

The realisation that our knowledge is socially constructed has led to a debate of whether it is possible to know if there exists an objective world that we can grasp with our knowledge. If we depend on language and our cognitive constructions to experience the world, how can we know that the external world is real? Some have drawn such drastic consequences from social constructivism that they argue there is no such thing as reliable knowledge about the world; everything is our subjective experience. The so called postmodernists are the most prominent among those who have maintained this view. From this view derives that we ourselves, as the producers of words and texts, are also the producers of reality.

A dilemma concerning this view is that it cannot be true if what it claims is true. If we maintain that there are only subjective experiences and no objective knowledge about the world, this assertion cannot be true either. In academic terms, we call such a theory self-referentially inconsistent. By presenting itself as knowledge of the non-existence of objective knowledge, we cannot take it seriously in terms of knowledge. The logical problem is of the same kind as this more humorous one: If a person claims that all Londoners lie, and this person is from London, the statement is self-referentially inconsistent because if it is true that all Londoners lie it follows that it is a lie when a Londoner claims that all Londoners lie.

Another way of approaching this issue is to state that the doubt whether we can possess objective knowledge about the world assumes that there is such a thing as objective knowledge. In doubting that objective knowledge about the world exists, we assume a division between such knowledge and knowledge that is not objective (Malnes, 2012). We do not need to believe that we possess objective knowledge about the world. We may very well think that our own knowledge is incomplete and insufficient. What we defend is the logical assumption that something like objective knowledge can exist. We may very well regard completely objective knowledge as an ideal it is difficult or even impossible to achieve in practice. However, we still hold on to the ideal. From this perspective Popper's belief in testing and falsification as a scientific approach makes sense. We cannot regard our knowledge to be final and reliable; it is always possible that new observations can contradict our experiences and so disprove our beliefs. Yet through systematic testing we can at least develop our knowledge to make it become better and more reliable.

In our practical world of action, we take a lot for granted. When I wake up in the morning, I look out of the window and check the weather to decide whether I should bring an umbrella to keep dry when walking to work. I take it for granted that I obtain knowledge about the weather by this simple observation. If in doubt, I can check the weather forecast or bring the umbrella anyway. However, I never doubt there is something out there that I can observe. In our everyday actions, we take at any time many things for granted. Otto von Neurath talks metaphorically about knowledge development as similar to rebuilding a boat while on the water (Neurath, 1932). We cannot change all the parts at the same time because then the boat will sink. Transferred to the matter of knowledge: If we doubt everything at the same time, our boat will sink in the sense that we are no longer able to orient ourselves in the world. Still, we can focus on one weak point at a time and do something about it. This is where systematic scientific approach comes in. Using scientific methods requires us to clarify what it is that we take for granted, what we are testing, and how we are doing it.

Another approach to this discussion is to differentiate between theories about how we gain knowledge about the world, and theories about what the world is like. This is equivalent to the philosophical division between epistemology and ontology. Epistemology is the study of knowledge and knowledge formation, while ontology is the study of what the world is like and what is in the world. In the sections above, I have dealt with epistemology or the philosophy of knowledge. The main point has been that we construct our knowledge linguistically and socially, but these constructions are not arbitrary. It is possible to assess whether an argument or proposition is better or more probable than another. The theory of social and linguistic constructivism is thus an epistemological theory, having to do with how we achieve knowledge about the world and what are the conditions for knowledge production. It is not an ontological theory, that is, a theory of what is or is not in the world (Ferraris, 2014; Hacking, 1999).

From an Understanding of Knowledge to Social Science Practice

Scientific knowledge is knowledge of statements and propositions and should have a testable form. We test general statements by comparing them with observations. Yet such an approach is not without pitfalls, because our observations depend on our frames of understanding. Language as well as our cognitive frames is between the world and us. Thus, our knowledge is socially constructed. Yet social constructivism has to do with the way we gain knowledge; it is not a proposition that reality too is an arbitrary construction. How to develop valid and useful knowledge under these conditions is a general challenge as well as a challenge for science. In the following, I will describe how social scientists proceed in practice when they attempt to develop new knowledge about a social phenomenon.

References

Apel, K.-O. (2003). Wahrheit als regulative Idee. In D. Böhler, M. Kettner, & G. Skirbekk (Eds.), *Reflexion und Verantwortung. Auseinandersetzungen mit Karl-Otto Apel.* Frankfurt am Main, Germany: Suhrkamp.

Berger, P. L., & Luckmann, T. (1967). *The social construction of reality: A treatise in the sociology of knowledge.* London: Penguin.

SCIENTIFIC KNOWLEDGE AND PRACTICE 27

Ferraris, M. (2014). *Manifesto of new realism.* Albany, NY: Suny Press.

Gilje, N. (1987). *Anomalier i moderne vitenskapsfilosofi* (Vol. 7). Bergen, Norway: Sentret for vitskapsteori.

Habermas, J. (1999). Wahrheit und Rechtfertigung. Zu Richard Rortys pragmatischer Wende. In J. Habermeas (Ed.), *Wahrheit und Rechtfertigung.* Frankfurt am Main, Germany: Suhrkamp.

Hacking, I. (1999). *The social construction of what?* Cambridge, MA: Harvard University Press.

Kuhn, T. S. (1996). *The structure of scientific revolutions.* Chicago: University of Chicago Press.

Lakatos, I. (1978). *The methodology of scientific research programmes* (Vol. 1). Cambridge, UK: Cambridge University Press.

Malnes, R. (2012). *Kunsten å begrunne.* Oslo, Norway: Gyldendal akademisk.

Neurath, O. (1932). Protokollsätze. *Erkenntnis, 3,* 204–214. https://doi.org/10.2307/20011678

Popper, K. R. (1992 (1959)). *The logic of scientific discovery.* London: Routledge.

Rorty, R. (1967). *The Linguistic turn: Recent essays in philosophical method.* Chicago: The University of Chicago Press.

Rorty, R. (1999). *Philosophy and social hope.* London: Penguin.

Rorty, R. (2000). Universality and truth. In R. Brandom (Ed.), *Rorty and his critics* (pp. 1–30). Oxford, UK: Blackwell.

Searle, J. R. (1995). *The construction of social reality.* London: Allen Lane.

Skirbekk, G. (2003). Wahrheit und Begründung. Überlegungen zu epistemischen Begriffen und Praktiken. In D. Böhler, M. Kettner, & G. Skirbekk (Eds.), *Reflexion und Verantwortung. Auseinandersetzungen mit Karl-Otto Apel.* Frankfurt am Main, Germany: Suhrkamp.

Skirbekk, G. (2004a). Striden om sanningen. In G. Skirbekk (Ed.), *Striden om sanningen* (pp. 7–28). Göteborg, Sweden: Daidalos.

Skirbekk, G. (Ed.). (2004b). *Striden om sanningen.* Gøteborg, Sweden: Daidalos.

Tranøy, K. E. (1986). *Vitenskapen – samfunnsmakt og livsform.* Oslo, Norway: Universitetsforlaget.

Truncellito, D. A. (2007). Epistemology. In J. Fieser & B. Dowden (Eds.), *The Internet encyclopedia of philosophy. A peer-reviewed academic resource.* iep.utm.edu/epistemo/.

Wellmer, A. (2003). Der Streit um die Wahrheit. Pragmatismus ohne Regulative Ideen. In D. Böhler, M. Kettner, & G. Skirbekk (Eds.), *Reflexion und Verantwortung. Auseinandersetzungen mit Karl-Otto Apel.* Frankfurt am Main, Germany: Suhrkamp.

Wittgenstein, L. (1953). *Philosophische Untersuchungen.* Oxford, UK: Basil Blackwell.

CHAPTER 3

Social Science as Reconstruction of Social Phenomena

Social science is the study of social facts and phenomena. When studying such phenomena, we need an understanding of social acts from within as well as an external explanation of social patterns and processes. In general, we can regard social research as a form of systematic reconstruction of social facts and phenomena. We have established a convincing reconstruction when there is a congruence between, on the one hand, the ideas and analytical frames we have in our heads when studying a social phenomenon, and on the other hand such data as have been collected and analysed through systematic use of scientific method. The last part of this chapter introduces the building stones of this reconstruction. What characterises scientific concepts, theories, models, and data, and what role do they play in the research process?

THE STUDY OF SOCIAL FACTS AND PHENOMENA

It does not follow from social constructivism that the world is a product of our subjective conceptions (Hacking, 1999). Yet there is an important division in the world between facts created by nature and social facts. Facts created by nature, such as mountains, seas, snow, and ice, exist independent of our impressions of them. John Searle (1995, 2008) calls such nature-created facts "raw" facts. That there is snow on Mount Everest is true even when there is nobody there to observe. Ferraris (2014) talks about the unchangeable nature of these facts. When an event has happened,

© The Author(s) 2019
O. Bukve, *Designing Social Science Research*,
https://doi.org/10.1007/978-3-030-03979-0_3

29

or a mountain lies where it always has, we cannot change these facts by the force of our thoughts. Even if we wish the event had never happened, or that the mountain was not exactly there, we cannot think away this type of facts.

On the contrary, social facts and phenomena are created by humans. Yet they exist outside the individual. Take the phenomena money, governments, or families: Such phenomena have a physical side; families and governments are made of real persons and money comes in the form of paper notes, metal pieces, or plastic cards, just to mention a few variants. But we do not understand what a government is by referring to Angela Merkel, or what money is by looking at a small, round metal piece. Social facts are, according to Searle, produced through mutual agreements between people to accept something or someone as something.[1] The banknote is not a social fact because it is a tree trunk converted to paper but because we accept it as a means of payment or exchange. We understand and trust that the banknote we accept as payment for a service today can be used to buy food tomorrow. We can say that social facts are created through collective agreements that something or someone has a meaning or function. The money functions as means of payment, the government as a supreme body for governing society, and families as units for reproduction and the socialisation of human beings. Thus, social facts entwine in extensive patterns. If I want to explain to you what money is, we both need to be familiar with other social phenomena such as payment and exchange. In order to understand the explanation of what a family is, it would be useful to know concepts such as reproduction and socialisation.

Even though social facts are created by humans, they form meta-individual contexts for our existence. Thus, they are objective facts although we cannot touch them or exhibit them. We do not doubt that money or families exist. Yet they only appear through the forms of social embeddedness and practices that they shape. Social facts are only maintained or reproduced through our compliance, that is, when we behave as if they exist and are meaningful. If people lose their trust in money as a

---

[1] There is a dispute between philosophers of science what the defining characteristics of social facts are. Ferraris (2014) agrees with Searle's division between different types of facts, calling them unchangeable and social. He insists that it is the registration or enrolling that constitutes social facts, through either the writing down of formal rules or the informal "writing" in the memory of those who establish an agreement.

means of payment, the system of payment will collapse. Such a trust can be lost for instance if the government prints so much money that the value of each note decreases. In this way, social facts are interdependent, because they knit together in patterns and influence each other.

Social sciences deal with the analysis of social facts, the way they are established, and how they appear and work as contexts for human action. Social facts constitute a form of action rules or rules of the game for social life. We should understand them as rules, not as inviolable laws of nature. Jürgen Habermas emphasises that we can see every act from two different standpoints (Habermas, 1982, 1990). We can try to look at it from within, which means that we try to understand the act as a meaningful statement by the actor. When Habermas talks about acts he includes speech acts as a form of action. We can also look at the act from the outside as an objective fact. From this point of view, we can explain the act by looking at it as the product of a social system of rules, as an element of a repetitive or changing social pattern. With this as his point of departure, Habermas understands social science as a reconstruction process, as a historical analysis of how structures and patterns in society develop and are connected. Still, we cannot stop there, with the reconstruction of patterns and connections in a social action system. The fact that we can point out statistical connections and regularities in a material does not give us the full explanation of the mechanisms that are the basis of the regularities. This is possible only when we can point out the logic of action behind the practices of social actors and the actual mechanisms that mediate between structural conditions and social practice. Understanding of social action from within and external causal explanations are complementary, not alternative ways of doing social science (Bukve, 2003).

The next couple of examples will serve to illustrate why an element of understanding is necessary when reconstructing a social system. We know that a British government has to resign if it is defeated in a vote of no confidence in Parliament, which has happened several times in the last decades. We can understand why it happens only through knowledge of a set of institutionalised rules that have become custom and practice. Further: Without knowledge of the institutional context, we cannot understand what it means that a government resigns, or for that matter what a government is. Only when we identify the rule system that governs a set of actions, we can distinguish between "correct" and "incorrect" actions related to a given system of rules. Thus, actions derive meaning from a given social context. If social science researchers do not understand this context, they may consider actions under study as irrational even if they are understandable from the actor's context. A classic example is Pierre Bourdieu's analysis of the Kabyles in Algeria (Bourdieu, 1990). Economists found that the Kabyles behaved irrationally by not saving or using money in a way that could improve their standard of living. What Bourdieu showed was that the way the Kabyles used their money for gifts was completely rational when taking into consideration that theirs was a culture of honour; giving gifts was a matter of honour granting social status. An act that seems irrational in one system of social rules can be completely rational in another social context.

Explanations in Social Science

In general, we can define an explanation as an answer to the question of why something happens or why some people behave as they do. The answers can refer to single incidents as well as relatively permanent phenomena in society. In the former section, I introduced a distinction between internal and external types of explanations, also called intentional and causal explanations. Below, I will say a bit more about these explanation types. I will also discuss how we can use functional explanations to analyse interrelations in society.

In order to understand the concept of social action, we need intentional explanations, also called purpose-oriented explanations. The basis of such explanations is that the actions build on rationales and reasons that the actors can account for, rather than on external causes that force the actors to act in certain ways. In order to give an intentional explanation, we need to know what a person knows and believes in. Said differently, we must *understand* the person. Further, we must assume that the person is rational in the sense of being able to judge different action alternatives. The Bourdieu example from the section above can serve as an example. An act that is understandable in light of a culture of honour can seem incomprehensible when interpreted externally from the researcher's western culture. An explanation of understanding tries to understand the actions of a social actor applying the actor's own premises. The explanation must take its starting point in the actors' motives for their actions, that is, what they wish to achieve or communicate.

When attempting to establish an understanding explanation, it is a challenge that we do not have direct access to people's motives and intentions. We have to interpret their intentions by means of the reasons they give

SOCIAL SCIENCE AS RECONSTRUCTION OF SOCIAL PHENOMENA   33

through their communicative acts. Such an interpretation is, however, not a straightforward one. We need to know the context of an action as well as how the actor perceives the context in order to be able to understand why any given action is meaningful. In much of what we humans do, we follow certain rules of action or established norms of conduct. Such compliance with rules can create stable social patterns; however, these patterns are not the result of unbreakable natural laws. Even creatures of habit can make new choices, thus establishing new patterns. Moreover, social actors may act strategically and cover up the real motive for an act, which may complicate the interpretation of social acts. Still, the main point is that an internal explanation means that we reconstruct an act as meaningful from a certain context.

There are different opinions on the use of causal explanations in social science, and the disagreement relates to a discussion in the theory of science about what a cause is. When dealing with causal explanations, we explain the phenomenon through one or more previous occurrences that have produced it. However, the agreement stops at this point. We can identify a division between those who adhere to a covering law perspective on causes, and those who see causes as complex mechanisms.

Causal explanations are often presented on this form: "if x (the temperature reaches the boiling point), then y (the water boils)". Such an explanation can be termed a covering law or general law. Causal explanations of this kind are common in the natural sciences; they give us the ability to control nature by being able to predict the effects of certain interventions or conditions. When we have established a law that says that water boils at 100 degree centigrade, we can use this knowledge to produce steam by heating the water. Covering law explanations try to isolate the effects of individual factors, which in their turn are given the status of the causes that something happens. To isolate such effects, we must keep the other factors constant. For instance, in order to be able to predict the right boiling temperature for water, we must keep the atmospheric pressure constant and make sure the water is quite pure.

When realising that social facts and frameworks constitute rules of the game for social action and not unbreakable natural laws, we understand that the idea of general laws is not a suitable way of arriving at social science explanations. Social sciences try to find more or less regular patterns in society. These patterns concern what is probable rather than what is bound to happen. A typical formulation could be that "it is unemployed, socially excluded youths from a minority background who are recruited by the IS." To understand this as a feasible explanation we do not need data showing that all youths with these three distinguishing marks—unemployed, socially excluded, and from a minority background—and only these youths enlist in the IS. It suffices that we have data showing that in a sample of youths of this category a larger number are recruited to the IS than in a sample of youths with other characteristics. Such explanations build on the probability of a certain result rather than on a deterministic law. To establish these explanations, we need statistical analyses securing a representative selection of data and making sure that we draw the right conclusions about the probability of a certain result in the various samples. Yet what covering law explanations and probability explanations have in common is that they focus on the connection between *causes* and *effects*.

Mechanism explanations try to grasp the totality instead of isolating individual factors the way causal explanations do. Mechanism explanations build on an interaction between different elements or factors that are necessary to produce a particular result. The film *Jihad*, in which Deeyah Khan interviews foreign fighters, is an example of this strategy (Khan, 2015). She asks what makes young men brought up in the west become foreign fighters and identifies the feeling of exclusion and alienation as a common feature in the interviewees. However, she also shows that the social backgrounds of the Jihadists vary and that there is an elite or top echelon of active champions for recruitment. Thus, the explanation she gives is complex. Several concurring factors create the conditions for Jihadism. Separately, social exclusion or contact with active recruiters does not necessarily make people into Jihadists. Yet together these two factors may form an important explanation; active recruiters who offer a particular interpretation of the mentioned exclusion and additionally offer a community for the excluded may add up to a strong *social mechanism* (Beach, 2016; Cartwright, 2006; Mayntz, 2004). Using a metaphor, a mechanism is like a machine; the components of a machine work together; they do not produce an observable result individually. For a car to have forward thrust demands an interaction between engine, transmission, and wheels. We cannot understand the mechanism by isolating the individual elements of the system (Beach & Pedersen, 2014).

Important to realise is that this type of explanation looks at causes by tracking down the conditions of a result rather than predicting effects. That means unwinding the causal chains from their beginning; we try to understand the *conditions* for something happening as it did or for somebody acting as they did. It is also important to note that mechanism explanations entail studying social facts and phenomena in context as well as the way the different factors interact. The actors' frames of understanding and their interpretations interact with external conditions; the factors in combination produce the effect. The focus of such explanations is on social mechanisms and systems. Another point is that mechanism explanations deal with a particular case or a particular class of events rather than universal generalisations.

Explaining connections in society often has to do with reconstructing the relationship between regular patterns and single acts. Such connections are complex. Social patterns create the conditions for single acts but are also maintained or changed by such acts. Functional explanations as well as mechanism explanations focus on such relationships.

Compared with causal explanations, functional explanations mean that in a way we reverse the sequences of cause and effect. A functional explanation of a social phenomenon means to explain the phenomenon by its *consequences*. A function is the same as a beneficial and positive consequence of a phenomenon. Functional explanations can only explain why a phenomenon continues, not why it happened in the first place. Such explanations are common in biology, where we presume that many phenomena originate through random mutations, but that those persisting survive because they have a positive function. Thus, a requirement concerning functional explanations is that we can demonstrate a feedback mechanism. We can for instance explain the long neck of the giraffe by the better access to food it gets from being able to graze in the treetops where it has no competitors. In the same way, we can explain a growth of productivity in a sector exposed to competition by the fact that businesses that increase their productivity have a better chance of survival.

The presentation in this section has shown that explanations in the social sciences may take different forms, which I will concretise in the next sections.

Social Science as Reconstruction of Social Patterns and Processes

An important argument in the former chapter was that our knowledge is socially constructed; it is a re-presentation or reconstruction of the world around us. Here, the question is what this entails regarding the development of knowledge about phenomena and patterns in society. What do social scientists do in practice when they analyse society and create reconstructions of social phenomena and patterns? We can say, generally speaking, that they make a systematic effort in order to establish a match between general ideas and theories about a class of phenomena on the one hand and collected data regarding these phenomena on the other (Ragin & Amoroso, 2011).

As shown in the first chapter it is a necessary condition, for scientists as well as for others who study society, to employ as a point of departure some provisional ideas and theories about the particular phenomenon they aim to study. Such frames of understanding may be quite different depending on the topic under study and the discipline where the researchers work. The common denominator is that in one way or another these frames form the starting point for stating something about properties of phenomena or connections between phenomena.

Let us take a closer look at the latter type of statement, that is, statements about connections between phenomena. Some relevant examples could be "knowledge differences are reproduced across generation borders"; "formal organisation limits are obstacles to health personnel cooperating to help patients"; or "high raw material prices will lead to an increase in production and a decrease in prices." The examples stem from the disciplines sociology, organisation theory, and economics. The first proposition results from a general image of society as defined by class structure and social inequality. The second relates to classical organisation theories and their image of organisations as mechanisms for division of labour and direction of the members' focus towards specific tasks and duties. The third proposition has its starting point in theories about markets characterised by free competition. Behind these theories, we find other even more general constraints, such as the idea that market actors act to increase their profit, that organisation actors experience a delimitation of their cognitive capacity, and that structural conditions in organisations and society determine individual behaviour. Thus, assertions about specific connections between phenomena link to general perspectives on society, organisations, and markets. What we need to do in a research project is to account for the theoretical framework that our investigation takes its starting point from, and the fundamental assumptions the research is based on.

To a greater or lesser extent, such general ideas and theoretical assertions as mentioned above can govern our observations and data production. Let us say that we collect data on price development and production level for coffee and oil, about grades for pupils from different social backgrounds, or on the follow-up of patients who underwent heart surgery in different organisational contexts. Departing from such data, the researcher can ask how theoretical ideas and empirical statements coincide. Do the theories give us a good understanding of connections and variation? Should we question some aspects of the theory, for instance that there are situations where it is not usable? Do we need to revise or discharge the whole theory, or are there reasons to doubt such observations that do not match with the theory? There are many possible outcomes of our scientific work, and there are different approaches or methods to arrive at the result or the best representation of our findings. Neither does research always start with the most general ideas. The starting point could very well be observations and data for which we do not have a good explanation, and hence need to try various theories to find how they fit, or construct new theories built on new ideas and premises.

Social science research does not always establish knowledge about connections between phenomena; sometimes the goal is to establish a deeper knowledge of characteristics or qualities related to a social phenomenon. What happens when pupils learn? How do participants from different health professions interact in teams? Such open questions can be the starting point of research too. Even then, the principles remain the same. The researcher arrives at a representation or reconstruction of the researched phenomenon, at the intersection between collected data and theoretical ideas that more or less explicitly steer the data collection.

When social researchers study social action, the reconstructions are about understanding the actors' actions as meaningful, which is to say that the researcher tries to reconstruct the reasons the actors have for acting in particular ways. In such instances, it is easy to understand that social research is about re-presentation of a social phenomenon. My point here is that, in principle, the same happens when we explicitly design the investigation as a systematic testing of theories and explanations. Theoretical statements and observations of the world around us are neither totally independent of each other nor identical. They play different roles in the production of knowledge, in other words in the researcher's representation of society.

Figure 3.1 is an attempt to sum up the main ideas of this section. The researcher's representation or reconstruction of social phenomena and connections revolves around the establishment of congruence between theoretical frameworks and empirical data concerning a social phenomenon. Depending on purpose, the researcher can do this in various ways. Within

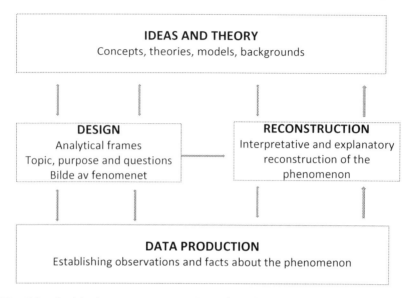

Fig. 3.1 Social science as reconstruction of social phenomena

the framework presented above, we can design research projects in many ways; they can have different designs. It is the research design that governs how we carry out the reconstruction of the phenomenon.

The Elements of Reconstruction

Figure 3.1 depicts the social science research process as a reconstruction in which we work with two types of elements or building stones that are to be adapted to each other. In the figure, I label one type of building stones for ideas and theory. Ideas and theories correspond to what Chap. 2 also referred to as generalisations and categorical statements. They say something about groups or classes of phenomena and connections between them. More specific we can say that such generalisations can take the forms of concepts, theories and hypotheses, models and backgrounds. The background is the most general framework of understanding. We do not usually question these frameworks, but they are present as conditions for our analysis. The other forms of ideas or generalisations are, however, active in the research process. They are used, tested, supported, revised, or discarded resulting from comparisons with data.

Data are the other form of building stones in the research process. They correspond to what we also call observation statements. The research process is about comparing the two forms of statements, in order to determine whether there is congruence or contradiction. In the next sections of this chapter, I account for the role that the different building stones have in the research process. In the next chapter, I introduce the approaches and inferential rules we use when comparing general theories and ideas with observations and data.

BACKGROUNDS

Behind the concepts and theories used by a researcher or a team of researchers there will always be some basic ideas and assumptions that we do not question in our academic work. Such assumptions are called backgrounds, paradigms, or cognitive frames (Kuhn, 1996; Searle, 1995). Some of the diversity and contradictions within the social sciences stem from the fact that scholars host different background assumptions. Some work from an assumption of social actors being ruled by their personal interests; others may see altruism as a fundamental human quality. Some understand the market as a perfect mechanism for distribution; others see it as a source of differences in living conditions and power. When researchers discuss such issues, the discussions will usually have a different character than discussions within a particular community of researchers. It is not easy to agree on valid arguments across paradigmatic borders, which is why they often take the form of hegemonic struggles between different scholarly communities. Below, it is not the discussions at this level that are presented, but the so-called normal-scientific knowledge development within a scholarly tradition or a research programme (Kuhn, 1996; Lakatos, 1978). The use and development of concepts, theories, and models is the central content of the next sections.

CONCEPTS

Let us begin with the concept of "concept". We can understand a concept as a mental perception of a phenomenon in the world. Ogden's semiotic triangle (Fig. 3.2) is a much-used starting point to understand what a concept is and does. The semiotic triangle separates the object or thing from the sign or symbol that refers to the thing, and from the concept defining the thing. The sign or symbol that refers to the thing can be

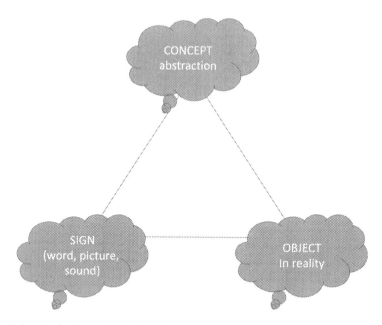

Fig. 3.2 Ogden's semiotic triangle

words, images, or sounds. We can write the word "boy", "Knabe", or "garcon", we can say the sounds these words correspond to, or we can show a picture. Thus, different signs can refer to the same phenomenon and express the same concept. The role of the concept is to define the thing. We can define a boy as a "male person not yet grown up", or a horse as "a four-legged hoofed mammal". The concept derives meaning through its use. The question is whether the concepts are usable or adequate, not if they are true or false. We can say that concepts have a normative aspect; they say something about how a thing or phenomenon should be in order to be the thing or phenomenon we call them.

In everyday life as well as in research we apply concepts to categorise phenomena in the world around us. In this sense, the concepts are theoretical tools to grasp the world; attempting to say something about what the world is like. The important thing in research is that we are able to look beyond the words or signs and to the concept itself. For instance, the sign "institution" refers to a number of different concepts, dependent on context or tradition. In everyday usage, it usually refers to organisations such as schools, hospitals, or prisons, in other words organisations that to

SOCIAL SCIENCE AS RECONSTRUCTION OF SOCIAL PHENOMENA 41

a large degree control the lives of their participants. In institutional organisation theory, an institution usually refers to an organisation infused by values and ideas, in other words an organisation whose function not only depends on formal rules. Political scientists usually see institutions and ideas as complementary; they consider institutions mainly as formal organisations. Concepts exist in contexts; they build on and refer to other concepts. In a sense, concepts are theoretically charged. They build on and presuppose ideas about characteristics of the world and about social phenomena. When doing research, we should clearly state these presuppositions; we should account for our understanding of central concepts and for the scientific perspectives to which they relate.

Another aspect of scientific work is the development of new concepts. This may have to do with creating new concepts to define new and unknown phenomena, or concept development could mean looking at familiar phenomena in a new way. "Social media" is an example of the former, whereas an example of the latter is the changing of the concept of institution by new institutionalism to include the concept of normative and cultural aspects of an organisation. One of the most striking examples is the concept of "wicked issues" (Rittel & Webber, 1974), used in recent years to describe problems with no definite solution because they involve actors with different perspectives and values. Using this concept, we have changed the way we analyse a number of issues, earlier seen as a matter of coordination.

Concepts and the creation of concepts are just as important elements in scientific work as is method (Collier & Mahon, 1993; Sartori, 1970). Despite this, social scientists have shown less interest in developing concepts and in the role of concepts in the research process. One exception is Gary Goertz (2006) with his book on the use of concepts in social science. Goertz maintains that most important scientific concepts are multidimensional as well as having several levels. He describes three levels in the development and use of concepts. On its most fundamental level, a concept refers to main properties of a phenomenon, that is, the distinctive mark of the phenomenon. One example is the concept of democracy, which we can define as representative government. Another concept is organisation, often defined as a goal-oriented cooperation between humans.

When we use concepts to form theoretical propositions about connections between phenomena, we operate at this fundamental level. On this level, according to Goertz, the concept is a noun to which we can connect adjectives. For instance, we can talk about parliamentary democracy or consensus democracy, or we can talk about loosely coupled versus hierarchical organisations.

At the second level, the multi-dimensional aspect of the concept emerges. Here, we can start talking about democracy having different dimensions or characteristics such as citizen rights and elections involving competition between candidates. Researchers will often disagree or debate what dimensions are sufficient or necessary in constituting a concept. It is therefore important that we account for the dimensions of the concepts we apply in our research. It can often be useful to look at how other researchers have made use of the concept, and to clarify our own standing. How, for instance, should we define the concept of family? Historically seen, our understanding of this concept has clearly changed. We can do without further definitions in everyday conversations; usually, use and context make our meaning clear. Still, if we plan to carry out a comparative research project about living conditions in families it will be important to clarify what units we include.

The third level of a concept is, according to Goertz, the indicator level or data level, also called the operational level. At this level, we define how to collect and measure data on various aspects of the concept. The operationalisation must permit us to decide whether a concept fully or partially covers a given phenomenon. Goertz emphasises that most important scientific concepts are continuous and vary on a continuum. The difference between democracy and non-democracy, for instance, is not clear-cut; there are several in-between forms on the scale between a perfect democracy and a totalitarian regime. Exactly where to place the division between states that are democracies and those that are dictatorships relates closely to our definitions of the concepts. Sometimes we need to make this division clear, but other times it can be useful to show the full scale.

When designing a research project, we need to know whether our goal is to use or to develop concepts. In the former case, we collect data to decide whether we can use a given concept or one of several different concepts to understand a phenomenon. In the latter case, we collect data to find whether we need to define the concept more precisely or develop it through new definitions and dimensions. Perhaps we even need a new concept in order to catch a new phenomenon. In any case, it is essential to be both theoretically and methodologically transparent. Theoretically, by clarifying the definition of the concept and what dimensions we include in it; methodically, by being clear about how we measure the observed phenomena in relation to the concept.

Theories and Hypotheses

While concepts in the social sciences define social phenomena and facts, theories deal with the relationships between phenomena. Said differently, theories are concept structures (Sohlberg & Sohlberg, 2013) because they focus on how various scientific concepts relate to each other. Using the terminology from the section above, we can say that theories are systems of categorical statements or generalisations, pointing to relationships between classes of phenomena rather than to individual phenomena. We can generalise at different levels of abstraction. Some theories aim at explaining phenomena that are relatively restricted in time and space; other generalisations can lay claim to a wide area of use.

So far, most scholars will probably agree on the definition of what a theory is, although some will probably use the theory concept mainly about larger explanatory systems in which the theory explains a number of partial relations. Organisation theory is an example of a discipline with a number of such theories with competing as well as complementary features. Some branches of organisation theory see organisations as strategic actors in fields marked with conflicts and competition, while other branches see them as cultural systems marked by the common values and perceptions of the participants. From their starting point in these assumptions, the theories then develop more specific ideas and theories about the functioning and development of organisations. We can understand theories as complementary by being suitable in different contexts and situations, but we can also regard them as competing when they explain the same phenomenon in different ways.

Other scholars maintain that a theory should point out a precise and observed connection between two phenomena. The ideal of such use of the concept is that a theory should state "if x, then y". "If the electoral system in a country is built on single-member constituencies, the country will develop a party system with fewer parties than in countries with proportional representation." We can test this proposition against data on the electoral system and party system in various countries. Usually, we call such a proposition a hypothesis. A hypothesis is an assumption about connections between phenomena, not yet tested against data. If tested against data in a systematic way without falsifying results, we can see the hypothesis as an established theory. Said otherwise, a hypothesis is a prediction based on a theoretical model (Clarke & Primo, 2007).

If a theory comprises only relatively broad and vague ideas about relationships between phenomena, it will be difficult to test it against data. If an organisation-theoretical assumption claims that "the organisational structure influences the way the organisation functions," testing or disproving the theory will not be easy. If on the other hand we assume that "divisional organisation of a large group gives better conditions than a linear organisation in terms of strategic adaptation to its environment," we can study it by comparing the development of organisations organised in those two ways. If theories are to be tested and developed based on empirical research, the theories need to have such a form that we can develop testable assumptions. Another question is whether such testing should be the only or the most important purpose of social research. Some will say that it is first and foremost new models and ways of understanding, not a detailed testing of theories, that give science its forward thrust.

MODELS

We can understand a model as a systematic representation of one or the other aspect of the world. The model is always a simplified representation, as it does not display all aspects of reality. We use different kinds of models for different purposes. Mathematical models apply a formal, mathematical language to describe an object or relations between objects. Graphic models visualise relationships, for instance in a figure or a three-dimensional model. Conceptual models specify the relationships between scientific concepts. Clarke and Primo (2012) argue that we should conceive models as objects. A property of objects is that they cannot be judged as true or false. What we can do is to evaluate them in terms of how useful they are for a given purpose.

A map is a type of model with which most people are familiar. The map is not identical to the terrain that it depicts; rather, it forms a re-presentation of the terrain. In this sense, the map is not true or false; it is, on the other hand, more or less useful for a specific purpose. A map that is meant to be useful for finding specific addresses in a city is different from a map used for climbing mountains or planning a journey to countries along the Silk Road. The usefulness of a model relates to the question of its purpose. We can also say that the usefulness of models reflects the interests of those who create and use them (Giere, 1999).

If we understand models as systematic representations of one aspect of the world, they are not directly falsified or strengthened by observations coherent with or contradicting the models. We do not prove or refute the model itself, but rather the assumptions about the world that the model leads to (Clarke & Primo, 2007, 2012). The model is a tool for developing and testing theoretical assumptions. It is, however, the theoretical assumptions derived from it we are testing, not the model in itself (Fig. 3.3).

Tests of model-based assumptions are about comparing one system with another, by comparing the model system with the system in the world that the model tries to say something about. In science, we deal with two different types of models: theoretical models and empirical models. Theoretical models structure the relationships between theoretical concepts, whereas empirical models structure the relationships between observations.

An example of a theoretical conceptual model can be a model of relationships between types of education and the reproduction of social inequality. We can find relevant theory for creating such a model in the literature on social stratification, learning, group dynamics, and the development of verbal competence. A possible hypothesis to derive from this model is that an educational system built on student activity in groups reproduces social inequality to a larger degree than an educational system based on traditional blackboard teaching and individual exercises. We can

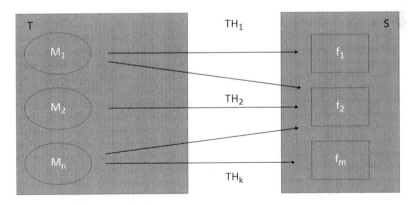

Fig. 3.3 The relationship between a theory, the models of the theory, and a system in the world. According to Clarke and Primo (2012)
A theory T comprises n models, M, and k theory-based hypotheses, TH. A system in the world, S, comprises m properties (f) that can be modelled

then compare whether this hypothesis is coherent with observations of the actual educational system.

"Social inequality" and "educational system" are theoretical concepts that we cannot measure directly. For an empirical investigation, we would have to define empirical indicators that we use to evaluate the theoretical model. First, we would need to operationalise the causal variable "social background". We could for instance use the family income or the parents' education and jobs. Thereafter we would have to operationalise the effect variable. A simple way of studying it would be to perform observations in the classroom. We could for instance observe how teachers divide their attention between pupils from different social backgrounds, and how pupils from different social backgrounds involve themselves in the class and the group. Another strategy could be to compare the grades of pupils from different social backgrounds to the type of education they participated in. These research strategies can be visualised by empirical models. Social background is a causal variable that we can operationalise as indicated. Participation in the classroom, grades, choice of education, and work are operationalisations of the effects, in other words the social inequality variable.

The theoretical model can direct our data collection in various directions, and we can evaluate observations and findings in light of the model. Vice versa, we can use the findings from empirical investigations to build general theoretical models. We could for instance have started with studies in the classroom and observed differences in attention and participation. Finding a correspondence between these findings and the pupils' family background, we would have been able to formulate a theoretical model of reproduction of social differences. According to Clarke and Primo (2012), it is gives no meaning to say that we falsify or verify a theoretical model when we test it against empirical findings. Testing a generalisation means judging the congruence between two types of models: one observation-based or empirical model, and one theory-based model. When testing, we confront the two models to see how well they match with each other. What we really do in this operation is to evaluate the usefulness of the theoretical model with some specific purpose in mind. The model is useful when the match between the theoretical model and our systematised observations is good. However, the confrontation goes both ways; we also need to judge whether such observation data as we have are sufficient to evaluate the theoretical model.

SOCIAL SCIENCE AS RECONSTRUCTION OF SOCIAL PHENOMENA   47

Models are useful in different ways. Clarke and Primo (2012) distinguish between several different ways of using models. We may use theoretical models as a point of departure to generate empirical investigations—in terms of confronting the models with data and consequently develop our knowledge in a particular field.[2] Theoretical models may also be synthesising or structuring, in that they sum up and generalise findings from different empirical investigations. Third, they can be explorative in that they identify processes and mechanisms that may have explanatory value. Finally, there is the predicting role that is about predicting what will happen under given conditions.

Empirical models are also useful in several ways. We can use them for prediction as well as for testing or confrontation of theories. They also have other purposes by being used to measure and characterise empirical phenomena and connections, in other words the descriptive aspect of the models. Thus, models play many different roles in research processes.

If we regard models as mere tools for designing predictions and falsifying testing, we lose important aspects of the use of models. Some examples can illustrate this. The theoretical model stating that water freezes to ice at zero degree centigrade will be only approximately confirmed by our everyday observations. If the water contains salt, the freezing temperature changes. Sometimes frost in the ground may make rain freeze to ice on the ground even at temperatures above zero. Still, this model is precise enough to be useful to me when I consider taking the flowers from the porch into the house because it seems to get quite cold. I decide after learning from the weather forecast that the temperature will probably go down to zero.

In political science, Anthony Downs' model of party competition in a two-party system is well known and much used (Downs, 1957). The model predicts that parties in such a system will become more alike, because they compete for the same voters in the centre. Voters on the wings will not in any case move to the other party. This model shares light on the dynamics of party competition, among other things how this will change in a multi-party system with wing parties that participate in the

---

[2] Clarke and Primo (2007) state that generative models are those that are useful for generating interesting claims and so stimulate new research. Downs' spatial model for party competition is one example. Game theories and theories about rational choices are other examples of areas where this type of model construction is important, and such models are used extensively in economics.

competition for voters. The model has inspired and been used in a number of projects and studies; yet the empirical effect indicated by the model has never been observed in practice. Taken to its logical conclusion, the prediction inferred from this model is that the two parties will become identical, both taking up the standpoint of the median voter. We have never seen this occur in reality; still, the model has been quite useful to research on political parties. Prediction is just one of the various interests that we researchers may have for using models, and just one of the ways we can use models.

An alternative way of employing theoretical models is to use them as starting points to structure future investigations. The usefulness of the model lies in clarification of what connections we want to test. If we systematise possible connections in a concept model, we can use the model as a basis for collecting data. Then we can test whether the data is coherent with the connections specified in the model. It is possible to describe the model in words, yet often a graphic figure may serve to make clear what relations will be of interest for further research.

We can also use models in an explorative way. In the process of reading and thinking about the topic for our project, we form thoughts about connections and mechanisms that could be relevant for further research. Creating a concept model can then be useful, outlining the mentioned aspects of the object of study and comparing the model to new data.

Another application for models is the synthesising, or—using Clarke and Primo's words—structuring application. In a field where we have empirical data from a number of projects, we can construct models that synthesise or generalise about connections based on the given empirical data. As a next step, we can use the model to structure new projects that in their turn may produce new evidence for evaluating the usefulness of the model.

A common trait of models is that we use them to connect or mediate between theory and data. In the design phase of a research project, it can often be useful to create a model for analysis that displays the concepts and connections we want to discuss in the project. Such analytical frames use elements from the model types discussed. If an extensive literature exists that we can employ when designing the project, our model of analysis can for instance structure the findings from the literature and focus on possible connections that have not yet been so well explained. In Chap. 11 about the design process, I return to the design of analytical frames to be used as tools in the design process.

The point of view promoted in this book makes me regard theories and models as tools in the social scientist's representation of social phenomena and relations. Theories and models are not directly mirroring reality; they are abstractions in the sense that they disregard certain aspects of reality and emphasise other aspects. What they emphasise are the aspects regarded as most important to understand and explain social phenomena.

DATA CONSTRUCTION

Social constructivism maintains that we cannot observe the world directly; language and cognitive frames stand between us and the world. In this sense, data and observations are socially constructed too. The section above mentioned that we confront theory-based hypotheses with real systems in the world. However, this does not take place directly. What we really do is to confront theoretical models with models of data. Data are reconstructions too. In social science, we distinguish between two main strategies for data construction. One is to divide the phenomena under study into single components that we usually label variables. Then we try to isolate the effect or causes of each variable in order to detect connections. The other strategy is to regard the object of study as a whole or as a system of mutually influencing components, which is the case strategy for data construction. I will return to these two strategies in Chap. 5.

FROM THE BUILDING STONES OF RECONSTRUCTION TO THE LOGIC OF RECONSTRUCTION

This chapter has introduced an understanding of social science as the reconstruction of social patterns and processes. Through such reconstruction we develop knowledge about various aspects of social phenomena and facts: knowledge about society. We can say that we possess knowledge about society when we have established a congruence between ideas and theories on the one hand, and observations and findings on the other.

Social phenomena and facts are paradoxical, because humans create them through social action and they simultaneously constitute the rules and frames for such actions. In social science research, we therefore combine internal explanations of social actions with external explanations of patterns and regularities. We need to combine the two ways of explanation to understand change and reproduction in social patterns and processes.

The last part of this chapter took a closer look at the theoretical tools of a social science researcher. On the most general level, there are the paradigmatic frames and presuppositions, also called backgrounds. These are the fundamental perceptions and assumptions that we do not question within the frame of a research programme. The most basic tools for social science researchers are scientific concepts that point to specific characteristics of a phenomenon. We can understand theories as concept structures since they specify the relationships between scientific concepts. Models are tools for presenting and establishing congruence between theoretical statements and observations of the world.

Data are also socially constructed; we are not able to observe the world in a direct way. The case strategy and the variable strategy are the two strategies for data construction that social scientists can use in a project. The former means looking at an object of study as a whole; the latter involves reducing it to a set of basic components.

After this introduction of the building stones in a reconstruction of social facts and phenomena, the next topic is to account for the specific tools used for the reconstruction. What kind of logic can we use to establish and evaluate the congruence between theoretical generalisations and observations of the world?

References

Beach, D. (2016). It's all about mechanisms – What process-tracing case studies should be tracing. *New Political Economy*, 1–10. https://doi.org/10.1080/1 3563467.2015.1134466

Beach, D., & Pedersen, R. B. (2014). *Process-tracing methods: Foundations and guidelines*. Ann Arbor, MI: University of Michigan Press.

Bourdieu, P. (1990). *The logic of practice (Orig: Le Sense Pratique)*. Oxford, UK: Polity Press.

Bukve, O. (2003). Forståing og forklaring i samfunnsvitskapen (Understanding and explanation in the social sciences). *Tidsskrift for samfunnsforskning, 44*(3), 391–415.

Cartwright, N. (2006). Where is the theory in our "theories" of causality? *The Journal of Philosophy, 103*(2), 55–66.

Clarke, K. A., & Primo, D. M. (2007). Modernizing political science: A model-based approach. *Perspectives on Politics, 5*(04), 741–753. https://doi.org/10.1017/S1537592707072192

Clarke, K. A., & Primo, D. M. (2012). *A model discipline: Political science and the logic of representations*. Oxford, UK: Oxford University Press.

Collier, D., & Mahon, J. E. (1993). Conceptual "stretching" revisited: Adapting categories in comparative analysis. *The American Political Science Review*, *87*(4), 845–855. https://doi.org/10.2307/2938818

Downs, A. (1957). An economic theory of political action in a democracy. *Journal of Political Economy*, *65*(2), 135–150.

Ferraris, M. (2014). *Manifesto of new realism*. Albany, NY: Suny Press.

Giere, R. N. (1999). Using models to represent reality. In L. Magnani, N. J. Nersessian, & P. Thagard (Eds.), *Model-based reasoning in scientific discovery*. New York: Kluwer Academic/Plenum Publishers.

Goertz, G. (2006). *Social science concepts: A user's guide*. Princeton, NJ: Princeton University Press.

Habermas, J. (1982). *Zur Logik der Sozialwissenschaften*. Frankfurt am Main, Germany: Suhrkamp.

Habermas, J. (1990). Reconstruction and interpretation in the social sciences. In *Moral consciousness and communicative action* (pp. 21–42). Cambridge, UK: Polity Press.

Hacking, I. (1999). *The social construction of what?* Cambridge, MA: Harvard University Press.

Khan, D. (Director). (2015). *Jihad: A story of the others* [Documentary film]. Oslo, Norway: Fuuse Film.

Kuhn, T. S. (1996). *The structure of scientific revolutions*. Chicago: University of Chicago Press.

Lakatos, I. (1978). *The methodology of scientific research programmes* (Vol. 1). Cambridge, UK: Cambridge University Press.

Mayntz, R. (2004). Mechanisms in the analysis of social macro-phenomena. *Philosophy of the Social Sciences*, *34*(2), 237–259.

Ragin, C. C., & Amoroso, L. M. (2011). *Constructing social research*. Thousand Oaks, CA: Pine Forge Press.

Rittel, H., & Webber, M. (1974). Wicked problems. *Man-Made Futures*, *26*(1), 272–280.

Sartori, G. (1970). Concept misformation in comparative politics. *American Political Science Review*, *64*(04), 1033–1053.

Searle, J. R. (1995). *The construction of social reality*. London: Allen Lane.

Searle, J. R. (2008). Language and social ontology. *Theory and Society*, *37*(5), 443–459.

Sohlberg, P., & Sohlberg, B.-M. (2013). *Kunskapens former: vetenskapsteori och forskningsmetod*. Stockholm: Liber.

CHAPTER 4

The Logic and Methodological Rules of Reconstruction

A main issue in all research is how to establish and test the correspondence between on the one hand theoretical ideas and analytical frames, and on the other hand observations and data. What rules and approaches do we use when trying to understand and explain observations by help of theory, or when changing the theories as a result of new observations and ideas? Throughout history, philosophers of science have been divided into two different camps concerning these questions. One tradition, also called the positivist tradition, emphasises the alternation between on the one hand observations and the formulation of general theories, also called laws, and on the other hand testing of theories through new observations. The rules for how to draw conclusions from observations to generalisations, then again from generalisations to expected observations, are usually called the hypothetical-deductive method. The other tradition has a special emphasis on interpreting and understanding social actors' intentions and reasons for actions, and how social action gets to be understandable and meaningful in light of the social situation and totality that the actors are part of. This tradition is commonly known as the hermeneutic tradition. We could say that the positivist tradition focuses on external explanations of social phenomena, whereas the hermeneutic tradition is interested in understanding and in internal explanations. These traditions are often considered to be competing with contradictory views of what social science is about. However, the tendency in today's social science is that the two traditions

© The Author(s) 2019
O. Bukve, *Designing Social Science Research,*
https://doi.org/10.1007/978-3-030-03979-0_4

53

54   O. BUKVE

are perceived as complementary; they support each other by giving access to different aspects of social phenomena and patterns.

A further question is whether the two traditions, through their self-understanding and explanations of their own practice, are able to give an adequate understanding of what researchers do when they exercise their craft. What does it mean in reality to establish connections between general or categorical statements on the one hand, and observations or data about individual phenomena or acts on the other? Many philosophers of science today would say that it means making visible the particular mechanisms (Cartwright, 2006; Mayntz, 2004) that mediate between an underlying cause and its effects, rather than concluding from a general law to a specific effect. This view will be concretised in the following section.

HYPOTHETICAL-DEDUCTIVE RESEARCH LOGIC: EXPLAINING BY LAWS

In the first chapter I made a distinction between observation statements and categorical statements. Observation statements deal with real phenomena or conditions: "The apple falls to the ground." "Labour lost the British parliament election in 2010." "The sale of electric cars is, relatively seen, larger in Norway than in any other country." Categorical statements are, on the other hand, general; they have to do with what a number of phenomena have in common: "Gravity makes loose objects fall." "Parties on the left suffer losses when the share of the working class in the population decreases." "Norwegians are the most environmentally friendly nation."

The strategy of concluding from the first type of statements to the second is called induction. Induction means that we draw conclusions from a number of individual cases to the whole universe or population. If we make a sufficient amount of observations of falling apples, losing left-wing parties, or the choices of car buyers, we have a basis for formulating generalisations. At the entrance to modernity, in the sixteenth century, Francis Bacon advocated the inductive method as the road to reliable knowledge. Inductive thinking is no doubt an important part of scientific knowledge development; however, as we have seen, science philosophers found that the inductive method alone cannot give us reliable knowledge. There is always a possibility that new observations may falsify a generalisation; thus, inductive reasoning can only make a categorical statement probable, but it cannot prove it. Moreover, inductive thinking shows little understanding of the role our cognitive frames play in the way we form our generalisations. As we have seen in the first chapter, our pre-understanding contributes to characterising what we observe. Inductive logic has little to say about this phenomenon.

Deductive logic is about making deductions from a general or categorical statement to what must happen in individual cases. If gravity works, the apple will fall when I drop it. If left-wing parties decrease when the working class decreases, we can predict future election results in a country, based on data about the composition of classes in that society. And if Norwegians are the most environmentally friendly nation, we can predict what they will do when buying a car as well as their behaviour in other areas where choices influence the environment. If a general statement is reliable, it can be used to predict what will happen in individual cases covered by the generalisation. This is the starting point of hypothesis testing, that is, that we formulate a general statement of what will happen under certain assumptions and then study whether the law predicts the right result.

Hypothetical-deductive thinking is probably the most well-known form of research logic and the one which is most frequently used when we explain how researchers think. As research logic it is related to a theory of science approach that had its golden age between the two world wars and is called logical positivism (Johansson, Kalleberg, & Liedman, 1972). The positivist programme was about building a unitary science; the positivists did not acknowledge the special characteristics of social science that I outlined in the first chapters. Still, they have played an important role in the development of the theory of science.

In short, the hypothetical-deductive method entails an alternation between an inductively based formation of hypotheses and a deductively based testing of hypotheses and theories. The knowledge development is cumulative through a merger of hypotheses about closely related phenomena into more extensive syntheses or theories. The logic of the hypothetical-deductive method is illustrated in Fig. 4.1. Good theories are those that resist multiple and systematic attempts at falsification. The case of gravity influencing objects so that they fall to the ground is an example of a theory that has resisted many attempts at falsification. The statement that Norwegians are more environmentally friendly than others has hardly been tested as extensively. It is possible to envision various forms of testing this claim. One way of testing is collecting data from a number of various social areas, for instance data on general consumption patterns, environ-

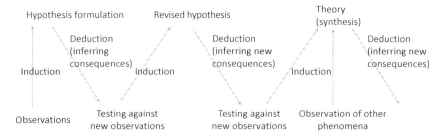

Fig. 4.1 Hypothetical-deductive research logic

mentally friendly travel, the amount of energy used for various purposes. Data indicate that the general assumption of Norwegians being the most environmentally friendly nation would get a shot across the bow. Norwegians would not score especially well in other areas than the purchase of electric cars. The interesting question in the next round is, then, why car purchase is the area where Norwegians are apparently environmentally friendly. We would need to dig deeper into this field, by collecting data about tax policies and prices, the right to use public-transport lanes, and so on. We could also ask car buyers why they choose a particular type of car. In this way we can form a more nuanced picture of what mechanisms are in force when Norwegians choose their type of car. I have not performed such an investigation. But from what I know, it is easy to envisage some probable hypotheses. It could be true that some Norwegians buy an electric car primarily for environmentally friendly purposes, others could be more interested in purchase price and operation costs, while others again are primarily interested in getting rid of long queues since they will have access to the public-transport lanes.

What can be seen from the last examples is that there will often be a need for external as well as internal strategies of explanation when we study complex social phenomena. The examples indicate that it will be useful to apply both hypothetical-deductive and interpretative research logic to analyse and draw inferences about the phenomena we study. The two logics support a perception of causal explanations and intentional explanations as complementary rather than competitive. In order to explain why social patterns emerge and are reproduced we need both the external approach of the hypothetical-deductive method and the internal explanations that are directed towards explaining individual acts and occurrences. About the latter, the abductive and the hermeneutic research logics have more to offer than positivism.

Abductive Research Logic: Uncovering Social Mechanisms

Hypothetical-deductive philosophy of science has often presented phenomena in nature and society as the product of general laws. Scientific activity is about uncovering the laws that cause individual phenomena in nature and society. But do such laws really exist, or are they mere abstractions? Let us take gravity as an example. Newton's law states that gravity influences objects with a constant force. From a hypothetical-deductive method this law is then proved through multiple observations of falling objects. But, says science philosopher Nancy Cartwright, is this really what we observe (Cartwright, 1983)? Our daily observations show us that objects fall in quite different ways. Leaves fall very slowly to the ground, and a gust of wind can make them move upwards as well as downwards. Flags can hang down, or horizontally in the wind, whereas heavy objects fall quickly. In other words, Newton's law is an abstraction that does not tell us very much about what really goes on around us. What goes on in reality is the product of many cooperating factors and specific mechanisms that influence the actual object. General laws are abstractions; they do not express specific causal relations.

Cartwright doubts the usefulness of hunting for general laws rather than uncovering the specific causal relations that we can approach (Cartwright, 2006). What should interest scientists is trying to trace the specific mechanisms that lead to an observed result. The wind, the specific weight and the form of the falling object, the gravity at that particular place—all these factors cooperate to create a falling movement. So too with the purchase of an electric car. The pattern we can observe is produced by actors with different reasons and frames of understanding as the cause of their choice. We should try to grasp the mechanisms of these specific causal relations (Beach, 2016; Mayntz, 2004).

It is debated what could constitute an adequate uncovering of mechanisms. One understanding is that the explanation of mechanisms involves finding the intermediate variables between cause and effect. Another understanding is that mechanisms should be seen as cooperating, making up parts of a total system. The sum of the factors in a given context makes up the mechanism (Beach, 2016; Beach & Pedersen, 2014). I will return to this in the discussion of case studies in Chap. 7. In the present section I discuss the logic we follow when trying to uncover mechanisms.

In science as well as in everyday life we often reflect on possible explanations of a phenomenon without following formal logic. When I get up in the morning and observe that the lawn is wet, I think that it must have rained. This is an "as if" explanation, where I think of a few conditions of the kind that if they are correct, they would have resulted in the observation I make. The reasoning I made about the purchase of electric cars in the section above is of the same kind. If it is so that people are interested in the economical side of owning a car, it could be a good reason for choosing an electric car. If they wish not be stuck in traffic jams, that could be a good reason for choosing an electric car. And if they wish to be environmentally friendly, that too can be a good reason for choosing a car that does not drive on fossil fuel. By creating such possible explanations of an observed phenomenon, we develop specific hypotheses that we can test through new inquiries and the collection of new data.

This type of methodical reasoning is called abduction. Interest in abductive logic has increased strongly among science theorists in recent years. Yet the idea is not new. The first scholar to account for abductive reasoning was the American philosopher Charles Saunders Peirce around 1900 (Peirce, 1972). He alternatively used the concepts abduction and retroduction as terms for this type of creative development of "if then" explanations (Hookway, 2016).

In abductive thinking, the relationship between premises and conclusions is different from what it is deduction. In deduction we know that if the premises, in the form of a hypothesis or a law, are true then the conclusion will follow from the premises. In abductive thinking, however, we go backwards from an observed conclusion and form premises and causal mechanisms of a kind that if they were true, the conclusion would be reasonable. So far, we are talking about a reasonable or possible connection, not a connection that is logically necessary. Through abductive thinking we can develop different possible explanations of one and the same phenomenon. Thus, such thinking also opens up for different forms of testing of ideas through practical testing or production of data that are relevant for the testing of connections and relations. In many ways the description of abduction is a description of an approach to practical problem solution. When facing a practical, everyday problem, we start with guessing at possible causes for the problem before trying to solve it through specific measures.

Peirce claimed that researchers often used abduction in actual scientific practice, but also that philosophers of science presented an insufficient explanation of this practice when they explained scientific thinking as the use of a hypothetical-deductive method. What Peirce actually did was describing the approach of science understood as representation or reconstruction of phenomena in society and nature. By practising abductive thinking, we are able to bridge theoretical frames of understanding and real observations and at the same time outline specific data collection inquiries that may contribute to testing the reliability of the hypothetical connections. Abductive thinking focuses on specific and context-dependent explanations rather than general laws. Abduction as a research logic is oriented towards finding which one of competing theories is the most usable, rather than testing an individual theory. However, theory testing has its place also within an abduction-based research logic (Fig. 4.2).

Hermeneutic Research Logic: Interpretative Understanding of Social Phenomena

While positivist research logic is closely linked to natural science research and presents it as a model for social science as well, hermeneutic research logic is oriented towards the specific characteristics of research dealing with society and human beings.

Hermeneutics was developed as a method for Bible interpretation with the aim of interpreting texts written in another time and language, making them understandable in the present time while maintaining the original meaning. From that point hermeneutics developed into a general method for philological text interpretation with the purpose of fully understanding the intention of the author. In the nineteenth century the German philosopher Wilhelm Dilthey called attention to hermeneutics as the right

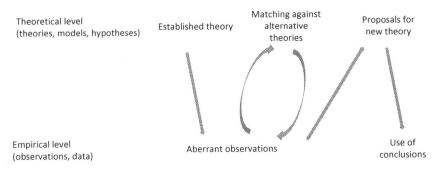

Fig. 4.2 Abductive research logic

method for the humanities, opposed to the focus on the positivist method in the natural sciences. To Dilthey, hermeneutics was not only a method for text interpretation, but for studying social phenomena in light of their historical and social contexts. Based on Heidegger's philosophy, hermeneutics was given an existentialist angle in the twentieth century with Hans Georg Gadamer as an important name. Gadamer regarded human beings as active makers of meaning. We are in constant dialogue with the world around us to understand and interpret it, and this interpretative dialogue is regarded as a fundamental characteristic of human behaviour (Gadamer, 1997/1960).

Hermeneutics is built on the belief that people connect meaning to their acts and statements. We cannot understand this meaning by studying social acts through an external research strategy. If we explain individual acts by looking at external causes, we reify socially constructed rules and pre-suppositions by considering them as inviolable natural laws.

Instead, we must look at re-presentation and reconstruction of social phenomena mainly as a matter of interpretation in order to understand. Many hermeneutically oriented researchers believe that the essential goal of social science is to interpret social phenomena for the sake of understanding, not to work out general laws or predict occurrences based on such laws. Interpretative understanding stems from looking at the individual phenomenon in its particular context. Social actors act on the basis of certain frames of understanding. To make these acts appear meaningful to us, we have to see them in the light of the context that makes the actors act the way they do.

Based on his concept of knowledge interest, Jürgen Habermas developed his critical version of hermeneutics. Scientific interpretation is supposed to free us from ideologies and false forms of understanding (Habermas, 1974/1968). In a later phase of his work Habermas distinguished between the different interests we can have in relation to the world: communicative, strategic, and expressive interests (Habermas, 1984), and he emphasised unconstrained communication as the ideal.

Paul Ricoeur is often considered the last of the great hermeneutists. He criticised Habermas' ideas of social science as ideology criticism by saying that nobody can claim a point of view outside the ideologies; we will always approach the world from a particular point of view or position (Ricoeur, 1988a(1986)). One of Ricoeur's key points is that what is said or written will have its own life, independent of the intention of the author. With his own formulation: "What the interpreter says, is a re-saying that reactivates what is said in the text" (Ricoeur, 1988b(1986), p. 64). To Ricoeur, hermeneutics is primarily a method of text interpretation, not of dialogical understanding of the author's intentions.

Ricoeur developed a set of methodological rules for such an interpretation, among other things, creating the expression "the hermeneutics of suspicion". This entails that a text should also be judged as a strategic act, not only as a specific interpretation of the world. Ricoeur's hermeneutics is an important starting point for discourse analysis, which will be introduced later in this chapter.

The raw material for modern hermeneutic analysis is usually, in line with Ricoeur's philosophy, understood as a text. Texts can be verbal statements from one or more persons. They can also be descriptions of acts, phenomena, or connections. Lastly, we can view gestures and symbols as material for hermeneutic analyses.

Broadly stated, we can distinguish between three ways of interpreting a text using the hermeneutic logic (Westlund, 2009). First, we may want to get at what the author or the speaker really says and what it is directed at; what is the real message in the text? The text is seen as a message or communication from sender to receiver. An interpretation from this perspective is usually called existential hermeneutics. Westlund (2009) gives an example of an utterance that can be interpreted from such an angle, by citing a pupil's statement broadly like this: "I am so tired of always having to do homework in the weekends." Applying existential hermeneutics, the message of this statement could be either that the pupil is frustrated and gives vent to emotions, or that this pupil claims there is too much homework, and that teachers who give such a workload are unreasonable. To judge the two interpretations against each other, we must know the context in which the statement was uttered. In other words, we need to know the totality of the utterance.

The other orientation of a hermeneutic interpretation is that which we can call the hermeneutics of suspicion. What does the speaker really wish to achieve with what she says? An interpretation using this perspective could for instance find that the pupil tries to influence the teacher to give less homework. From this perspective, we judge the speaker as a strategic actor. This perspective, like the one mentioned above, depends on knowing the actor's position in a social context. How is the speaker positioned in a social field, and what are the interests of the actor in this position? Is she a conscientious pupil who feels overloaded by homework and is crying for help? Is she a pupil who is not so interested in school work and only wants it to be as easy as possible? Or does she have other plans for this weekend and sees the homework as ill-timed, therefore she tries to influence her teacher to act to her advantage? (Fig. 4.3).

The third orientation in hermeneutics concerns the general interpretation of the situation in which the utterance or text is given. Let us say that the topic of the analysis is not so much the individual statement, but rather the statement seen as an element in understanding the situation of lower secondary school pupils in 2018. In this case, it will be necessary to combine various texts and utterances about lower secondary school to give a total picture. The way we approach this issue is defined by the underlying knowledge we have of the entire education system and what goes on in this area, in addition to our assumptions about teaching and pedagogy in more general terms. This interpretation has several layers. While existential hermeneutics often interprets on the background of everyday knowledge and does not build on specific theories, hermeneutics as a general study of interpretation requires researchers to clarify their main frames of understanding and the ideas they base their work on.

Fig. 4.3 The hermeneutic circle

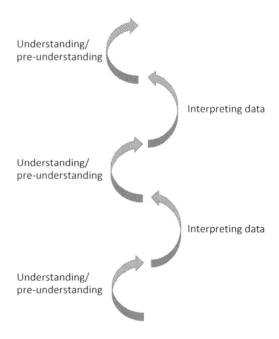

What the various levels of interpretation have in common is an alternation between interpretation of singular acts and re-evaluation of our understanding of the totality or context where the acts are taking place. This alternation is often called the hermeneutic circle. We could just as well call it the hermeneutic spiral, because a hermeneutic interpretation can also lead to a re-evaluation of the frames of interpretation or the pre suppositions. The principle is that each statement or each text element is interpreted as part of a whole. In the research process we alternate between constructing a holistic understanding that complies with the individual element that is being interpreted and finding out whether new individual elements can be interpreted on the basis of the understanding of context we already have. This can be compared to looking at a piece from a puzzle and trying to imagine the whole picture that will emerge when the puzzle has been put together, or with having almost finished the puzzle but wondering if the piece we just picked up really fits into this puzzle. Can it be fit in or do we need to make a new puzzle to fit it in? When the pieces do not fit in, that is, when we find text elements that are opposed to the main content of the text, our interpretation is challenged. One of the most important features of hermeneutic interpretation is that we are open to such contradictions; we should not overlook the individual elements that do not fit into our pre-interpretation.

Hermeneutic method is often criticised from the side of positivism for not being interested in or suited for developing generalisations. We can say that positivists regard hermeneutic-oriented studies of an event, a text, or a phenomenon as generalisations based on a single observation, hence less reliable. However, the hermeneutic spiral can also be interpreted in another way. If in a hermeneutic study the researcher alternates between on the one hand establishing a context understanding from individual elements and on the other hand interpreting individual elements in light of the context, this process can be regarded as a series of single observations following each other, thus giving a basis for critical revision of established interpretations. In this way, well-constructed studies founded on hermeneutic method may give a basis for statements with a wider range than for that specific case.

CRITICAL THEORY

The three levels of hermeneutic interpretation introduced above are not the only division into different levels and forms of interpretation. Critical theory, for instance, sees triple hermeneutics differently. Here, the division is between the active actor's interpretation of the world, the researcher's interpretation of the actor, and on the third level the interpretation of the unconscious processes, the ideologies, the power, and dominance relations that make the actor interpret the world the way she does (Alvesson & Sköldberg, 2000, p. 144). Critical theory is rooted in Marxist social analysis and was developed by a group of German social scientists and philosophers of the so-called Frankfurt School. Critical theory is critical in that it aims to disclose the unconscious assumptions in our way of interpreting the world. In critical theory, conventional hermeneutics is criticised for postulating a common framework of understanding and thus seeing social harmony as an ideal.

The strength of critical theory is that it may make us aware of alternative interpretations and so give those a voice that are not otherwise heard. Yet critical theory can be criticised too, for assuming a point of standing where only the researcher is free from ideological bindings and tunnel vision (Ricoeur, 1988a(1986)). This criticism is largely the starting point of discourse analysis, which is introduced in the next section.

DISCOURSE ANALYTICAL RESEARCH LOGIC: HEGEMONIC AND ALTERNATIVE FRAMEWORKS OF UNDERSTANDING

Discourse analysis is the youngest of the research logics presented in this book. As a research logic, it is a legitimate child of linguistic-social constructivism. The focus of discourse analysis is how language discourses constitute the world for us as well as how we constitute the world through language.

A discourse can be understood as a particular way of talking about and understanding the world (Winther Jørgensen & Phillips, 1999, p. 9). A little more detailed and technical we could say that the discourse is a system of producing statements and practices that constitute the world to those who are the bearers of the discourse (Neumann, 2001, p. 177). The latter definition emphasises that we as individuals as well as our understanding of the world are formed by the discourses we are included in. The discourses contribute to producing our self-perception or identity. We could say that the discourses supply ready-made subject positions for us (Neumann, 2001, p. 177). When a specific framework of understanding is dominant in the social context we are part of, we tend to take these frames for granted; we understand ourselves as well as the surrounding world with such hegemonic discourses as the starting point. So far, discourse analysis is in line with critical theory, which is its source and which it also criticises. But discourse analysis is more complex because it takes into account that discourses and subject positions are not necessarily unambiguous.

One example of discourse is the discourse about nurses. It forms our understanding of what it is to be a nurse. But we can see that this discourse is not unambiguous; there is an ongoing debate about what it is that constitutes nursing as an academic field and as a profession. Within this discourse there is a discourse of evidence and a discourse of care. The evidence discourse understands nursing as a scientifically based field, where we base care and development of new practices on evidence that is analysed using hypothetical-deductive logic. Contrary to that, the care discourse emphasises that the direct relations between nurse and patient and the encounter with the patient as a person are the starting point for giving assistance.

Discourse analysis offers some concepts for analysing such situations. The main concepts are discourse order, hegemony, and discursive practices. The concept of discourse order, originally formulated by Norman Fairclough, can be understood as the sum of the types of discourses that are present within a social field or a social institution (Winther Jørgensen & Phillips, 1999). Between the different types of discourse there can be contrasts and contest about which discourses give the correct understanding of that particular field. We can say that these discourse types fight for the hegemony (Gramsci, 1973; Laclau & Mouffe, 2001) or authority (Weber, 1971/1922) within the field. This fight takes place through discursive practices. Depending on what relations the discursive practices have to each other, discourse orders can be more or less open.

We can describe a discourse order by looking at what discourses are present in a field, how they construct reality through their discursive practices, what interdependent positions they have (discourse positions), and to what degree a position is hegemonic (Dunn & Neumann, 2016; Neumann, 2001). When a form of discourse or representation of the world dominates in such a way that it appears to be more or less self-evident, we can talk about a hegemonic state. However, such hegemonic conditions do not last on their own accord; they must always be reconfirmed through language, through our linguistic or discursive practice. In other words, they need discursive work. For a long time, the care discourse had such a hegemonic discourse position in the nursing discourses. Only in the last decades has the evidence discourse become a contender. It may be that this discourse has come to the fore because the field of nursing is no longer the definite point of reference for nursing discourses. While the fields of nurses and physicians used to be hierarchically divided with the doctors at the top, both professions are today included in a discursively constructed health field with several professions relating to each other. In this context, evidence discourse becomes an alternative discourse in order to give nurses a more powerful position in the field.

Discourses, and in particular hegemonic discourses, are enshrined or institutionalised in social institutions, thus gaining a material existence. Discourses on nursing may become an integral part of institutions that educate nurses, in accreditation agencies and curriculum-producing agencies, in professional organisations, in professional journals, and in the public authority agencies that regulate the profession and its activity in the health care sector. According to Neumann (p. 177), institutionalising a discourse means formalising the statements and practices that constitute the discourse. This is done in the type of institutions mentioned above. These institutions authorise certain discourses and discursive practices as the possible, correct, and normal ones. Other discourses are out-defined through the formalisation and routinisation of practices that take place in the institutions (Fig. 4.4).

Macro analyses from a discourse analytical position usually investigate the relations between discursive practices in a social field and the institutions. Their starting point can be a social institution or a social field with the aim of investigating what subject positions and discursive practices are produced and accepted in that context. The other way around, we can study how discursive practices in a field will lead to institutionalisation. If such fields are studied over time, we can see how different discourses compete for hegemony with more or less success, and how through this the field is institutionalised or deinstitutionalised (Neumann, 2001; Schmidt, 2008).

Discourse analysis can also be micro-oriented. In that case, the discourse analyst is interested in analysing texts, how they have been formed as part of discursive practices, and how such practices are dependent on and influence other social practices and institutions. Main concepts for the analysis of texts are statements, intertextuality, and monuments. A statement is the smallest building stone of a text. Intertextuality shows that texts merge into each other, that a text builds on other texts by referring to them. Neumann shows that within a number of discursive fields a few texts will gain status as monuments; they become reference texts that we refer to when describing how the field is constituted (Neumann, 2001).

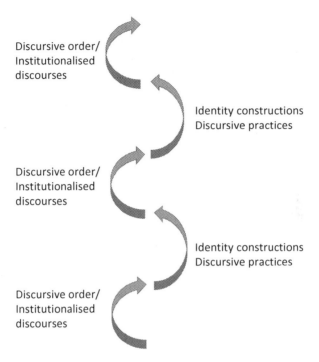

Fig. 4.4 The discourse analytical logic

Neither are texts the only possible starting point for discourse analysis. We can also use events and processes as starting points. Other starting points may be that we organise the analysis around an object or a subject position. In the latter case the main issues will be for instance: How do individuals construct their identity? What identity repertoire do they activate, and can they activate from a given position?

Critical ambition is a common ambition for discourse analysts. An essential question is what is being excluded by the dominant discourse type in a field. Whose voices are not heard when a type of discourse is more or less taken for granted? Discourse analysis can be used to get at alternative perspectives of reality, to see that another world is possible. Researchers can join a discursive field as participants; they are not placed outside society but can influence it by virtue of their ways of re-presenting social phenomena.

Methodically, discourse analysis is a developing field. Thus, it is not possible to refer to an authoritative version of the way it is supposed to be performed. A basic piece of advice is to choose the method in accordance with the topic and level that are to be analysed, and to use method books suitable for such topics and levels. Another piece of advice is based on the fact that for discourse analysts, theory and method are intertwined. It is therefore important to study the content of relevant theories and the context of the field we want to research. It is a mistaken belief to think that we may enter an empirical field without any presuppositions. It is therefore a sound piece of advice to make this pre-understanding as solid and explicit as possible. Directing our interest towards changes, breakdowns, and open fields can also serve as advice for finding an interesting topic. Michel Foucault, the founder of discourse analysis, wrote no methodology book himself. However, he gave advice. For instance, about being open to several methods. And about learning the method through observing it in use rather than through recipes. In other words, getting to know other researchers' analyses and learn from them.

A Comparison of the Research Logics

The research logics presented in this chapter have different purposes and foci for the analyses. The differences are summed up in Table 4.1. Nevertheless, there is a common feature of all research logics, namely the question of how to establish a correspondence between theoretical ideas and empirical data. Yet the different logics give different answers to how the reconstruction takes place.

Hypothetical-deductive research logic builds on the controlled experiment as an ideal, and on falsification of established hypotheses and theories as the road to success in research. We need many observations of similar cases and of results coherent with our theory in order to be convinced of the robustness of some theoretical ideas. The logic of hypothetical-deductive reasoning is directed at testing theories to find out whether they are valid. It has less to say on the development of new ideas and theories.

The other research logics are more about how to proceed in order to eliminate rivalling ideas and theories as far as possible. They build on a more pluralistic basis: that there usually are several possible explanations for and interpretations of social patterns and events. The task of social

Table 4.1 Comparison of research logics

Research logic	Main purpose	Analytical focus
Hypothetical-deductive	Effect analysis and prediction	Testing of hypotheses in controlled conditions
Abduction	Explaining the conditions for an observed result	Tracing possible processes or chains of events
Hermeneutics	Text interpretation Contextualised interpretation—the whole in light of the element and the element in light of the whole	The content of an utterance The actor's purpose with the utterance The situation that the utterance is part of
Critical theory	Ideology criticism	The actor's interpretation of the world The researcher's interpretation of the actor The researcher's interpretation of the structures that govern the actor's interpretation
Discourse analysis	Uncovering our reconstruction of the world through language and discourse	Discourse order and discursive practices in a field Institutionalisation of discourses How texts and events are produced and how they influence discursive practices and institutions The subject's construction of identity

scientists is to use available data to support a claim that some of these explanations are more probable than other ones, or to build a probable explanation that we may later test in more detail.

Presenting different interpretations and theories as well as testing them against each other is a more fundamental logic than the falsification logic. Falsification observations alone do not create new knowledge. New knowledge occurs when we have presented a more convincing explanation of the phenomenon or connections we observed. Thus, scientific work has to do with assessing rivalling theories and hypotheses against each other and not only with falsifying or verifying individual hypotheses (Campbell, 1984; Lakatos, 1978). If we accept that theory development and theory testing are necessary parts of the reconstruction of phenomena and connections in society, it also makes sense to understand the presented research logics as complementary rather than alternatives that we cannot combine.

70   O. BUKVE

A property of the research logics, apart from the hypothetical-deductive logic, is that they are focused on the study of social facts and phenomena in a given context or situation. The interaction between the specific context and the phenomenon is in focus. For instance, the focus of analysis in hermeneutics is either an utterance in light of a given situation or an utterance in light of the actor who makes the utterance and wishes to achieve something. In discourse analysis, we study how a given discourse order produces specific discursive practices and thus the actors' interpretation of the world, or how subjects are constructing their identity in a given discursive context.

These logics also focus on the mutual interaction between phenomenon and context. Strategic actors can change a given situation, and discursive practices can produce new frames of understanding and orders of discourse.

We can say that hermeneutics and discourse analysis are concerned with the production of contextualised and situational explanations rather than with abstract generalisations that ignore time and space. Such explanations utilise and may contribute to developing a so-called middle range theory (Boudon, 1991; Merton, 1968).

The following chapters will show how the different research logics are relevant for and used in various research designs.

REFERENCES

Alvesson, M., & Sköldberg, K. (2000). *Reflexive methodology. New vistas for qualitative research.* London: Sage.

Beach, D. (2016). It's all about mechanisms – What process-tracing case studies should be tracing. *New Political Economy*, 1–10. https://doi.org/10.1080/1 3563467.2015.1134466

Beach, D., & Pedersen, R. B. (2014). *Process-tracing methods: Foundations and guidelines.* Ann Arbor, MI: University of Michigan Press.

Boudon, R. (1991). What Middle-Range Theories Are. [Robert K. Merton: Consensus and Controversy., Jon Clark, Celia Modgil, Sohan Modgil; Puritanism and the Rise of Modern Science: The Merton Thesis., I. Bernard Cohen, K. E. Duffin, Stuart Strickland; "After Merton": Protestant and Catholic Science in Seventeenth-Century Europe., Rivka Feldhay, Yehuda Elkana; The Focused Interview: A Manual of Procedures., Robert K. Merton, Marjorie Fiske, Patricia L. Kendall; L'Opera di R. K. Merton e la Sociologia Contemporanea., Carlo Mongardini, Simonetta Tabboni]. *Contemporary Sociology, 20*(4), 519–522.

THE LOGIC AND METHODOLOGICAL RULES OF RECONSTRUCTION   71

Campbell, D. T. (1984). Foreword. In R. K. Yin (Ed.), *Case study research. Design and methods.* Beverly Hills, CA: Sage.

Cartwright, N. (1983). *How the laws of physics lie.* Oxford/New York: Oxford University Press/Clarendon Press.

Cartwright, N. (2006). Where is the theory in our "theories" of causality? *The Journal of Philosophy, 103*(2), 55–66.

Dunn, K. C., & Neumann, I. B. (2016). *Undertaking discourse analysis for social research.* Ann Arbor, MI: University of Michigan Press.

Gadamer, H.-G. (1997/1960). *Sanning och metod: i urval (Orig. Wahrheit und Methode).* Göteborg, Sweden: Daidalos.

Gramsci, A. (1973). *Politikk og kultur: artikler, opptegnelser og brev fra fengslet* (Vol. F255). Oslo, Norway: Gyldendal.

Habermas, J. (1974/1968). *Vitenskap som ideologi (Orig. Technik und Wissenschaft als "Ideologie")* (2. oppl. ed.). Oslo, Norway: Gyldendal.

Habermas, J. (1984). *The theory of communicative action* (Vol. 1). Boston: Beacon Press.

Hookway, C. (2016). "*Pragmatism*". *The Stanford encyclopedia of philosophy* (Summer 2016 ed., Edward N. Zalta, Ed.). URL = .

Johansson, I., Kalleberg, R., & Liedman, S.-E. (1972). *Positivism, marxism, kritisk teori: riktningar inom modern vetenskapsfilosofi* (3. uppl. ed.). Stockholm: Pan/Norstedts.

Laclau, E., & Mouffe, C. (2001). *Hegemony and socialist strategy: Towards a radical democratic politics.* London: Verso.

Lakatos, I. (1978). *The methodology of scientific research programmes* (Vol. 1). Cambridge: Cambridge University Press.

Mayntz, R. (2004). Mechanisms in the analysis of social macro-phenomena. *Philosophy of the Social Sciences, 34*(2), 237–259.

Merton, R. K. (1968). *Social theory and social structure* (Enl. ed.). New York: The Free Press.

Neumann, I. B. (2001). *Mening, materialitet, makt: en innføring i diskursanalyse.* Bergen, Norway: Fagbokforl.

Peirce, C. S. (1972). *Charles Sanders Peirce. Selected texts by I. Gullvåg.* Oslo, Norway: Pax.

Ricoeur, P. (1988a (1986)). Hermeneutik och ideologikritik. In *Från text till handling: en antologi om hermeneutik (Orig.: Du texte à l'action, Essais d'hermenutiques)* (Vol. 1). Stockholm: Brutus Östlings bokförlag Symposion.

Ricoeur, P. (1988b (1986)). Vad är en text? In *Från text till handling: en antologi om hermeneutik (Orig.: Du texte à l'action, Essais d'hermenutiques)* (Vol. 1). Stockholm: Brutus Östlings bokförlag Symposion.

Schmidt, V. A. (2008). Discursive institutionalism: The explanatory power of ideas and discourse. *Annual Review of Political Science, 11*, 303–326.

72 O. BUKVE

Weber, M. (1971/1922). *Makt og byräkrati: essays om politikk og klasse, samfunns-forskning og verdier (Orig. Wirtschaft und Gesellschaft, part III, ch. 1)*. Oslo: Gyldendal.

Westlund, I. (2009). Hermeneutik. In A. Fejes & R. Thornberg (Eds.), *Handbok i kvalitativ analys* (pp. 62–80). Stockholm: Liber.

Winther Jørgensen, M., & Phillips, L. (1999). *Diskursanalyse som teori og metode*. Frederiksberg, Denmark: Roskilde Universitetsforl. Samfundslitteratur.

CHAPTER 5

Design of Research Projects

This chapter takes its starting point in the definition of research designs that I presented in the introduction: A research design is a plan for how to carry out a research project. This plan or structure has two parts. One is the purpose of the project, in other words what knowledge we want to develop about what. I distinguish between different purposes that can govern the research interest in a research project: Theory testing, theory development, theoretical interpretation, and lastly an intervention orientation.

The other element in the design has to do with how we construct data to answer our questions. I here distinguish between variable-centred and case-centred strategies as two main forms of data construction and show how they point to different approaches in the production and analysis of data. Used for different research purposes, these two basic strategies for data construction constitute a number of designs discussed in the next two chapters about variable-centred designs and case designs. We can also combine the main strategies for design in various ways. Depending on the purpose, such combinations are the basis of integrative designs, comparative designs, and intervention-oriented designs, all of which are introduced in Chaps. 8, 9, and 10.

© The Author(s) 2019
O. Bukve, *Designing Social Science Research*,
https://doi.org/10.1007/978-3-030-03979-0_5

Research Purposes, Data Construction, and the Phases of the Design Process

A research design can be understood as a plan for how to organise a research project to make sure we get from questions to answers (Yin, 1984, p. 28). In this plan we work out and make visible the logical structure of the project (De Vaus & de Vaus, 2001). In other words, we create a design to think through and make sure we answer our questions with the best arguments we can find. Working out the logical structure of a project entails accounting for the two different parts of the research process and the connection between them.

- The first task of a research design is clarifying the purpose of our project. We could also call the purpose a knowledge goal. Generally, research has to do with finding new knowledge. It is for instance possible to test established theories and concepts against new data to find out whether they match or to find out in which contexts and faced with what phenomena they have explanatory power. Further, we can aim at developing theories and concepts that explain empirical findings better than the explanations we have today. Yet another type of knowledge goal can be about using established theories and concepts as tools to understand and explain the phenomenon or phenomena we are studying. Clarifying the conditions for purpose-directed change of social phenomena could also be a goal for our research.
- The second task in working out the design is forming a strategy for data construction. A strategy for data construction combines the choice of a basic perspective on data production with a specification of what methods and techniques we want to use for selecting, collecting, and analysing such data that the project needs.[1] What a good strategy for data construction is depends on what kind of information we need to answer our questions in an adequate way. When concretising the strategy, it is also necessary to address methodical questions related to the selection, collection, and analysis of data.

---

[1] This totality of perspective on and techniques of data production is sometimes called a research methodology. This concept is used to distinguish between a complete methodology for data construction, and the technical questions belonging to the method (Gobo, 2008). I prefer the concept of strategy for the simple reason that it is more easily kept apart from the concept of method, and because a common use of the strategy concept is to regard strategy as an approach to realise a given goal.

DESIGN OF RESEARCH PROJECTS   75

Regardless of the research purpose in a given project, we have to make some clarifications during the first phase of the design work. We have to delimit our topic in order to clarify what phenomenon or connections we focus on in the project. We also need to search the relevant research literature to clarify the current knowledge status regarding the topic we want to study. Only after such introductory work can we decide about the need for new knowledge, and thus what questions are relevant for the project. The knowledge goal will also be a decisive factor in how to use existing theories and concepts in the project. Chapter 11, which is about the design process, discusses in more detail how to conduct the first part of the research design. In the present chapter, I limit the discussion to making clear the differences between the types of design. If this book is used as a handbook while working with your own project plan, it can be useful to look at Chap. 11 already at this point; it will give you a better overview of the work tasks that need to be performed in the different phases of the design work.

The other main phase of the design work includes finding and concretising a strategy for data production. As mentioned in the introduction, I distinguish between a variable-centred and a case-centred perspective on data construction. Basically, the variable-centred perspective is reductionist, meaning that we seek to decompose the objects of study to single elements or variables. The strategy for data production will thus be providing data to analyse covariance and being able to draw conclusions about causal relations between the variables.

The case-centred perspective, on the other hand, is holistic. We regard the object of study as a holistic system in which the components are interdependent, acting together in complex ways. Typically, the strategy for data production will be oriented towards studying this interaction or these processes in detail, but also towards uncovering regular patterns of stability and variation.

When concretising the strategy for data construction, we encounter methodological questions. The next chapters cover different designs in more detail and refer to relevant methods and techniques. However, as the ambition of this book is limited to being a general guide to research design, I do not discuss the specific methods and analytical techniques in detail.

Introductory books about method usually make a main distinction between qualitative and quantitative methods. Many of these books also tend to present the choice between these two types of method as the most important choice when making a research design. This is a view I cannot share. In my view, the fundamental choice in a design strategy is between a variable-centred and a case-centred perspective on data construction. The literature about quantitative methods may be the most relevant when the task is to specify the technicalities of data collection and analysis within a variable-centred perspective; however, a mechanical use of quantitative methods can also prevent us from seeing the complexity in the interaction between the variables that are present in an analysis. When concluding from correlation between variables in a data material to causal relations and explanations, it is often beneficial to include knowledge of methods developed in the literature about process tracing and the analysis of social mechanisms. Vice versa we could need quantitative techniques when analysing data on social patterns and variation across cases. I will return to this. The point here is that the choice of method is not the first thing we do in the design phase; we should rather regard this choice as a step in the concretisation of the strategy for data production.

Neither can we reduce the making of a research design to making a work plan or schedule for the project. It is not only about placing the various work tasks in sequence; it has to do with working out a logical structure for what we need to do. On the other hand, when we have finished the design work it can be useful to make a work plan that makes it clear what we must do when, and how much time we need to allocate for each task.

RESEARCH DESIGNS AND PURPOSES

A specific research purpose always relates to the phenomenon or the connections we are going to study, and to the knowledge that already exists. Thus, the purpose is unique for each research project. The purpose also relates to concepts and theoretical ideas that govern our research interest and questions, and in the next round the strategy for data production. Even though knowledge goals and questions are uniquely concretised in each project, we can talk about types of research purpose. The purpose types dealt with in this book are theory testing, theory development, theoretical interpretation, and intervention-oriented types.

This classification of research purposes is not self-evident. Conventional books on methods usually distinguish between on the one hand explanatory and on the other hand interpretative purposes and questions. Explanatory purposes are seen as oriented towards finding the causal relations between phenomena, whereas interpretative purposes are oriented towards understanding a phenomenon in depth. These conventional presentations often see interpretation and explanatory purposes as related to different research logics. They understand explanation as the development of generalisations through a hypothetical-deductive research logic, using observations to test hypotheses and theories about connections. A sound testing of hypotheses requires representative data about a great number of cases. Therefore, a quantitative method is the most suitable when explanation is the purpose. Interpretation requires uncovering the meaning that social actors give to acts and events, understanding them via a hermeneutic research logic. Interpretation is oriented towards the unique in a social phenomenon or case rather than towards generalisation.

A problem with this classification is that it keeps up an unfounded division between interpretative and explanatory research purposes. In my opinion, it is more productive to take our starting point from a division between internal and external explanatory types as shown in Chap. 2. When establishing an internal or understanding explanation, one needs to examine how social actors construct the social fields that they inhibit. An external explanation seeks to identify causes and effects to find out what creates and maintains rule-governed patterns in society. Seen like this, the two explanatory types are complementary tools rather than a product of alternative perspectives on the world.

A second problem with the conventional classification is that it establishes different standards for good research. If we maintain that interpretative research is only oriented towards understanding a phenomenon as unique, it will be impossible to see social research as an activity where scientific knowledge is developed by adding new elements to what we already know, and at the same time reject theories and hypotheses that are not up to the mark when confronted with data. In the past decade, many philosophers of science and social researchers have taken an interest in what could be a unitary standard for scientific knowledge. King, Keohane, and Verba launched a much-debated answer to this question in their book *Designing Social Inquiry* (King, Keohane, & Verba, 1994). Their view builds on a hypothetical-deductive research logic. They claim also that case studies should be designed from a variable-centred perspective. Since its publication in 1994, their book has influenced much of the debate about standards of scientific knowledge. Implications of this view of case studies are primarily developed by John Gerring, who discussed various designs of case studies and their strong versus weak sides from a reductionist perspective (Gerring, 2004, 2006).

An alternative view has also been proposed in this debate. This view claims that holistic case studies have their strength in exploring complex social mechanisms and processes, and that they constitute their own set of strategies and methods for the development of research-based knowledge. Based on this view, case studies may be tools for systematic knowledge development and testing of hypotheses (Brady & Collier, 2010; Eisenhardt, 1989; Levy, 2008; Yin, 1984). Writers belonging to what can be termed the comparative-historical school emphasise that we can develop theory through case studies and additionally test the theory through systematic comparison of cases (Lange, 2013). The literature about the tracing of social processes, often involving mechanistic explanations, has seen a growth in recent years (Beach & Pedersen, 2014, 2016; Bennett & Checkel, 2015; Collier, 2011; Mahoney, 2015; Rohlfing, 2013). These writers agree with the idea that there should be a common standard for scientific knowledge. Still, this is a standard at the philosophy of science level; it does not entail a common standard at the methodological level (Mahoney, 2008). We may use different methods to produce testable knowledge. The present book shares this view.

There are more shortcomings with the dichotomy of explanatory and interpretative projects and designs. This dichotomy does not really invite a reflection on the relationship between theory testing and theory development. As shown in the former chapter on research logics, the testing of an established explanation and the development of a new explanation require different research logics and approaches. One of the weaknesses of conventional hypothetical-deductive research logic is that it has little to say about developing new concepts and theories through scientific thinking. It views theoretical change mainly as a necessary adjustment when new observations disprove an existing theory and says little about how to reach new theoretical ideas and frames of understanding. The emphasis on concept and theory development as a distinct purpose for research projects is therefore an important development of the conventional dichotomy. To develop good designs, we need to make clear the division between theory testing and theory development purposes—and how these purposes can be realised through different research designs and methods. In the sections below, I therefore distinguish between theory testing and theory development purposes.

Another shortcoming of the dichotomy explanation/interpretation is that it ignores the role of theory when we focus on interpreting or understanding phenomena. As shown in Chap. 1, we never understand a phenomenon without activating our presuppositions. Such a presupposition is, however, in itself a form of generalisation. Thus, generalisation and interpretation of individual phenomena intertwine in more complex ways than the dichotomy of explanation and interpretation lets us understand. Here, the point is that an interpretation of a social phenomenon always depends on theoretical frames, either explicitly or implicitly. When the purpose of a project is interpretation in light of theory rather than testing or developing theories, I will refer to it as a theoretical-interpretative purpose. As will be shown later, such an interpretation is often about tracing the conditions of an observed phenomenon or outcome, and about considering the case as an example of a larger class of phenomena.

A type of research purposes not commonly discussed in the design literature concerns projects that are part of or evaluate interventions into social conditions. The goal of interventions is to create desired changes. Conventional books on methods usually regard such interventions as something outside the research process itself. Yet we should not forget that its potential value for practical interventions often guides research. Evaluations and action research are examples of research with this type of motivation. Mainstream literature on methods mostly ignores such research strategies; they are covered in a specialised literature on evaluation and action research. This literature does not discuss the relationship between conventional research purposes and research where implementation and assessment of interventions are the declared purpose of the project. I consider this lack of discussion of intervention-oriented research a weakness of the conventional literature, not least in a society that increasingly uses research as a guide for policy and organisational practice (Naustdalslid & Reitan, 1994). Consequently, I include intervention-oriented designs as a separate category in this book.

In the following sections, four different types of purpose are included as a starting point to discuss project designs. The first type is theory testing. The second is theory development, and the third is theoretical interpretation of a social phenomenon. Finally, I include intervention assessment as a separate purpose. The distinction between these groups is based on the overall knowledge goal of a project, and on how we ask in order to find the knowledge we want.

We need to be aware that in a given project different types of questions may be mixed and interacting. The usefulness of discussing pure research purposes is that we can show clear-cut types of research questions and purposes rather than developing complete templates for the design of

80 O. BUKVE

projects. Real designs often build on a combination of purposes. These complex projects will also usually have an overall purpose to which we relate the particular questions of the project.

Theory- and Hypothesis-Testing Purposes

In a *theory-testing* project, the research purpose is to *test an established theory—or a hypothesis of connections between phenomena*—in order to judge how they match when encountering new data and observations. Theory-testing projects need a well-structured design. It is important to be clear about what theoretical statements are to be tested and to design the data collection in such a way that the testing will be real. We should be as critical as possible to the established theory or interpretation that we take as our point of departure. Theory testing usually relates to projects where we collect data about many cases. Even so, Chap. 7 shows that it is also possible to test a theory through designs where we go in depth into one or a few phenomena or cases. For both, the design and the criteria for selection of cases are decisive for critical testing (Andersen, 2013; George & Bennett, 2005). In such projects, new knowledge means that our theories are strengthened, rejected, or modified to be valid only under certain conditions.

Concept- and Theory-Developing Purposes and Questions

In theory-developing projects, the research purpose is to arrive at *new interpretations of a phenomenon* or *new ideas about the connections* between phenomena. Creativity and reflection will then play a more important role than in theory-testing projects; still, methodical techniques can be useful to systematise our data collection and analysis of the findings as well as the theorising around them. The design should be more flexible in such projects because researchers need to be open to new interpretations and connections as they go along. The design can be oriented towards new interpretations of cases. Attempting to uncover specific mechanisms that convey connections between condition and effect is another example of theory development.

A concept and theory development purpose can be appropriate when the project is dealing with a new social phenomenon that has still not been studied in full. It can also be appropriate when established explanations and interpretations are insufficient. When we have a finding that we cannot explain by use of established theory, the challenge is to find new explanations and concepts to interpret the phenomenon. One requirement for researchers starting research projects with this purpose is that they know the field of research well and possess an overview of the knowledge status of the field. Researchers should not confuse the fact that they personally lack the understanding of a field or a topic with the fact that the collective research community lacks such knowledge. Therefore, it is most often experienced researchers who succeed with projects that develop interesting new concepts and theory. For novices in a research field, common project purposes are often to test the scope of established theories and hypotheses or use theoretical propositions and ideas to analyse and interpret the phenomenon or the phenomena they are studying.

Theoretically Interpretative Purposes

In theoretically interpretative projects, the purpose is to use theories and scientific concepts as a framework to analyse and render meaning to the phenomenon or phenomena we are studying. The ambition is not primarily to develop new concepts and theories but to use those theories that best help us interpret the data, and to place them in a context. Many social science projects have such a purpose. This is also the case with many master's degree and PhD theses. Hence, how to design such projects in order to develop new knowledge is relevant to many readers of this book.

It is possible to distinguish between two main strategies for implementing theoretically interpretative projects. One strategy builds on a structured framework with the collection and analysis of data based on previously specified theories. We can label such projects *theory-informed* projects. They are informed by theory and are explicit about the theoretical basis all the way from the design of the project. The main question is whether there is a match between the patterns of the data material and what we would expect based on the theory. In theory-informed projects, we can use several theories as a framework for the interpretation. It is then necessary to clarify whether we see the theories as competing explanations or as complementary in the sense that they can support each other to give a more adequate representation of phenomena and connections.

The other kind of the theoretically interpretative design is more empirical in the sense that the project starts with the data collection, after which the researcher, based on the findings, attempts to judge what concepts and theories will give the best understanding and interpretation of the data. The frames of such a project are usually flexible. Researchers need to prepare for the possibility that the data material may lead them in other directions and to other interpretations than they envisaged at the beginning. Interpretation takes place by using familiar concepts and theories and not by developing new ones. We can label the strategy of such projects *interpretative reconstruction*.

INTERVENTION-ORIENTED PURPOSES

Intervention-oriented projects are different because their research purpose is practical rather than theoretical. The practical purpose can be to solve a specific task or problem, or to enable a change or an improvement measure. In such projects, the hallmark of a good explanation or interpretation is that we can use them for practical interventions. The theories are primarily a tool to support practical interventions. Even so, theories play an important role in intervention-oriented projects. Every intervention, whether in society or nature, rests on an implicit or explicit theory that explains connections and processes around the phenomenon we try to influence or change. This theory is the starting point of conceptions of how the phenomenon may undergo change through intervention. We can say that interventions build on a *theory of action*. The theory of action may be implicit, or it could be explicitly thematised. When through formative evaluation projects and action research we give advice to those who are to carry out an intervention, we either explicitly or implicitly relate the advice to a theoretical framework. Many interventions in social conditions build on previous research that has established a scientific foundation for the interventions, although this foundation is not always clear to those who implement the change. Thus, a role that intervention-oriented research could take up concerns making the underlying action theory explicit and assessing its usability.

Neither is the action theory at all times clear and well established. Starting a reform or a project, in other words an intervention, may itself influence the actors involved. For instance, groups that are important for the implementation may feel sceptical about the result and for that reason be unwilling to participate. Action research and formative evaluation research may contribute to developing an understanding of how interventions influence the actors' construction of meaning and action, which in its turn may change the conditions for implementation.

The other way around, after an intervention-oriented project we may be interested in generalising beyond that particular case. Why did one type of intervention fail while another intervention was a success? The goal is to explain the relationship between interventions and actual effects. Experiments and effect evaluations are examples of such intervening or explanatory projects. In an experiment, we construct a situation in which we can keep constant all other factors than the one whose effects we want to explore. In this way, we can make predictions that provide a basis for other interventions. Evaluations with the use of control groups follow the same logic; they establish a quasi-experimental design by comparing the intervention cases with a control group.

If we do not have the right theoretical understanding of the processes in which we want to intervene, we risk giving the wrong advice or intervene in ways that create unwanted results. An essential criterion for assessing interventions is whether it builds on usable action theories. Thus, the answer to how to implement the intervention should build on other types of questions oriented towards clarifying what type of phenomenon is present and how it comes into existence. The purpose of the first type of question is to describe the phenomenon; the purpose of the other is to interpret or explain it. When we talk about types of project purposes, it can be useful to categorise intervention-oriented projects as a separate category.

Mere Description?

Descriptive projects describe a phenomenon or a group of phenomena without interpreting them through explicit theoretical frames (Andersen, 2013). Sometimes, descriptive purposes and projects are called a-theoretical. Yet as we have seen above, there is no such thing as descriptions without presuppositions and interpretative frameworks. When researchers perceive a project as a-theoretical, a possible pitfall is that they become blind to their own underlying frames of understanding, perceiving them as the obvious perspective from which to view the phenomenon. The danger exists of smuggling one's own assumptions into the description. For that reason, we should regard such projects as implicitly theory informed, and projects may benefit from making this frame of understanding explicit as the basis of approaches and descriptions in the project. This is why this book does not include descriptive purposes as independent purposes for research projects.

Still, descriptive questions play an important role in complex research projects by constituting necessary steps in projects where the main purpose involves testing, developing, or using theory. In variable-centred designs, we need to describe the distribution pattern for individual variables or covariation between variables in a set of data. In case designs, a detailed description of actions, events, processes, and patterns is more often the starting point; however, it is usually followed by a matching with established theories and concepts or by attempts to develop new ones. Where previous research-based knowledge is scarce, we may justify a mainly descriptive or exploratory approach. In general, however, descriptions structured in accordance with the main interest of the project are one of several steps in a complete research design.

Purpose and Design of an Analytic Frame

When designing a research project, it is important to clarify the type of purpose represented by the project, because the purpose has consequences for the design of the analytic framework of the project. If the purpose is testing of theory or theory-informed analysis of a social phenomenon, we need a precise and well-structured analytic frame before starting the data collection, and we should stick to it during the project. Testing a theory against data, or interpreting a set of data using theory, requires precise hypotheses or assumptions based on theory as well as good operationalisations of the theoretical concepts before carrying out the data collection. If the purpose is to analyse a set of data using various theories, it is important that we make clear the expectations concerning findings related to each individual theory we use. In such cases, we deal with multiple analytic frames. Intervention-oriented projects need a distinct analytic frame too, because the testing of the underlying action theory for the intervention is a vital part of the analysis. Structured frames may be visualised through analytic models that make visible the theoretical model as well as the data model we plan to use.

If the purpose of the project is theory development or theoretical interpretation of a social phenomenon, the purpose also entails that at the end of the project we hope to have more precise and complete concepts and ideas about connections than we had at the beginning. Still, we should make our point of departure clear, for instance because our literature review may have referred to interesting findings and patterns that have not been sufficiently analysed and explained. In such cases, we can structure our analytic frame by applying a data model to find underlying theoretical variables and patterns. Further, we could be interested in analysing phenomena or relations for which there is little previous research. Prior to the data collection, we may then have to content ourselves with referring to concepts and theories used to study similar phenomena and be prepared for unexpected findings that may lead us in new directions. In such cases, the analytic frame must be more open and flexible. A general piece of advice is to structure the analytic frame as far as possible in view of the purpose of the project and the status of knowledge in the actual field.

The analytic frame plays a vital role when designing a research project. The following chapters give a number of examples of such frames, and in Chap. 11 I return to a full discussion of the place of the analytic frame in the design process.

RESEARCH DESIGN AND DATA CONSTRUCTION

The view of social science as reconstruction or re-presentation of social phenomena entails that also our data are socially constructed. This does not mean that we may regard the world around us as arbitrary and malleable through our constructions. It does say, however, something about the conditions for establishing data. In our knowledge production, we depend on our cognitive frames and assumptions. Empirical science requires an awareness of these frames as well as a construction of data in ways that do not make us unduly dependent on our frames.

This book suggests a strategy where the choice of method is not our first choice when designing a project. Purpose and research questions must guide the choice of method rather than the other way around. Method is primarily a tool, and we should choose the tool in accordance with the work tasks. If we only have saws in our toolbox, we are ill equipped to hammer in a nail. It could in fact create problems for a project if the researcher adheres to a specific type of method from the outset or makes the decision about which methods to use before clarifying and refining the research questions. If it then turns out that the most relevant research questions actually require another approach, a limited methodical repertoire may function like a straitjacket.

This way of thinking entails that the choice of method is less fundamental for the design than what is usually the case in conventional method books. According to Gianpetro Gobo, method is a technique, and this technique must be subordinate to the purpose of the project and the theoretical assumptions of the researcher (Gobo, 2008). The method is what we choose to do when we have defined the research purpose and limited our research topic. According to Gobo, the choice of method is only a part of a comprehensive methodology. He emphasises that data are also socially constructed, and proposes a classification of research strategies by cognitive modes, or according to the way of sensing a research object.[2]

I find Gobo's concept of cognitive modes interesting because he makes it very clear that the purpose of the research must have precedence over the choice of method. Still, his detailing of cognitive modes leads to somewhat artificial divisions when it comes to his methodological propositions.

An alternative proposition for operationalisation of different cognitive modes that guide data construction is to distinguish between holistic and reductionist approaches to the object of study. These approaches point to different ways of seeing the research object. The holistic approach entails studying the phenomenon in its totality and in light of its context. We seek to establish data and knowledge about as many aspects of the phenomenon as possible. What are its main characteristics? How has it developed? What effects does it have? The reductionist approach, on the other hand, attempts to study a phenomenon as the sum of a number of components that may vary. It aims at studying how changes in one component or variable lead to a change of other characteristics of the phenomenon. The underlying assumption of a holistic approach is that the whole constitutes something more and different from the sum of the parts. Reductionism, on the other hand, assumes that we can explain a complex system by reducing it to its separate components.

We can also say that the holistic look constructs data as cases while the reductionist look constructs data as entities with variable characteristics. From the two ways of constructing data, we can distinguish between

---

[2] Altogether, Gobo categorises six types of cognitive modes: the listening, the inquiring, the observing, the reading, the operative, and the reflective modes. He relates them to six corresponding methodologies: the discursive, the survey, the ethnographic, the documenting, the transformative, and the speculative methodologies. Except for the survey methodology, he believes that the methodologies can be used for structured as well as unstructured data. However, his philosophy is complicated and it is not easy to identify specific research designs outside his special area, which is ethnography. For instance, it is not easy to understand that the listening, inquiring, and reading ways of assessing data should lead to different methodological choices on a more fundamental level. In practice, Gobo's detailed classifications reduce methodology to an approach for data collection.

case-centred and variable-centred research strategies. Case-centred strategies are holistic, looking at data as made up of cases that we have to study in their real context. The focus of the analysis is the conditions of observed effects, and the explanatory strategy is about uncovering the interacting factors or mechanisms that lead to a given result. Different from this we have variable-centred or reductionist strategies. They look at data as a population of units that we can describe through variable characteristics. The analysis is oriented towards isolating the factors or causes that, other factors given, produce certain effects.

In their pure form, we can consider these two research strategies ideal types in the Weberian sense. In a specific research project, it is possible to combine the two approaches in various ways. Such integrated strategies are discussed later in this book. Here, the purpose is to present the two types of strategies in their pure forms (Table 5.1).

VARIABLE-CENTRED STRATEGIES

When working from a variable-centred strategy our cognitive mode is reductionist. What we see in the set of data is a population of units with variable characteristics. Our interest is oriented towards all the varying characteristics that make up parts of a unit, rather than towards the unit in itself. In a quantitative inquiry into the quality of the service production in municipalities, the individual municipality is not in focus but how it can be placed along variables such as size, economy, access to professional knowledge, geography, and so on. We can study the connections between such variables and the service production by use of a variety of statistical methods.

The main purposes of variable-centred strategies are on the one hand to test theories and theory-based hypotheses and, on the other hand, to develop generalisations and theoretical models. When theory testing is the

Table 5.1 Ideal-typical approaches to data construction

Strategy	Case centred	Variable centred
Cognitive mode	Holistic	Reductionist
Perspective on data	Made up of cases	Made up of population
Causal view	Mechanisms	Causes
Analytic focus	Conditions of observed results	Causal effects
Level of generalisation	Contextualised	Abstract

purpose, we must begin with a theoretical model that makes it possible to develop theory-based hypotheses. The model governs what data are collected. Theories and hypotheses are strengthened if data collected through scientifically valid and reliable procedures match with the theory. Without such matching or coherence, we would face the challenge of changing or refining theories and hypotheses, or simply reject the data as unreliable.

With a variable-centred strategy, we could also go the opposite way with the purpose of developing generalisations and theories about phenomena we can observe but not explain. In such research, we start with collecting data and analysing them. In this way we can describe the properties of different phenomena and the way they correlate. Still, correlation between the elements of a data model is no theoretical explanation. To establish such an explanation, we have to assume that the variables in the data model represent and measure underlying theoretical variables and connections. We can then infer from the correlation in the set of data to causal connections, which we can formulate in a theoretical or concept model.

The next chapter discusses in detail how we can use varieties of variable-centred designs for theory testing and theory development, illustrated by examples.

Case-Oriented Strategies

In case-oriented studies, we regard the phenomenon or phenomena for study as parts of a whole. We consider a case as an instance of a class of corresponding phenomena. Case studies may be carried out as single-case studies as well as multi-case studies. These types of case studies give different challenges and possibilities for the choice of method. While single-case studies let one case represent the phenomenon under study, multi-case studies employ a number of cases that we can perceive as representing the same class of phenomena. Such an approach gives us several observations of the same phenomenon, and hence the ability to draw more reliable conclusions about the class of phenomena that the case belongs to. Said differently, multi-case studies build on a replication logic. An example of a multi-case study could be a study of network building in SMEs with global ambitions and the common characteristic that they commercialise academic inventions, when this study uses data from seven case businesses. The goal is primarily to characterise the phenomenon network building in such businesses (Witsø, 2014) and the variation between them is of secondary importance. The primary level of analysis is thus the type of business ("born global academic spinoffs") and its distinguishing marks, rather than the individual business. By using a multiple-case study, we can more safely draw conclusions about network building in this specific type of businesses. Variation between cases is primarily considered as a clue for developing more precise ideas on sufficient and necessary conditions for businesses of this kind to involve in network building.

We can approach cases in different ways and for different purposes. Case studies can benefit a number of knowledge goals. A common way of using them is to develop new concepts and theoretical ideas. It is more controversial how useful case studies are for testing theories. My view is that they can be useful under some conditions, especially when we design the inquiry in such a way that it is possible to study the match between observed patterns in the cases and patterns proposed by theories of the phenomenon represented by the cases. We can also perform case studies with the purpose of interpreting or explaining a case in light of established theory rather than testing or developing new theory. When the results are unexpected, such studies can give us challenges to develop new and more adequate theories.

COMBINATION STRATEGIES

Case orientation and variable orientation are two basic strategies for data construction in a research project. These two types may well be combined in a single research project. We can use different approaches to get a better basis for drawing conclusions. Moreover, the project may include a number of research questions that can best be studied using different designs.

There are several ways to make this combination. Here I distinguish between integrative designs, comparative designs, and intervention-oriented designs. The integrative element in integrative designs varies between types. Triangulation is a form of integrative design where the purpose is to use different sets of data and analytical strategies in order to make the research findings more robust. A second purpose behind integrated designs is to integrate theory development and theory testing in the same project, while choosing the better methods for both testing and development of theories. I discuss several design variants under this integrated design umbrella but pay particular attention to nested design. A third ambition behind combined strategies is to develop designs that are suitable for developing and testing theories about social mechanisms. A focus on social mechanisms is a main feature of the literature presenting itself as multimethod research (Goertz, 2017).

Comparative designs are still another class of combined designs. The specific purpose of comparative designs is, as the term indicates, comparing and studying variation. Recently, several writers have emphasised the fact that comparative research requires innovative thinking in matters related to design and method. The purpose as well as the data construction in comparative research is dealt with in recent literature on this topic (George & Bennett, 2005; Landman, 2008; Lange, 2013; Ragin, 1987; Ragin & Amoroso, 2011).

Ragin and Amoroso (2011) argue that comparative studies constitute a third form of research strategies in addition to qualitative and quantitative strategies. They regard comparative research as a strategy to study variation. Qualitative strategies are oriented towards finding common features and characteristics of phenomena, whereas quantitative methods are about the study of correlation. On this basis, the authors discuss how the three strategies may contribute to realising a set of primary research purposes. Ragin and Amoroso's book is one of the most interesting books on the construction of social research. In the presentation of comparative strategies, however, it focuses more on comparing cases than on how to analyse each of the cases included in the study. Ragin has also been pivotal in developing methods for variable-centred analyses of comparative studies with multiple cases (Ragin, 1987, 2000).

George and Bennett (2005), on the other hand, emphasise that comparative designs should combine a holistic analysis of the processes within each case and a comparison of the cases. For this reason, comparative case studies tend to utilise a combination of strategies for data production. One example, taken from comparative politics, is when we study the conditions for revolutions to take place. This means analysing social change processes in various countries and searching for factors that may have been influential for whether the processes result in a revolution or not. We then divide the countries into two groups, those with and those without a revolution, and use a variable-centred analysis to find out if the countries are systematically different on possible explanatory variables. In this way, we can uncover necessary conditions for social revolutions.

In my illustration below, I categorise comparative designs as a combination strategy rather than a third type of basic design. Comparative designs use a variable-centred strategy to compare the cases, while case strategies are used to analyse each case from within. Where comparison is based on just a few cases, the comparison of cases is usually done by developing types and theoretical typologies (George & Bennett, 2005). When comparing multiple cases in a many-N design, the comparison is mostly oriented towards uncovering necessary and sufficient conditions for specific outcomes (Ragin & Amoroso, 2011). I return to this in Chap. 9.

The third combined form is intervention-oriented designs, where there is often a need to combine studies of process and effect. Typically, the intervention processes are studied through case design while effects are traced through variable design. Such a combination of process and effect studies is particularly relevant when the purpose of the project is to develop knowledge about intervention in social conditions. In these cases, we want to find out about the result of a given intervention, in other words the effects. Moreover, we also usually want to find out *why* a measure was successful or unsuccessful in producing specific effects, in order to adjust the process when we fail or to carry on with the good measures when we succeed. For this purpose, process designs are often beneficial. Therefore, an intervention-oriented design often needs a combination of strategies. A complete programme evaluation thus comprises a combination of a case-oriented study of implementation processes and a variable-centred study of effects.

Figure 5.1 sums up the strategies for data production. The topic for the next five chapters is how the two pure strategies for data construction and the three types of combined designs produce different research designs in practice. First, I will introduce some general requirements of a good research design.

REQUIREMENTS OF A GOOD RESEARCH DESIGN

A good research design must be able to meet a number of requirements. An essential requirement is that the inquiry should be designed in such a way that the data can be used to draw conclusions about equivalent

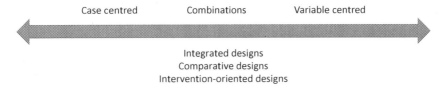

Fig. 5.1 Different strategies for data construction

92 O. BUKVE

phenomena, or about more general cases, in a reliable way. If inferences cannot be drawn from an inquiry, it has low validity. There are three types of validity requirements for scientific investigations.

One requirement is construction validity or concept validity, which is about whether our data do actually measure the theoretical concept we mean to measure (Cronbach, Meehl, & Dennis, 1955). We cannot measure theoretical concepts directly; we have to establish a set of empirical operationalisations or indicators related to the concept. For instance, we can operationalise the concept of social status through indicators such as income, property, education, job, or reputation. The measurement will easily become lopsided if we base our research on only one or two of these indicators. When constructing questionnaires and interview guides it is vital to judge how well the questions are suited to establish operational goals for the theoretical concepts we want to use. One of the advantages of a case design is that we can extend our understanding of the relationship between the theoretical concept and the operationalisation in the course of the project. New observations in the course of the project may give a reason for adjusting the operationalisation and the plan for the collection of data. This is not so easy in a variable-centred project where we collect standardised data across units, thus making it necessary to specify the indicators prior to the data collection.

Internal validity is about whether we have drawn the right conclusions about causal relations in the data material (Campbell & Fiske, 1959; Yin, 1984). It is a matter of how good our arguments are for stating whether our theoretical model fits the patterns of observations on the one hand and the data on the other. If a theoretical concept model is the starting point of our investigation, the key question is whether it is possible to say that the data are in accordance with or contrary to the theoretical statements. If we start from a set of empirical data and connections, the important question is whether we can construct a theoretical model that explains these connections. A good research design needs to be consistent when specifying the relation between the set of data and the theoretical model. How to establish this relation may vary, depending on whether the project aims to test or develop theories.

External validity is about whether conclusions about causal connections in our material can be generalised from the actual investigation to other situations (Yin, 1984, pp. 38–40). External validity is thus a matter of how representative our data set is for the class of phenomena it is part of. If our data set has been collected in the third form of a particular school we cannot be sure that we can generalise our findings to other pupils or to third-form pupils in general. In the literature on method, we learn about strategies to judge whether a set of data is representative. We base our judgement of variable-centred designs on statistical representativeness, regarding the set of data as a selection from a larger population and using statistical methods to judge whether the findings from the selection can be generalised to the entire population. In case designs, we assess external validity by judging whether the cases are theoretically or strategically representative. The criteria for theoretical representativeness can vary: in certain designs we may for instance want to have a case that is typical for a class of phenomena; in other designs we want an extreme case. Strategic representativeness is about selecting cases that vary on the empirical variables for which we want to investigate the effect or the conditions. We can also base our inquiry on theoretical saturation, which means that we study new cases until the addition of a new case no longer gives relevant supplementary information. Consequently, in a good design we need to reflect whether and how we can get representative data, either from a logic based on statistical representativeness or from a logic based on theoretical or strategic representativeness.

Reliability is about whether an investigation gives robust results. The empirical indicators and connections are in focus, rather than the relation between theory and data. The research is reliable when other people can perform the same inquiry again and reach the same results.

Ringdal (2013) refers to an inquiry that illustrates the distinction between reliability and validity in a way that is easy to understand. In an American small town, the museum had very good attendance, interpreted by the management as an indicator of high cultural interest in that town. It turned out that the attendance fell steeply when the city established a public toilet right beside the museum. This investigation has a problem of validity, not reliability. Using the number of tickets sold as a measure of the number of visitors was reliable enough; the number of visitors was estimated in a sound way by using the ticket sale as the indicator. The problem was that it was not correct to use the sale of tickets as an indicator of the theoretical concept cultural interest, because there was a systematic source of error. The indicator measured another need and was affected when from a given time that need could be met in another way.

From Design as Concept to Design Variants

This chapter has discussed the concept of research design. I regard design as the logical structure of a research project or as a plan for how to get from questions to answers in the project. Two aspects of the research design are especially important. First, we must ask what the main purpose of the project is. In other words: What do we want to know? Based on the literature in this field I distinguish between purposes of theory testing, theory development, theoretical interpretation, and intervention orientation. The other important aspect is how to construct the object of the research, what perspective we have on the data. I here distinguish between the holistic and the reductionist perspective as constitutive for the two basic forms of research strategies: case-centred and variable-centred strategies. I have also discussed some combined forms of design.

Thus, this chapter has developed two typologies: one for knowledge goals and the other for strategies for data construction. Further, I have stated that a research design is developed through a certain combination of knowledge goals and strategy for data production. This I intend to concretise in the following chapters. As seen above, there may be gliding transitions between different knowledge goals in a given project, at the same time as relevant strategies for data construction combine the two basic forms. This diversity does not make it easy to organise the presentation of the various research designs in a systematic way. If I combined the two typologies in a matrix with four types of purposes and five types of strategies, I would get to a detailed classification that disregards the complexity we may need in a specific project design. The organisation of the following parts of this book into five chapters on designs is consequently made with a basis in the five strategies for data construction presented in Fig. 5.1. I show how these strategies are the basis of different design variants depending on the main purpose of the project.

The next chapter discusses the properties of variable-centred designs and how they can meet the requirements of good design. The main types of variable-centred designs are discussed: cross-sectional designs, time designs, and experimental designs. Chapter 7 discusses case designs, focusing on pattern-matching designs, process tracing, and interpretative reconstruction as the important variants. Chapters 8, 9, and 10 deal with the combined strategies. I first look at integrated designs that aim at combining case analyses and variable-centred analyses in various ways. I then introduce comparative designs, pointing to the characteristic feature of comparative designs in that they combine strategies for analysing individual cases with strategies for comparing the cases. Finally, I introduce intervention-oriented designs that combine process and effect analyses, discussing designs for evaluation and action research and how to develop intervention-relevant knowledge.

REFERENCES

Andersen, S. S. (2013). *Casestudier: forskningsstrategi, generalisering og forklaring*. Bergen, Norway: Fagbokforl.

Beach, D., & Pedersen, R. B. (2014). *Process-tracing methods: Foundations and guidelines*. Ann Arbor, MI: University of Michigan Press.

Beach, D., & Pedersen, R. B. (2016). *Causal case study methods: Foundations and guidelines for comparing, matching and tracing*. Ann Arbor, MI: University of Michigan Press.

Bennett, A., & Checkel, J. T. (2015). *Process tracing: From metaphor to analytic tool*. Cambridge: Cambridge University Press.

Brady, H. E., & Collier, D. (2010). *Rethinking social inquiry: Diverse tools, shared standards*. Lanham, Boulder, New York, Toronto, Plymouth, UK: Rowman & Littlefield Publishers.

Campbell, D. T., & Fiske, D. W. (1959). Convergent and discriminant validation by the multitrait-multimethod matrix. *Psychological Bulletin, 56*(2), 81–105. https://doi.org/10.1037/h0046016

Collier, D. (2011). Understanding process tracing. *PS: Political Science & Politics, 44*(4), 823–830.

Cronbach, L. J., Meehl, P. E., & Dennis, W. (1955). Construct validity in psychological tests. *Psychological Bulletin, 52*(4), 281–302. https://doi.org/10.1037/h0040957

De Vaus, D. A., & de Vaus, D. (2001). *Research design in social research*. London: Sage.

Eisenhardt, K. M. (1989). Building theories from case study research. *The Academy of Management Review, 14*(4), 532–550. https://doi.org/10.2307/258557

George, A. L., & Bennett, A. (2005). *Case studies and theory development in the social sciences*. Cambridge, MA: MIT Press.

Gerring, J. (2004). What is a case study and what is it good for? *The American Political Science Review, 98*(2), 341–354. https://doi.org/10.2307/4145316

Gerring, J. (2006). *Case study research: Principles and practices*. New York: Cambridge University Press.

Gobo, G. (2008). *Doing ethnography*. Los Angeles, CA: Sage.

Goertz, G. (2017). *Multimethod research, causal mechanisms, and case studies: An integrated approach*. Princeton, NJ: Princeton University Press.

King, G., Keohane, R. O., & Verba, S. (1994). *Designing social inquiry: Scientific inference in qualitative research*. Princeton, NJ: Princeton University Press.

Landman, T. (2008). *Issues and methods in comparative politics: An introduction* (3rd ed.). Milton Park, Abingdon, Oxon, UK: Routledge.

Lange, M. (2013). *Comparative-historical methods.* Los Angeles, CA: Sage.

Levy, J. (2008). Case studies: Types, designs, and logics of inference. *Conflict Management and Peace Science, 25*(1), 1–18. https://doi.org/10.1080/07388940701860318

Mahoney, J. (2008). Toward a unified theory of causality. (Author abstract) (Report). *Comparative Political Studies, 41*(4–5), 412.

Mahoney, J. (2015). Process tracing and historical explanation. *Security Studies, 24*(2), 200–218. https://doi.org/10.1080/09636412.2015.1036610

Naustdalslid, J., & Reitan, M. (1994). *Kunnskap og styring: om bruk av forskning i politikk og forvaltning.* Oslo, Norway: TANO: Norsk institutt for by- og regionsforskning.

Ragin, C. C. (1987). *The comparative method.* Berkeley, CA: University of California Press.

Ragin, C. C. (2000). *Fuzzy-set social science.* Chicago: University of Chicago Press.

Ragin, C. C., & Amoroso, L. M. (2011). *Constructing social research.* Thousand Oaks, CA: Pine Forge Press.

Ringdal, K. (2013). Enhet og mangfold. *Samfunnsvitenskapelig forskning og kvantitativ metode. 3. utg.* Bergen: Fagbokforlaget.

Rohlfing, I. (2013). Varieties of process tracing and ways to answer why-questions. *European Political Science, 12*(1), 31–39.

Witsø, S. B. (2014). *International networking strategies in academic spin-off companies: A study of international network building processes and the roles of the top management team and board in influencing internationalization speed and international network range.* (Master thesis), Norges teknisk-naturvitenskapelige universitet, Trondheim.

Yin, R. K. (1984). *Case study research. Design and methods.* Beverly Hills, CA: Sage.

CHAPTER 6

Variable-Centred Designs

Below, I first introduce the basic properties of a variable-centred design, followed by the requirements necessary for such designs to contribute to knowledge development. I then discuss how theory testing and theory development place different demands on the set-up of a variable-centred inquiry, before ending with an overview of main variants of variable-centred designs. Experimental designs, cross-sectional designs, and time series designs are discussed.

WHAT IS A VARIABLE-CENTRED DESIGN?

Variable-centred designs are often called quantitative designs. Such designs are commonly defined as building on quantitative data and on data from multiple units. As a description this is adequate. The basic property is, however, the underlying reductionism that decides how we produce and organise data in a variable-centred design.

The potential research objects in a variable-centred design can be understood as a population, a population made up of units with varying properties. Typical kinds of units are individuals, groups, families, organisations, states, or societies. Consequently, the units are on different levels. They can be described by use of variables. A variable is *a characteristic, a property, or a dimension of a unit for analysis*. For instance, an individual can be described using variables such as gender, age, education, beliefs, and political views. We can describe states through variables such as per

© The Author(s) 2019

O. Bukve, *Designing Social Science Research*,

https://doi.org/10.1007/978-3-030-03979-0_6

capita national product, degree of economic equality, form of government, and level of political conflict. Each variable has a set of values that can be measured. The operationalisation of the variables—in other words building good measures and indicators to describe the variation on a variable—is a main question in variable-centred designs. I discuss this further in the next section.

In a variable-centred design, we will usually not collect data about the entire population. Therefore, to make our analysis reliable we need methods to ensure that the included data set is representative for the whole population. Randomised samples are the most common method to achieve this.

When we have collected the data, we organise them in a data matrix as shown in Table 6.1. The values of each variable are registered in a cell in the matrix. These values are the building blocks of the data matrix. Each cell represents an observation, and we can increase the number of observations either by adding more units or by collecting more information about each unit, thus increasing the number of variables. When we analyse data from a variable-centred project, the variation in the values of a variable and the covariation between the values of different variables are in focus. This is the reason why I characterise the variable-centred design as reductionist: the sum of the observation values defines a unit.

The data in the matrix are usually registered as numbers. However, the numbers are often codifications of differences that are qualitative rather than quantitative. For instance, gender is usually encoded as a dichotomous variable, that is, a variable with two values. Sometimes the data matrix can contain text that the researcher encodes into categories that can be symbolised by signs. We can for instance ask managers what they believe are important leadership qualities and ask them to answer with one sentence that describes these qualities. The researcher can then interpret

Table 6.1 The data matrix of variable-centred designs

	Variable 1	Variable 2	Variable 3	Variable 4	Variable 5	Variable n
Unit 1						
Unit 2		Observation				
Unit 3						
Unit 4						
Unit 5						
Unit n						

the answers by categories such as "caring", "performance oriented", "controlling", and allocate numerical values to them. Such quantification can be an arbitrary way of representing properties of the units; we cannot easily range the units on the basis of the numbers. It is also possible that the categories are derived from a theoretical model; then the ordering of data depends on the model.

The data matrix is the starting point for placing data in a data model or empirical model of analysis. This makes it possible to study the match between the data model and the theoretical model in the project. Which one comes first or last of data model and theoretical model depends on the purpose of the project.

Let me introduce two imaginary inquiries that I intend to use as examples in the discussion of variable-centred designs. I begin by concretising what the data matrix would look like in each of the two inquiries.

The first inquiry is about learning in school. We are interested in what factors influence pupils' learning. In such an investigation the units will usually be pupils. Instead of unit 1-n we can write pupil 1-n. Some of the variables in this investigation will be those that measure learning, whereas others measure the underlying factors that influence learning. Grades are a much-used goal for learning, thus we could use this variable in our inquiry. We can find several factors that influence learning, for instance how proficient the teacher is academically as well as pedagogically, what kinds of teaching methods are used in a particular course, and the number of pupils per teacher. These factors are registered as variables in the data matrix.

The second investigation is about how the choice of governance model in municipalities influences aspects of their policies. Elected politicians can be a relevant source of information. We could send them a questionnaire asking about their background, their political positions, what they think of the governance model, and so on. The questions represent the variables in the investigation while the politicians are the units.

Let us look more closely at how these inquiries meet various requirements of validity and what to do to create a good design around the type of questions that the mentioned inquiries are dealing with.

CONSTRUCTION VALIDITY AND KNOWLEDGE DEVELOPMENT

If variable-centred designs are to contribute to knowledge development, they must meet the requirements for validity and reliability introduced in Chap. 5. External validity and reliability can be regarded as methodical questions related to the choice of data and a systematic implementation of the investigation, while internal validity is related to the analysis of data. Construction validity, also called concept validity, has, on the other hand, to do with the relation between the theoretical model and the data model included in the project. Thus, questions related to construction validity are important in the design phase.

Construction validity has to do with actually measuring the theoretical concept we plan to measure. We cannot measure theoretical concepts directly; it has to be performed through observations. Thus, construction validity has to do with the relation between observations and theoretical concepts, consequently between data models and theoretical models.

The first-mentioned example above comprises theoretical concepts such as learning, teacher qualifications, and teaching methods. When operationalising learning, we often use grades as a measure. However, it is possible to imagine other measures; if we inquire into learning in a specific subject such as mathematics or English, we could give the pupils a standardised test and use the test result as a measure of learning. In this way we can prevent varying practices of grading from influencing the way we measure learning. If, on the other hand, we believe that grades are a too limited measure of learning we could attempt to measure the pupils' general development and maturity, their creativity, and so on. This could be done by giving them other tasks than those used for determining grades. The teacher's qualifications could for instance be operationalised by measuring how many credits she has achieved in her studies in the subject she teaches. Teaching methods can also be operationalised in various ways. We could for instance register the time allocated to instruction in class, individual guidance, group work, and individual exercises; or we could register whether the teaching is based on problem-based learning or on traditional methods. These examples show that good goals or operationalisations of a concept are dependent on the purpose of the inquiry.

In the investigation of municipal governance models, we could register the model by looking at the difference between consensus-based and majority-based executive bodies. With the first type, party and groupings in the elected body are represented by their relative strength in the council; with the second type the majority controls the administration. Relations of power within the two types could be registered by asking the politicians how much power the various political bodies have, whether there are political A teams and B teams, and by asking how they perceive their own influence in political matters. The reader can easily imagine possible operationalisations of other variables that a change of governance model could influence.

In order to create a project with high construction validity, we must meet some demands. For one thing, we must know the field of study and the concepts used there. We must consult the literature of the field of study and become familiar with concepts such as governance model, power, learning, teaching methods, and teacher qualifications. We must learn how others have used and operationalised the concepts in their investigations. We can learn a lot from other researchers' operationalisations, use of concepts, and findings. Next, we must think through the purpose of our investigation while we operationalise; because the purpose of the project influences construction validity. Last, but not least, we must be critical and creative. Can the measurements be done better than what the others have done? Do we have good proposals for new operationalisations? Why are our proposals good, or even better than those formerly used?

In a variable-centred design, we use all the observations on each variable in order to describe it. The literature on method deals with how we do this. Descriptive statistics focuses, among other things, on measure level, frequency distributions, averages, medians, and distribution patterns of a variable. The analysis of variable data will start with such descriptions. From there the question is whether the purpose of our investigation is the testing or the development of theory-based explanations. The next sections introduce the design requirements of the two mentioned purposes.

THEORY TESTING IN VARIABLE-CENTRED DESIGNS

If testing a set of theoretical statements against data is the purpose of a variable-centred design, then the formulation of a theoretical model or a concept model is the starting point of the choice of design. In the following sections, the terms "concept model" and "empirical model" are used, and these terms are equivalent to the terms "theoretical model" and "data model" used in Chap. 3.

In our first example, such a model could for instance specify the relation between two independent variables and one dependent variable. The independent variable would be the teacher's academic qualifications and the teaching methods used. The dependent variable is the pupils' learning. This can be visualised in a concept model such as the one shown in Fig. 6.1.

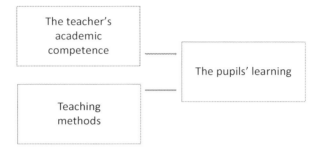

Fig. 6.1 A concept model for the relationship between the teacher's academic competence, teaching methods, and the pupils' learning

The first question we should ask in connection with this design is why this is an adequate theoretical model. Why are just these variables interesting? We have to use our knowledge of the specific literature and the field of study to give reasons for that. Based on the literature, specific statements or hypotheses about the relations between the variables can also be formulated. "High academic teacher competence gives better learning for the pupils." "Problem-based teaching gives a better learning result than traditional classroom teaching." In this way we have created a theoretical or concept model.

The next step is to find good operationalisations or empirical goals for the theoretical variables, seen in relation to our purpose. This has to do with construction validity. Based on the operationalisations we can create an empirical model in which we replace the theoretical concepts by measurable variables. In practice, we often place the theoretical model and the empirical model in the same figure by putting both the theoretical concepts and the measurable variables into one analytical model as shown in Fig. 6.2.

A corresponding model based on our second example would have only one independent variable, but several dependent variables. The independent variable is the governance model. Possible dependent variables could be power relations, distribution of accountability, control of the administration, the division of work between politicians and bureaucrats, and the legitimacy of the governance model. The relations between the variables are shown in Fig. 6.3. Based on the literature in the field of study we can formulate statements about the connection between a political governance model and such variables.

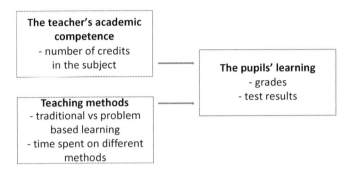

Fig. 6.2 Combined concept model and empirical model for the connection between the teacher's academic competence, teaching methods, and the pupils' learning

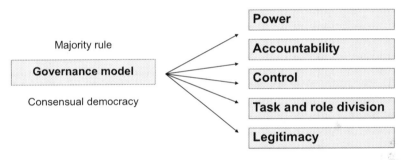

Fig. 6.3 Concept model to study effects of an independent variable

When using a variable-centred design, there are two main strategies to control for factors that are not included in our causal model. One strategy is to carry out an experiment in which we can control all contextual conditions and keep them constant. This is rarely possible in social research. True, there is an increase in laboratory experiments in social sciences too, but normally we depend on the other control strategy, which is to use statistical methods to control for the influence of variables that are not part of the causal model. In our first example we could for instance say that the social and ethnic backgrounds of the pupils are a type of factor that could influence their learning. If our purpose is to explore the effects of academic competence and teaching methods and not of the pupils' ethnicity or social background, we could include these data about the pupils in the design and treat social and ethnic backgrounds as control variables. In this case, the model must be extended with two control variables. There may be a number of relevant operationalisations of the concepts of social background and ethnicity (Fig. 6.4).

The literature on methods further discusses what kind of statistical methods we can use to explore the connection between causal variables and effect variables and to control for the effect of other factors, so-called control variables. What method is the best depends on the purpose of the project as well as our data. In our example we could for instance want to compare the learning of pupils who have used problem-based learning methods with those pupils who have been given traditional classroom teaching. To do this, we could divide the pupils in the research into two groups and then compare the groups—controlling for different social backgrounds in the groups and for teachers with different academic competence. In our second example we could want to compare the results of the dependent variables between municipalities with different governance models. Methods for variance analyses have to do with how to perform such analyses (Ringdal, 2013; Roberts & Russo, 2014). If we need such a method for our purpose, we should look closely at the conditions for using the method and operationalise in ways that are suited to the method.

Regression analysis is the most used method among social scientists for exploring connections between independent and dependent variables (Allen, 2004; Midtbø, 2007). Techniques for multivariate regression anal-

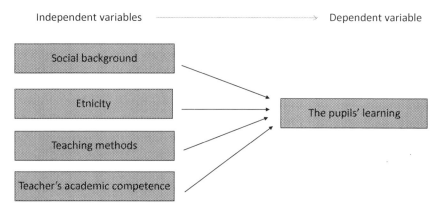

Fig. 6.4 Concept model to explain the causes of a phenomenon

ysis make it possible to explore the effect of a potential causal variable while at the same time controlling for variation in other variables. In this way, we can test causal explanations by isolating the effect of one variable and meeting the demand for keeping the contextual conditions constant. The simplest regression models deal with linear connections, while more advanced forms of regression analyses explore non-linear connections (Faraway, 2016). There are also other techniques than regression analysis for analysing connections with multiple independent variables (Clausen, 2009; Hjellbrekke, 1999; Kim & Mueller, 1978).

An important aspect of our choice of method is that we use a method adapted to the set of data we have or plan to collect, and that we have a plan for the modelling. Increasing the number of variables in a project is of little help if the result is a model that is too complex to allow for reliable conclusions from a limited data material. Technically, it is easy to perform complex regression analyses using statistic packages; it can be more difficult to assess the quality of the statistical methods in use. Some statisticians believe social scientists too often use a rather limited set of statistical tools without taking into account the conditions for using them (Schrodt, 2014).

The final element of the design is external validity, that is, the conditions for concluding from our set of data to the entire population. The standard answer to this in variable-centred designs is to make randomised selections. How we should perform this and how large the selection should be is dealt with in the method books. It is important in the design phase to consider both the size of our data set and how to select it in order to secure representativeness. Further, it is important to consider what population we are interested in generalising to. Referring to our example again: Is the population pupils in general, is it pupils in that particular school, or is it all third-form pupils? The sample should correspond reasonably to the population.

Employing a model-based way of thinking that regards social research as a reconstruction of phenomena and connections in society, we draw conclusions about our theoretical model—based on the degree of matching with the empirical findings that we analyse by means of an empirical model. If the findings do not match the model, we should first ask if the investigation was performed in such a way that it is reliable. If we find no reason to doubt our data, the question is whether we can use the findings to develop our model, or if we should start hunting for alternative hypotheses and theory-based explanations.

Theory Development in Variable-Centred Designs

Theory development can be one of the goals of variable-centred designs. The starting point will often be data that are organised around a set of empirical variables that have not been selected or designed based on theoretical concepts and models. Our goal then is to arrive at connections and patterns in the material that we can use to develop theoretical generalisations. We thus seek in the opposite direction of the cause-effect relations we want to explain (Fig. 6.5). The working model can be illustrated as follows:

Easily observable in our empirical material is correlation, that is, covariation between empirical variables. A strategy to proceed is to create an empirical model for analysis, such that some of the variables in our data set are supposed to influence other variables. Let us say that we have data for how the inhabitants in a sample of municipalities judge the quality of the government services. We could then build an empirical explanatory model where the size of the municipality, its revenue, and characteristics of the local inhabitants contribute to explaining the assessment of the services. Using a regression analysis, we can then find how each of the independent variables influences the quality assessments. In this way, we can establish some empirical connections as probable, and then control them for representativeness or external validity in the usual way.

Still, we have not yet given a theoretical explanation to why the inhabitants judge the government services the way they do. Municipal size is for instance an empirical indicator in this investigation. But for what causal factor is it an indicator? Is it about proximity, that is, how accessible—geographically as well as socially—the government services are? Is it rather about professional expertise, that large municipalities systematically have better or weaker employees than small ones? And what about revenue as an indicator? Should we relate revenue to expertise because municipalities with high revenues are more competitive in recruiting qualified workers? The way our inquiry is constructed gives no clear answer to this. Thus, the construction validity is low. Data extension,

Fig. 6.5 Model for theory development

using indicators that are poorly suited for measuring the theoretical concept that the indicators refer to, is a common problem when developing theory from this type of analyses (Collier & Mahon, 1993; Sartori, 1970).

In order to justify theoretical generalisations from this type of design, we need other forms of reasoning as a supplement. One solution is to use abductive reasoning where we consider what possible mechanisms bind together the variables municipality size and quality assessments. Through such reasoning we can develop new ideas about connections that in their turn can be tested on new data. We could for instance collect data not only about quality but also about geographical and perceived proximity to the services. We could also collect data about expertise. Another strategy could be to design the investigation in such a way that we can use methods for data reduction. These methods organise groups of empirical variables according to their covariation. Explorative factor analyses (Kim & Mueller, 1978) are the most common.

Still, we could be led astray when implementing this type of analyses. If we include variables with no other reason than that we have data on them, there is a risk that the models for analysis identify a covariation that is haphazard or spurious. We could also be tempted to include too many variables for a limited set of data to give reliable conclusions. A steady hand is needed if we want to formulate theoretical generalisations from data that have not been constructed for the purpose. We must take user guidance in method books seriously, and maybe we should be content with ascertaining that we have found interesting empirical patterns. The next project can then proceed from there.

VARIANTS OF VARIABLE-CENTRED DESIGNS

In a laboratory experiment, it is possible to have only two variables in the data matrix: one causal variable and one effect variable. All other variables are kept constant. Such controlled experiments are, however, unusual in social research. Usually there are multiple factors that vary. Moreover, it is a question whether it is feasible to generalise from the units we possess the data for to all possible units of the same kind. This is a question about whether the data permit generalising from the sample to the population.

In variable-centred social research the answer to these problems is using statistical methods of analysis. Such methods are used to judge whether a sample of units is representative for the whole population, and to analyse whether findings based on a sample can be generalised to entire populations. Regression-based analyses are used when we want to control for the effect of and the interaction between causal variables. Variance analyses are used to examine whether differences between two or more groups can be generalised. Factor analyses and correspondence analyses are usually used as tools to reduce data complexity and to build generalisations. The technical aspects of these analyses can be studied in the method books; here, the aim is to give a brief overview of possible designs, thus providing a basis for choosing a suitable design that will be able to answer the research questions in the project. I distinguish between different types of experimental designs, and between cross-sectional and longitudinal designs. As shown below, these types of designs are suited for a number of purposes and for a variety of questions.

Table 6.2 sums up the variants of variable-centred designs introduced and their uses.

Table 6.2 Variants of variable-centred designs

Types of design	Questions	Purposes
True experiment	Do the results on the effect variable match with the theoretical statement?	Testing hypotheses and theoretical models
Quasi-experiments and natural experiments	Are our observations in accordance with the statements in the theory? Can we find a theoretical explanation that complies with the observations? Can we generalise from the sample to the population?	Testing and developing theories and theoretical models
Cross-sectional designs	Is there a variation between units or groups? How do phenomena correlate? Can the correlation be interpreted as the result of a causal connection?	Describing variation and correlation Testing theory
Longitudinal designs	Is a phenomenon stable, or does it vary over time? How do phenomena correlate? Can we interpret the correlation as the result of a causal connection?	Describing stability and change Analysing causal connections—testing theory

Experimental Designs

Experimental designs can be divided into three groups: true experiments, quasi-experiments, and natural experiments (Ringdal, 2013). Already Chap. 2 discussed the conditions for a true experimental design. In a true experiment, we must be able to keep constant the contextual conditions that could influence the result of a variation in a causal variable. We can do this by controlling the contextual conditions, by matching, or by randomisation.

If we want to perform an experiment to find whether water boils at 100 degree centigrade at a normal atmospheric pressure, we need to be able to control a number of such contextual conditions. We need to be sure that the water is not mixed or polluted with fluids that have a different boiling point. We need to know that the thermometer is accurate. And we need to be able to control the air pressure, which requires an airtight container or, at least, a correct barometer and a day with a favourable atmospheric pressure. Only when we can control the contextual conditions can we be sure that the investigated causal factor (heating water to 100 degree centigrade) and no other factors leads to the observed result (that the water boils). If the result fails to appear and if we are sure the contextual conditions are under control, it is a strong indicator that the theory is not good enough and should be rejected.

Controlling the contextual conditions is a strong strategy when we want to test a hypothesis. Yet there are disadvantages. For instance, we may have to perform the test in a laboratory. If we are to control the contextual conditions outside a laboratory, we can do so by choosing only identical units in the experiment. We can for instance investigate the effect of fitness training by choosing the test persons among those who never do workout. A high internal validity in the investigation can then be secured, since the control group has no training effect. It can, however, be more difficult to generalise the findings to other groups of the population, for instance those who are already fit. Thus, the external validity decreases.

An alternative strategy is to match the test persons in equal pairs where one variable is different and the other variables are constant. Studies of identical twins are a well-known example of this strategy. Still, matching is not always easy to perform in practice; thus, the most usual strategy for control is randomising, in other words that we select a random sample of units for our experiment.

True experiments are considered the gold standard in the study of causal connections (Ringdal, 2013); both because the experimental factor can be manipulated so that the cause is working in advance of the measuring of the effect, and because the researchers can control for other factors than the cause they want to study the effect of.

True experiments are rare in social sciences for several reasons, one being that social actors are able to act strategically to influence the result if they are aware that they are part of an experiment. This is so because in social sciences we study intentional actors rather than passive objects. The knowledge that you are part of an experiment can have an influence; this is known as the experimental effect or the placebo effect. It is well known that when the control group in an experiment is given a placebo medicine it has a positive effect on how they feel. In the field of organisation theory, the Hawthorne experiment is a standard example of something similar. A group of researchers who studied the effect of better lighting and other improvements of the working environment in a factory found that the workers reacted to changes with higher effort and productivity, and that this happened even when the physical conditions were actually aggravated by the changes.

Another reason is that when we try out new ideas, approaches, and models in an experiment we cannot prevent these ideas from having an influence in other places than where the experiment is carried out. Here we have to do with a contamination effect (Cook et al., 1979) or with sliding control groups that influence the experiment.

If we want to investigate a hypothesis about a specific causal connection but cannot perform a controlled experiment we have to base the experiment on a quasi-experimental design, the core of which is randomisation and statistical control. Randomisation means that we must collect data from a random selection of units in the population we want to generalise to. The sections above have shown how we can use statistical methods to secure internal and external validity in research projects; hence it will not be repeated here.

With natural experiments, we mean non-experimental situations that are similar to experiments. Two examples of this are political reforms and mass vaccination. In such situations we may get the chance to compare units that have implemented the reform or the measure with units that have not. In such a situation, we can organise a natural experiment. Another alternative is that we get the chance to carry out condition measurements before and after the actual reform or intervention. We could for instance get information about the number of influenza cases among elderly people who have taken a vaccine and those who did not, or we could collect data about the number of cases before and after the introduction of a new vaccine. This example shows two designs built on different principles. In the first case we have a cross-sectional design, in the second a longitudinal design. The next section discusses these two designs and their uses.

CROSS-SECTIONAL AND LONGITUDINAL DESIGNS

Cross-sectional designs involve a collection of the same kind of data from multiple units at the same time. It is the most common form of variable-centred designs, not least because it is easier to carry out in practice than designs that require data collected at different times.

The cross-sectional design is useful when our study focuses on the variation between units or groups of units. Back to our example: Do pupils' performances vary between schools, or between schools in different municipalities? Do teaching methods or teachers' academic competence vary between schools or between municipalities? This is a descriptive use of the cross-sectional design. Data established through a cross-sectional design are often used to study the way different variables co-vary. Is there a correlation between the teachers' academic competence and the pupils' performances? Is there a correlation between the teaching methods and the pupils' performances? As often as not we interpret such correlations as a proof of causal connections between the variables. The dilemma is that the design does not give us data that meet the main requirement for causality: that the cause should appear before the effect. If we collect data on academic competence and pupils' performances at the same time, we have, strictly speaking, no data to tell us whether academic competence is the cause of higher pupil performance.

A solution to this problem is that we have a good theory that is able to establish as probable that there is a causal relationship. In our case there are good reasons to maintain that high academic competence measured in 2015 will also be a good indicator of high academic competence in 2012 when our third-form pupils started school. If we can establish such a connection as probable on concept level, the cross-sectional design will be easier to accept as a relevant procedure. However, we cannot conclude the other way, from correlation to causality, on the grounds of the data set alone. The correlation could also be caused by a third variable that influences both of the observed variables. In such a situation we say that the relationship is random or spurious (Simon, 1954).

An alternative solution would be to create a longitudinal design, collecting data at different times. Longitudinal designs can be used to study stability and change in a given phenomenon. They are also stronger than cross-sectional designs when performing causal analyses, because we can get data on causes that are working before we collect data on their supposed effects.

Longitudinal designs can be retrospective or prospective. In retrospective designs we collect data afterwards; in prospective designs we collect data prior to the period we study as well as afterwards. If we collect data afterwards through interviews or questionnaires, faulty memory and styling of information will be a possible source of bias in retrospective designs. We do not encounter these problems if we use register data, however, because these data have usually been collected at different time points.

There are a number of variants also of prospective designs. If we collect data from different samples of the same population at different times, we have a design called time series study, or a repeated cross-sectional study. We could for instance have studied third-form pupils at the same schools in 2013 and 2015.

If we collect data from the same sample at different times, but without registering the time series for each individual in the sample, we have a cohort study. We could for instance have studied our third-form pupils over time and collected data about the same pupils as third-year pupils as well as when they are fifth-year pupils.

While we can use the cohort study only to analyse changes on group levels, a panel study can give information about changes on the level of individuals. We need to get data about the same persons at different times and identify them in such a way that we can study them over time. This makes it possible to study variation and correlation on individual as well as group levels.

References

Allen, M. P. (2004). *Understanding regression analysis*. New York: Springer Science & Business Media.

Clausen, S.-E. (2009). *Multivariate analysemetoder for samfunnsvitere : med eksempler i SPSS*. Oslo, Norway: Universitetsforl.

VARIABLE-CENTRED DESIGNS   113

Collier, D., & Mahon, J. E. (1993). Conceptual "stretching" revisited: Adapting categories in comparative analysis. *The American Political Science Review, 87*(4), 845–855. https://doi.org/10.2307/2938818

Cook, T. D., Campbell, D. T., Fankhauser, G., Reichardt, C. S., McCain, L. J., & McCleary, R. (1979). *Quasi-experimentation: Design & analysis issues for field settings.* Boston: Houghton Mifflin Co.

Faraway, J. J. (2016). *Extending the linear model with R: Generalized linear, mixed effects and nonparametric regression models* (Vol. 124). Boca Raton, FL: CRC press.

Hjellbrekke, J. (1999). *Innføring i korrespondanseanalyse.* Bergen-Sandviken, Norway: Fagbokforl.

Kim, J.-O., & Mueller, C. W. (1978). *Introduction to factor analysis: What it is and how to do it* (Vol. 13). Beverly Hills, CA: Sage.

Midtbø, T. (2007). *Regresjonsanalyse for samfunnsvitere: med eksempler i SPSS.* Oslo, Norway: Universitetsforl.

Ringdal, K. (2013). *Enhet og mangfold. Samfunnsvitenskapelig forskning og kvantitativ metode. 3. utg.* Bergen: Fagbokforlaget.

Roberts, M., & Russo, R. (2014). *A student's guide to analysis of variance.* London: Routledge.

Sartori, G. (1970). Concept misformation in comparative politics. *American Political Science Review, 64*(04), 1033–1053.

Schrodt, P. A. (2014). Seven deadly sins of contemporary quantitative political analysis. *Journal of Peace Research, 51*(2), 287–300. https://doi.org/10.1177/0022343313499597

Simon, H. (1954). Spurious correlation: A causal interpretation*. *Journal of the American Statistical Association, 49*(267), 467–479. https://doi.org/10.1080/01621459.1954.10483515

CHAPTER 7

Case Designs

In a case study, we study social phenomena in their real context. Also, we study the case as part of a larger class of events or cases. It is important to understand what constitutes the case in a case study and what class of phenomena it represents. A case study needs to be focused; that is, it must be oriented towards a specific type of research purpose, and it must have a focus that is relevant for the purpose. Further, the collection of data must be structured in such a way that the collected information can be used for theoretical interpretation of the case or be relevant for the development or testing of theories. In the following sections, I discuss in detail what these requirements involve, using them to introduce variants of case designs. Discussed are designs with critical cases, congruence designs, designs for process tracing, and designs for theoretical interpretative reconstruction.

What Is a Case Study?

A common definition of case studies is that they are intensive qualitative studies of one or a few research units (Andersen, 2013). As an approach to describing a typical case study there is nothing wrong with this definition. Most case studies are just that: They include one or a few cases, and they mainly use qualitative data.

© The Author(s) 2019
O. Bukve, *Designing Social Science Research*,
https://doi.org/10.1007/978-3-030-03979-0_7

Still, the question is whether this definition places too little emphasis on another essential aspect of case studies: that they attempt to study a social phenomenon in its entirety and in its context. Robert Yin's book about designs and methods in case studies, first published in 1984, was ground-breaking by making just this aspect the foundation of his understanding of what a case study is. According to Yin (1984, p. 23), a case study is an empirical inquiry that investigates a contemporary phenomenon within its real-life context, when the boundaries between phenomenon and context are not clearly evident, and in which multiple sources of evidence are used. Thus, the two constitutive features of a case study are that we study the phenomenon in its real context and that the boundaries are not clear. This delimits the case study from the experiment, where the ideal is an approach that keeps the researched phenomenon from being influenced by the context. In the experiment, the effect of the context is to be controlled and zeroed. This is impossible with most social phenomena. We have to study them the way they actually take place, as contextualised phenomena. The challenges involved constitute a particular issue for the social sciences. The strength of Yin's definition is that it is based on a realistic understanding of the conditions and delimitations that social researchers are faced with when studying a social phenomenon.

The part of Yin's definition that seems less justified is the delimitation to contemporary phenomena. Social phenomena take place over time; thus, the distinction between contemporary and historical phenomena is in my opinion artificial. A case design can just as well investigate historical phenomena or processes over time.

Importantly, Yin does not define a case study from the type of data but states that many types of data can be used to describe a case. Thus, it is also possible to make use of data in the form of numbers to describe the properties of a case.

Further, it is important to note that Yin does not mention anything about the number of cases in a case study. Case studies can be single-case studies or multiple-case studies; the number of cases is not decisive. This will become clearer in the following discussion of how to define and delimit what the case is in a given study. It is not unimportant what we perceive as the case in a case study.

What Is the Case in a Case Study?

According to Yin, the question of what constitutes the case is decided in the introductory research question (Yin, 1984, p. 34). Still, the research questions must, as discussed in Chap. 5, be related to the overall purpose or knowledge goal of a project. I therefore believe that it is more precise to define the case in relation to the purpose of the project. What constitutes the case depends on the purpose of the project or what kind of knowledge we want to develop.

Let us for instance say that we want to interview a staff of 20 teachers in a school about their perceptions of their principal as a leader. This can be regarded as a study with a single case. The 20 teachers are informants while the case is the principal as school leader. But by changing the approach a little, we can make the study into a multiple-case study. We could for instance get informants from four different schools, five teachers, and the principal from each school. Then we have a multiple-case study of the principal as a school leader, with four cases and 24 informants.

Using other research questions, we could employ the first sample of informants in a multiple-case study. We could for instance be interested in finding the characteristic features of the self-understanding of the teacher profession in Norway in 2016. We would use the data from the 20 teachers to construct a picture of the typical Norwegian teacher. The teachers are cases representing the phenomenon or the study object, the teacher profession. At the same time, we can see that the study will be more robust if we select cases from different schools.

In fact, we could regard this study as a study with far more than 20 cases. If we ask the interview objects to describe situations in which they feel success as teachers, and situations in which they feel they do not succeed, these situations constitute the cases in the study. If each teacher describes 2–3 cases, we will have 40–60 potential cases in the study.

Like single-case studies, multiple-case studies are oriented towards finding typical characteristics of a phenomenon. They also make it possible to spot variations between different types of phenomena. When we use multiple-case studies to discover variation, the next step can be the development of designs directly oriented towards comparison.

With yet another research question, our study of teachers may become a comparative case study where we compare contentment in various contexts. We could for instance ask if it is more stressful to work as a teacher at the lower secondary level than in primary school. Our starting point could be the hypothesis that working with older children who have reached puberty is more challenging than working with younger children. We would need a strategic sample of informants, constructed in a way that makes both groups part of the sample. "Lower secondary level" and "primary level" are the cases in the inquiry. In a comparative case study, we should be aware of relevant variation in the context when choosing the cases. Characteristic for comparative case studies is that we analyse at two levels. We analyse each case in the study to find case internal development traits and connections, and we also analyse similarity and variation across cases (George & Bennett, 2005). I discuss the characteristics of designs of comparative case studies in Chap. 9.

A common beginner mistake in case studies is that the definition of the case is not taken seriously; some only use case as another word for informant. That often makes problems after the collection of data has been performed. One possible problem is that we may not be able to keep the analysis of the data in focus. If we do not clearly know what phenomenon we are analysing, we will easily be confused in the analytical phase. And even if we manage to find an analytical focus after the data collection has been performed, a danger exists that we have failed to ask the questions that are necessary to understand the phenomenon we want to analyse. If the data collection is not clearly related to the research purpose, holes in the set of data can easily occur.

To sum up: What the case or the unit for analysis in a case study is depends on what class of phenomena we are studying and what the purpose of the project is. We have to decide what the relevant case is based on the phenomena we want to find out about, and it is important to define what level we are generalising to. Is it to the role of principal, to the teacher profession, to the type of teacher, or to the type of school? Depending on these choices, we can design our study as a single-case study, a multiple-case study, or a comparative case study.

CASE STUDIES AND KNOWLEDGE DEVELOPMENT

As we have seen, it is important to define the level that makes up the case. Further, through such a definition we are also saying something about the class of phenomena the case belongs to. The most recent contributions to the extensive literature on case studies emphasise that we should regard the case as *an instance of a larger class of events or instances* (George & Bennett, 2005; Gerring, 2004). This is not as clearly formulated in Yin's definition (1984). George and Bennett define what a case study is by focusing on the following: "We define a case as an instance of a class of events" (George & Bennett, 2005, p. 17). This can be seen as an extension of Yin's definition. Although Yin does not mention this element in his definition, it is inherent in his approach.

George and Bennett further state that "a larger class of events" refers to a phenomenon of theoretical interest. Regarding the case as an incident of a larger class, we place it in a theoretical and scientific context. We analyse it in the context of the concepts and theories of the field of study.

Returning to our imagined teacher study, we can concretise it. When we talk about the typical teacher or teacher profession in Norway it does not take place in a scientific or theoretical vacuum. Perhaps we wish to compare the self-understanding of today's teachers with a historical picture of the Norwegian teacher. Alternatively, we may want to relate our study to a general theory about professions and their typical characteristics, or we may want to relate to the self-understanding of other professions. In the mentioned multiple-case studies, the general phenomenon could be working life satisfaction or mastering in a profession; the teachers or the types of teachers could be seen as cases of this phenomenon. Studying a social phenomenon based on a case design we most probably want to be able to say something about a broader class of phenomena than just the case we are studying. In this way, a case study can contribute to providing new knowledge about a social phenomenon.

George and Bennett (2005) list two basic requirements of a case study that is meant to develop our knowledge: it has to be structured, and it has to be focused (p. 67). That a case study is *structured* means that we must ask a set of standardised and identical questions to all the cases in the class. In single-case studies, too, we must be so clear about what we are looking for that the approach can be repeated in new studies of other cases belonging to the same class of phenomena. Unless we structure the study, we cannot build and develop theories systematically.

That the case study is *focused* means that it is performed with a specific research purpose and with a theoretical focus that is relevant for that purpose. A case study is focused through our decision that a specific aspect of the case is to be placed in the centre of the analysis. An example to illustrate this could be a case study of a major political crisis such as today's situation in Syria. This imagined study is still not focused. We focus it by deciding what aspect of the Syrian situation we want to study. Do we want to study the situation as a civil war, as a humanitarian disaster, as part of an ongoing competition between superpowers, as a case of terrorism, or as a religious conflict? It is the focusing that links the case to a broader class of phenomena and thus makes it theoretically and scientifically relevant.

The requirements of a good case study are that researchers must place themselves in the relevant field of study and build on what other researchers have done, theoretically as well as empirically. A research project is a new argument in an ongoing debate in a field. If researchers only discuss with themselves they risk producing little that is of use to others.

How precise the design should be depends on the purpose of the study. If the purpose is to test an established theory, the analytical frame should be more structured than when the purpose is to develop new concepts and theories. I return to this in the discussion of different types of case designs.

Case, Context, Embeddedness

An important distinction when we carry out a case study is the difference between studies that focus on the case as a whole, and studies that regard the case as embedded in a context (Yin, 1984, p. 44ff). An analysis of embedded cases can be illustrated by a simple systems model, in which the case or the cases make up partial systems within a more extensive system (Fig. 7.1).

When studying the case as a whole, properties of the case and within-case relations are in focus, while context is less important. Taking a look at the examples on the previous pages, we see that the first examples are of this kind. When analysing the self-understanding of the teacher profession or the satisfaction among teachers, the phenomenon in itself is in focus.

When on the other hand we analyse the case or the cases as embedded in a context, the relations between the case and the context are the centre of interest. We can distinguish between two different strategies to analyse

Fig. 7.1 Analytical model of an embedded case

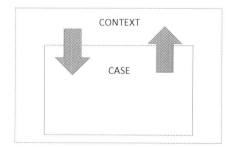

the relation between case and context. These two strategies may with some justice be regarded as the case design's versions of cross-sectional and longitudinal designs.

One strategy is the one discussed in the former section about regarding the case as an instance of a larger class of phenomena. Then the questions are how knowledge about the case can contribute to developing knowledge about the broader class of phenomena on which we base our study of the case, and the other way around, how knowledge about the broader class of phenomena can give us a broader perspective on the case. Congruence and deviation between theory and case are the centre of attention of the analysis.

The other kind of analysis of embedded cases looks at the interaction between context and case from a process perspective. How are stability, change, and various ways of development produced in the interaction between the case we direct our attention at and the environment it is part of? For instance, we could perform a study of adaptation strategies in the Norwegian oil industry after the big drop in oil prices in 2014–2015. At company level, we can imagine several feasible strategies: A company could choose to dismiss people, permanently or temporarily; it could restructure to new products, move its business activities to an area where it can produce with lower costs, or could lose money while waiting for better times. What a company chooses will depend on context factors such as industry, management, corporate culture, and financial capacity. Case studies can seek to uncover what factors are the decisive ones in each instance and build generalisations on this basis.

THEORY TESTING IN CASE DESIGNS

When creating a theory-testing case design, it is necessary to have as much prior knowledge about the case that we are able to justify why it is reasonable to regard the case as an instance of a class of cases. A case study of a social welfare office could be regarded as an instance of the class of vocational organisations, the class of service producing organisations, or the class of public administration bureaucracy. We can also choose to regard it as an organisation situated in the field of tension between these three types of organisations. To make such a case study into a real theory-testing case we need to read up on theories about the class or the classes of cases we plan to study. Decisive is that we specify what findings and observations would be in accordance with a given theory and then collect data that enable us to assess the findings against expectations and theory-based statements.

In case studies we need a holistic approach to each of the cases in an inquiry. This places practical limitations on the number of cases a case study can possibly comprise. In regard to theory testing, the essential question is whether it makes sense to subject a theory to real-term testing when it can only be tested on a limited number of cases.

An answer to that question is that we should do theory testing with the help of *critical cases*, that is, cases that have been selected with the specific aim of putting the theory to a real-life test (Eckstein, 1975; Levy, 2008). This is a controversial solution (Mahoney, 2008). A less radical view of theory-testing case studies is based on the view that social science theories are concerned with the probability of a result rather than with deterministic relations. Social scientists tend to formulate statements of the type "there is a greater probability for a person born in the west of Norway to use the language variant 'nynorsk' than for a person born in Oslo," rather than "those born in the west of Norway write 'nynorsk'".[1] Thus, there will be no critical case that can lead to a rejection of the statement.

However, we do not depend on critical cases to test theories by help of a case study. Case studies can for instance help us evaluate rivalling theories against each other. Let us stick to the case about the use of language norm but sharpen the research question to deal with the change of language norm when people who were born in the west of Norway move to Oslo. One theory would be that language norm depends on values and norms acquired in childhood and youth. From this theory we could formulate the hypothesis that young people from the west of Norway have been socialised into a "nynorsk" culture, and because they are characterised by this culture they will go on using this language norm even when they live in the city. Another theory could be that language use is influenced by rules and demands in people's jobs, what organisation theory calls institutional coercion. According to this theory, those who move to the city will feel the need to use the language variant "bokmål". A third theory could be that values and culture related to "nynorsk" are on the decline, so that those who move to the city will change their language norm even if they do not encounter formal demands to do so. We can

---

[1] Nynorsk (literally "new Norwegian") and bokmål (literally "book language") are two equated writing norms in Norway. Bokmål is used by the majority, nynorsk mainly in Western Norway.

operationalise these three theories. If theory 1 is the most plausible, we would assume that our informants would write "nynorsk" in their private lives as well as on the job. If theory 2 is the most plausible, we would assume that the informants write "nynorsk" in their private writings but use "bokmål" in their work. If theory 3 is the right one, we will find a change of language norm both in people's private lives and in connection with their jobs. This type of theory-based hypothesis can be tested through a *correspondence design* where the findings in a case study are compared to expectations based on different theories. Of course, a case is not a strong testing of a theory. But if we organise the study according to a replication logic (Yin, 1984, pp. 48–53), testing several similar cases, the testing would be stronger. We could also combine the congruence design with process tracing (Beach & Pedersen, 2014; Bennett & Checkel, 2015), searching for the specific mechanisms that lead to a possible change of language norms. I will return to this.

Interpretative Reconstruction and Theory Development in Case Designs

The discussion about case designs and theory development is many-sided. There are some who claim that the development of general statements and theories is not a goal for the social sciences. Social science is first and foremost a matter of understanding the unique, the individual case. The conventional definition of an understanding case study is that such a study interprets a case in order to establish a deeper understanding of the case and such phenomena that the case represents. An important question will then be what is typical or characteristic for the phenomenon. What distinguishes it from other phenomena? When researchers answer such questions, the concepts and theories of the discipline will always be present in the sense that they inform the interpretation of the data. Therefore, I have chosen to use the concepts of interpretative reconstruction or theoretical interpretation for a type of studies that are often just called interpretative or understanding.

Interpretation also means reconstructing meaning (Habermas, 1990). In order to understand what happens in groups, organisations, or communities, we need to understand the meaning social actors give to what they say and do. Such understanding requires an interpretation of each act or statement in light of the context in which they were articulated or produced. In other words, interpretative reconstruction requires a hermeneutic or discourse analytical research logic. Each act or statement is interpreted as part of a totality and thus reconstructed as meaningful in that context. We should ask what the reason is for the actor to do what she or he does. If we want to understand foreign fighters as a phenomenon without having to use stereotypes, we should try to understand their thinking and reasons and how they construct the social context that their acts are based on.

Interpretative projects may also encourage new and alternative interpretations of social phenomena (Ragin & Amoroso, 2011). Critical theory has a special interest in giving underprivileged groups, those who are not usually heard in the social debate, a voice by presenting a phenomenon from their perspective. The value of such critical interpretative projects lies in the possibility that they may change our view and the way we define groups and situations, thus providing us with another view of ourselves and others. As a result, our eyes may be directed towards new forms of intervention. How we understand the phenomenon of foreign fighters will influence the way we try to counteract it.

In naïvely interpretative projects the researcher aims to interpret a phenomenon as unique. A dilemma with such designs is that data will often be interpreted based on fairly general and vague concepts, since the data collection was not designed for clarifying or testing aspects of these concepts. This gives a weak foundation for the development of new and more precise knowledge from this type of projects.

If the implications of theoretical frames and observations are not made explicit, they cannot be challenged by new observations. Some researchers will defend themselves against such criticism by claiming that social science is not about developing general and abstract knowledge but rather about interpreting phenomena that are always unique. If this were the case, it would mean giving up the ambitions that scientific work should result in new knowledge in the form of more precise concepts and theories.

Others believe we could and should use case studies for systematic theory development. The issue of theory development by use of case designs has traditionally been linked to an inductive research logic. It has been presented as an ideal that data should speak for themselves without being restricted by pre-defined frames. From then on, it is up to the researcher to abstract from observations in the case to theoretical concepts and statements. Contrary to this, a more science-theoretically updated understanding is based on the belief that data do not speak for themselves. The researcher will always have a specific pre-understanding of the case, and there is an interest and a positioning behind this view. This view has been substantiated in the first part of this book. The researcher's understanding of the case can never erase the distance between the text and the reader; therefore, a theoretical interpretation will always be a reconstruction. The researcher reconstructs the case in an oscillation between frames of understanding and data. When interpreting, the reader becomes the author, according to Barbara Czarniawska (2004, p. 71). Apart from this, there are few detailed rules for the design of interpretative and theory development case studies; the design frames are volatile. Yet that does not make it less important to use adequate methodological approaches. Analytical narratives (Czarniawska, 2004), grounded theory (Glaser & Strauss, 1967; Kelle, 2007), and process tracing (Beach & Pedersen, 2014) are examples of methods that can be used in this type of design.

Variants of Case Designs

The literature on case studies describes several types of case designs. A case design can be used to ask different types of questions, and different variants of designs can be oriented towards different purposes. This is not the place to deal with the methodological approaches in detail. Nevertheless, this section offers a few remarks to various designs both as a starting point for choosing a design and as a gateway to the more detailed descriptions found in books on case design methods.

Table 7.1 presents an overview of the design types discussed in the next sections. I base the presentation on the main purpose of a given design, but the table also attempts to show how one and the same design can be relevant for a number of purposes.

Creating an overview of the various case designs is more complicated than introducing the designs in variable-centred research. This is partly due to the fact that the academic discussion on case methods is rapidly developing, and different authors may present different views. An established standard cannot easily be found. Partly, this has to do with the relation between overall designs and the selection of cases, which in a case design is different from variable-centred designs. In a variable-centred design the ideal is to find a statistically seen random selection of a given population. This makes overall designs and the selection of data two separate phases in the research process. With case designs, on the other hand, theoretical reasoning plays a role in the selection of cases. The cases must be relevant in terms of the ambition of testing and developing theory. This

126   O. BUKVE

Table 7.1 Variants of case designs

Design	Main questions	Purposes

Critical case design
  Most probable cases
  Least probable cases
	Can a theory be strengthened or weakened by being tested against a critical case?	Theory testing

Congruence design
(Pattern matching)
  One theory/multiple theories
  One case/several identical ones
  (replication logic)
	How do case observations correspond to theory-based expectations and statements?	Theory testing
		Theory-informed analysis of the case

Process tracing
  From theoretical hypothesis to case
  From result to mechanisms
  Deviant cases
	Can we identify the actuating causes and reconstruct the mechanisms that produce a given result in an instance or a type of instances?
	Why is the result in this case other than expected?
		Theory testing
		Theory-informed analysis of the case
		Theory building

Theoretical interpretative reconstruction
  Sensitising concepts
  Analytical narrative
  Grounded theory
	What happened in this instance? How can we reconstruct processes and actions?
	How can scientific concepts and theories be used to illuminate a case or a phenomenon?
	What does the case tell us about the phenomenon and the connections we are studying?
		Theoretical reconstruction of the case
		Theory development

makes the difference between overall designs and method less clear. Some researchers refer to this totality of design and method as methodology (Gobo, 2008). I, however, use the concept of design also in the subsequent chapters and sections, and, as will become clear to the reader, this concept often also involves the selection of cases.

CRITICAL CASES AS DESIGN FOR THEORY TESTING

The use of critical cases for theory testing is, as mentioned, controversial both in terms of the power of explanation of any single case and because it is difficult to identify one particular case to be used as a strong test of a theory or hypothesis (Gerring, 2006; Mahoney, 2008). The literature mentions two strategies for using critical cases to test hypotheses. One is the so-called most likely design; the other is the least likely design. These designs have become well known because of a classic article by Harry Eckstein (1975), where he recommends trying to disprove a theory by checking whether it holds water or not when applied to a case for which the theory regards it as most likely that it should, and vice versa that the theory is more plausible if it can explain a case for which it is least likely that it should be the right one.

In a "most likely design" we select a case that on all relevant independent variables corresponds to a certain result predicted by the hypothesis. The idea is that if the result does not correspond to the hypothesis in this instance, the hypothesis is least likely to predict correctly in other instances. Most likely designs build on a falsification logic, in other words that a critical case can disprove a theory.

In "least likely designs", on the other hand, we choose a case that on all relevant independent variables, minus one, should lead to opposite findings from what the hypothesis predicts. Let us imagine a tripartite hypothesis that predicts that small, sparsely populated, and affluent municipalities have the highest costs per inhabitant. We could then choose a case with a municipality that is small and affluent, but densely populated. If this municipality, against our expectations, has low costs per capita we can conclude that the critical variable for costs is not size or level of income but that the area is sparsely populated. If the small, affluent, and densely populated municipality has low costs, it is likely that also other densely populated municipalities have low costs per inhabitant.

Now the question is how wide-reaching the conclusions are that we could draw from this type of hypothesis testing based on single cases. I find John Gerring's criticism quite convincing. He is sceptical to the idea of critical cases from one specific reason: Falsifying a theory just from one case presupposes a deterministic view of the theory, which is rare for theories about society (Gerring, 2007). Theories about society usually operate with degrees of connections and interacting causes. In the case mentioned above, the level of income, the size of the municipality, and the settlement structure could all three have an impact on the level of costs in the municipalities. We could possibly say that a given hypothesis is more plausible if it is not disproved by a case and less plausible if there is a different result than what was predicted by the hypothesis. Yet we cannot say that a case study is a strong proof for whether a hypothesis is right or wrong. Theory testing through critical cases is not the main reason for performing case studies. However, unexpected findings will often be a stimulus for rethinking established theories. Is there a logical flaw in the theory, or should the theory be better delimited regarding the context where it actually fits?

Congruence Design: Case Analysis with Structured Frames

In the method literature, the analytical approach to establish congruence between theoretical frames and data in case studies is called either pattern matching (Yin, 1984) or the congruence method (George & Bennett, 2005). I have chosen the term *congruence design*. In a congruence design we establish a theoretical frame or model as well as expectations about findings before starting to analyse the case. Then we compare the findings to the already defined expectations or hypotheses. Congruence design can be suitable for various purposes. It can be used for systematic testing of theories. It can also be used for theory-informed analysis of a case, without the ambition of testing or developing new theory. In both cases, findings that are contrary to theory or hypotheses can give rise to adjustments and development of established theory.

As a *theory-testing* design, congruence design in its simplest form can be used for testing statements based on a theory by means of a single case. Congruence design used on a single case can be regarded as analogue to an experiment, whereas the use on multiple cases is analogue to carrying out several experiments of the same kind. Replication logic is the term Yin (1984) uses for the logic behind such repeated case studies. Theoretical statements supported by repeated cases can be regarded as more solid than those that are supported by only one case. The advantage of a well-constructed congruence design is also that the replication can be performed by other researchers studying new cases. By using a congruence design, even a small case study can be part of a broader scientific context. George and Bennett (2005) give sound advice about methods suited to analyse congruence in such studies.

A *theory-informed case study with structured frames* can be organised in various ways (Andersen, 2013). For one thing, we can study familiar phenomena using new theoretical frames and thus shed new light on the phenomenon. The other way around, we can use established theories to study new phenomena. We can also study the same phenomenon in light of different theories. One choice is to regard the theories as complementary, as tools to give a more comprehensive explanation than what a single theory can do. We can also analyse the phenomenon by using competing theories, making the approach similar to that of a theory-testing project.

When we analyse familiar phenomena with new concepts and theories our main goal is often to find new aspects of these phenomena, aspects we have not been aware of. A historic example is the shift from studying organisations as tools for the management to regarding them as cultures. Theories about organisational culture focus on other aspects of life in an organisation than what the tool theories do; they study established values, norms, and informal practices rather than formal structures. They can for instance make us understand why it is that the management fails in attempting to change certain aspects of the organisation, or why the management succeeds in getting support for major changes by concentrating on values. As organisation culture theories direct their attention towards other aspects of the organisation than the tool theories do, we often use the theories complementarily to illuminate factors that together form a holistic explanation. We can also imagine the theories being contrasted; we should then carefully specify what findings will be congruent with culture theory as opposed to tool theory. If we want to use the cases to evaluate and test theories, we should carefully define statements or expectations for what will happen if the one or the other theory proves to be correct.

Another strategy to develop new knowledge through a theory-informed case study is to use established theories as a framework to study new phenomena, or familiar phenomena in new contexts. Quite a few projects have investigated the use of economic incentives in organisations, and there are alternative theories about how such incentives motivate or change motivation. It is a relatively new phenomenon that some Norwegian municipalities give performance-based salaries; that the Norwegian health sector has started to use economic incentives in the form of diagnosis-related groups; and that Norwegian counties and larger cities have introduced parliamentarism. These are examples of familiar phenomena in new contexts. Such phenomena can be analysed by using familiar theories as complementary or alternative theories. This type of project can contribute to theory development because they produce new knowledge about the way the context influences the researched phenomenon.

Interpreting a set of data from a number of familiar theories can be done by regarding the theories as either complementary or competing. If we regard them as complementary, the point is to show that we get to discover a variety of aspects of the object of study by analysing it from several theoretical perspectives. Complementarity could mean that we study the same aspects of the object of study using a variety of theories but also that we use theories that focus on different aspects of the phenomenon. In both cases, the goal of the complementarity is to develop a more complete description and understanding of the researched phenomenon.

The theories we plan to use should be specified and justified before collecting the data in order to make sure that the data collection matches the need to analyse the data in light of a variety of theories.

Regarding the theories as competing rather than complementary, the question is what theory can best explain the phenomenon in its present form. To perform this in a good way, we should clarify in advance what kind of findings we expect from the one or the other theory. In other words, the theory should be linked to the object of study prior to the collection of data. If we are able to define relatively precise expectations with a basis in alternative theories, the project design can be developed into a theory-testing or theory development project. The development of theory will typically be performed on the basis of findings that are unexpected and cannot be explained by established theory.

The common feature of the different strategies mentioned above is that we attempt to establish a convincing congruence between a set of theoretical statements and a set of data. The statements have been developed in the design phase of the project and guide the collection of data. Structured, theory-informed case studies are often a suitable choice for inexperienced researchers who have a limited time frame for their project, such as a master's degree thesis. If such studies are well structured and the hypotheses sufficiently clear, it can also be possible to steer them towards theory testing and development.

Process Tracing

Process tracing can best be understood as a set of designs where the common feature is that we trace processes over time and relate them to theoretical models and explanations of how the processes play out. Within this frame, we can create designs for theory testing and theory development as well as theory-informed explanation of single cases.

The historical method is about explaining the processes related to historical events. Historians are first of all interested in explaining the individual event; they are not as interested in developing and testing theory. The narrative of a single case with no theoretical anchoring has also had its place in social science, but in the last decades social scientists' interest has been oriented towards how process analyses can be connected to theory-based explanations. The use of process analyses in theory development and generalisations has been a topic since the 1990s (Pettigrew, 1990, 1997). George and Bennett (2005) dedicate a chapter in their book about case methods to a discussion of how processes can be traced. Yet it is not until recent years that we have got a literature that systematises the approaches for tracing processes (Beach & Pedersen, 2014; Bennett & Checkel, 2015; Rohlfing, 2013).

There are two different views of how to proceed when tracing processes. One is the variable-centred and reductionist view; the other is system centred and holistic. The method literature usually regards process tracing as the search for the intermediary variables that lead from cause X to effect Y (George & Bennett, 2005). This has been clearly shown by Gerring (2007), who says that also in a case design we should opt for a variable-centred thinking and view the case as a series of repeated observations of relations between variables. We can then choose an iterative or step-by-step strategy, alternating between observations, preliminary proposals for theoretical interpretations and generalisations, new observations that we connect to these proposals, and so on.

Other scientists, on the other hand, think that the causal mechanisms we search for in process analyses have a system character (Beach, 2016). It is the interaction that produces the results rather than the isolated individual factor. Beach and Pedersen (2014) compare a mechanism to a machine that produces a result. The fuel, the engine, and the transmission chain need to cooperate to give a forward thrust to a car. It does not make sense to isolate the variable "engine", claiming that the engine causes the propulsion. The engine is a necessary condition for the process but not a sufficient condition; the factors in combination produce the result (Mahoney, 2008). In my opinion, this view makes sense: It is the interaction of factors and the actual context that produces the outcome of a historical process.

Based on this view, Beach and Pedersen (2014) discuss three variants of process tracing. One is theory testing; we first specify mechanisms based on theory, then select the case and analyse for congruence. This variety of process tracing is not much different from the congruence method discussed above. The other varieties of process tracing are the theory-developing and the result explanatory methods. What these have in common is that they start by going backwards in a process with the intent of uncovering more or less general mechanisms behind the process.

Theory development and result explanatory process analyses mostly use abductive reasoning, using reason to identify processes and mechanisms that would result in an observed outcome. Through process tracing we can develop hypotheses, generalisations, and explanations that can be tested in other situations.

An example of this is what it is that we want to know when we ask why a particular event or act could happen. In everyday life we often ask how-questions in such situations. Let us say that I arrive for lunch at my work-place with a swelling on my brow and a colleague at the same table asks, "How did this happen?" The brief answer could be, "I bumped into a door". This answer constitutes a descriptive approach to the instance. But the colleague is curious and asks, "How on earth could you do that?" He wants to know about the chain of events that led to the observed result. A possible answer is that I was preoccupied with thoughts and did not see the door; another possible answer is that somebody arrived at great speed and banged the door open and I could not get away. In this example we could have exchanged the how with a why; "why did this incident happen?"

When we ask with why, the attention is directed towards the decisive cause of an event. When we ask with how, we use a form similar to that of the detective or the explorer. How could this event happen? How did we get this result? That is the detective's way of asking, establishing what happened and giving it a description. The next step is to uncover the underlying events and processes that led to the result. Thus, questions beginning with how point to chains of decisions and actions, whereas questions with why point to actuating causes and chains of causes.

A common approach in the tracing of processes is to carry out a reconstruction of the decision processes and events that move a matter forwards and thus determine a result. The reconstruction of chains of decision and events is a form of process tracing. However, this is yet another reconstruction of a unique development. On the contrary, a theoretical reconstruction of the processes must be based on an identification of actuating causes that lead to a specific chain of actions and events (Rohlfing, 2013). Such a reconstruction is needed when the purpose is to develop an explanation or an interpretation that reaches beyond the individual phenomenon we are studying. Comparisons with other instances play an important role when the researcher wants to place an instance. Is the pattern of this instance similar to what we have seen in other instances, or are there special features that single it out? From here, we can try to find a concept that sums up the characteristic features of the instance, that is, a synthesising concept. Or we can try to develop hypotheses about what are the main drivers behind the emergence of the phenomenon and how it develops. The difference between process analyses for theory development on the one hand and theory-informed or explaining-outcome process tracing on the other is the ambition to build theory. Systematic theory-building studies will establish stringent and testable hypotheses about causal mechanisms, whereas explaining-outcome process tracing may utilise various types of explanations that the researcher finds relevant (Beach & Pedersen, 2014).

A special type of strategy to develop theory based on a case is to study a so-called deviant case. A deviant case is a case with an unexpected or deviant outcome on the dependent variable. The case is deviant in relation to the predictions of established theories. The problem of the study will then first and foremost be to explain why the deviation occurred. This is about tracing processes, about passing from observed results to possible causes. Such an explanation could then necessitate a change or clarification of the theory.

The abductive approach also involves proceeding from a contextual understanding to discussing contextual conditions for a phenomenon. What are the conditions for the type of interpretative frames and actions that characterise foreign fighters? In this instance, we use the detailed interpretation of the phenomenon to establish possible explanations by means of abduction, which means that we pass from interpretation of the unique case to theory development. In an interpretative project lies a potential for developing context-dependent generalisations from within. We could for instance carry out a project where we start out with the ambition of understanding young people who become radicalised and enlist as foreign fighters. This far, we aim to perform an understanding interpretation. Yet in the course of the process we may start asking questions that go beyond understanding each individual. Is radicalisation first and foremost a product of a context in which literal interpretations of Islam dominate? Or is it about young people who are marginalised in western societies and respond by adopting certain views that they believe to be the right form of Islam? In other words, context-related theory development means identifying the conditions for a phenomenon to emerge or become a lasting one. The interaction between contextual conditions and action patterns is in focus, but it is a contextual explanation rather than a universal generalisation.

Two Exemplifying Cases

Several well-known studies in the social sciences use process tracing as a strategy even if they do not always discuss their own method as a process tracing logic. One example is John Kingdon's study of why some questions and problems appear on the political agenda while others do not

(Kingdon, 1984). He asks, "How does an idea's time come?" To answer that, he interviewed actors in the health and transport sectors four times over a period of three years. He asked which topics had their attention at the different points in time, thus creating a picture of the way some issues become important on the political agenda while others were forgotten and nothing was done. Kingdon says that at any time there are plenty of candidates for issues and solutions to them. He notices that the attention to various types of issues changes when the general opinion and the political climate change. What he sees as the decisive factor is the way the connection between problem and solutions is made. He finds two decisive mechanisms or drivers. One is so-called political entrepreneurs: actors in politics, organisations, and public administration who are working hard to achieve solutions to an issue. The other connecting mechanism is the politics window. The politics window opens in periods where there is concurrence between a particular understanding of a problem and the general political atmosphere. Then well-known facts and information can be forefronted and given attention. Kingdon's process model can be illustrated as in Fig. 7.2.

The main explanatory strategy in this case is to account for the mechanisms that connect streams of problems and solutions. The mechanism thus helps raise a matter or a problem up on the political agenda.

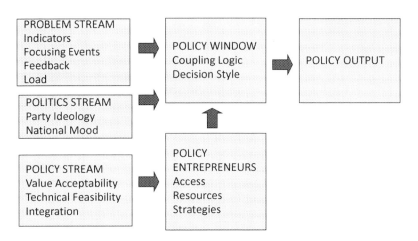

Fig. 7.2 Policy windows and policy entrepreneurs as connectors. (Adapted from Zahariadis, 2007)

When such a mechanism-based explanation is established we can use a congruence design to investigate whether one or more cases coincide with the theory. This was done in a master's degree thesis that studied how inter-municipal cooperation was put on the agenda in the municipalities of a Norwegian region (Neset, 2012). The student used two cases: one in the health sector and one in ICT. Both cases had been placed on the agenda in the municipalities, and inter municipal cooperation had been developed around them. By going through the two cases and setting up a data matrix that corresponds to the elements in Kingdon's model, the student found congruence between the model and the data set. He also found a variation between the cases. In one case professionals are the political entrepreneurs while in the other case we find an alliance of industry actors and politicians. This is how far the thesis goes. Yet in principle we could imagine that this variation would give the spark to a new question and a new project: What are the conditions for different groups to succeed as political entrepreneurs? Such a study could lead to a development of Kingdon's model as a typology for different forms of agenda setting.

THEORETICAL INTERPRETATIVE RECONSTRUCTION

Interpretative reconstruction is the type of design least controlled by strict guidelines. This design builds on flexible or volatile frames. Yet the researcher's concepts and theories are present as "sensitising concepts", making us observant by steering our interpretations in particular directions (Blumer, 1954). Interpretations are never theoretically "neutral", and it is an advantage that researchers are able to reflect on their own interpretative frames (Alvesson & Sköldberg, 2000). A common feature of the various approaches for interpretative reconstruction is that they regard reconstruction as an iterative or gradual process where researcher alternates between interpreting data in light of theory, and developing concepts and theory in light of new data. At the heart of this reconstructive process lies a bottom-up approach. A good interpretation of a social situation requires an understanding from within. Hence, interpretative approaches focus on the construction of meaning in social settings. How do social actors make sense and meaning to the world around them, as well as to their own actions and positions within a situated context? Interpretative research needs methods and data that give access to the actors' construction of meaning. Interpretative theory building also gives priority to context-dependent concepts and theories rather than to abstract generalisations (Schwartz-Shea & Yanow, 2012).

Even if a bottom-up approach characterises interpretative designs, it would be wrong to understand these approaches as purely inductive. Researchers always have some kind of pre-understanding of a situation, and they situate themselves within a community of researchers with its established concepts and ideas. This is why we can talk about interpretative reconstruction as an iterative process, where the researcher alternates between development of concepts and theories from data and interpretation of new data in light of concepts and theories. Both hermeneutic and discourse analytical research logics aim at uncovering the procedures for knowledge development used in interpretative reconstruction. Also, abductive research logics—underlining the change between the development of "if then" explanations and the matching of theories and concepts with new data—give guidelines for interpretative reconstruction.

The most basic form of interpretation of a situation is when we compare a new experience to something well known. What we do then is use analogies and metaphors. If we want to explain how crocodile meat tastes to somebody who lacks this experience, we might say that it tastes a bit like chicken. We are then using an analogy. Using metaphors is similar to using a picture. In a well-known introduction to organisation theory, Gareth Morgan compares different types of organisations to machines, organisms, brains, and internal prisons respectively (Morgan, 1998). Such metaphors can be useful because they let us see organisations from new angles and discover their various properties. The machine can be controlled, whereas the organism is programmed to survive in a particular environment. The brain uses information as a basis for acting, whereas internal prisons hold us back in established habits and thinking. A less well-chosen metaphor could, on the other hand, lead us astray. We should therefore try to proceed from metaphors to a more systematic development of concepts, for instance by following Goertz's strategy for concept development by presenting several dimensions to a general concept and investigate the relevance of the more complex concepts we will then arrive at (Goertz, 2006).

We could proceed from organisation metaphors to concept development for instance by asking what the relevant dimensions of the different variants of the concept of organisation are. Such a dimension could be the relation between the organisation and its environments. Is the organisation clearly marked off from its environments, enabling us to study it as a closed system? Or is it subjected to external influences, thus an open system? Another dimension could be the internal control of the organisation. Is the organisation a rational tool for reaching goals, or does it go in directions that can only be influenced to a limited degree by its managers? By help of the two dimensions we can identify four different types of the concept of organisation (Bukve, 1997). Chapter 9 about comparative designs returns to the construction of typologies.

Interpretative reconstruction can thus take place by development and differentiation of concepts. This form of concept development usually builds on synthesising studies where we start with existing studies and analyse cross-wise. Also, concept development is possible from case studies, often by combining different frames of understanding in the interpretation of the case (Andersen, 2013, pp. 81–83).

We can also use established concepts as a theoretical frame to interpret the case, with no ambition of developing or formulating new concepts; for instance, by using the organisation typology mentioned above to analyse and place one or more cases. The typology is a frame of interpretation, a model. It will not be falsified if we find cases that do not fit in. Like other models, typologies and concepts should be judged by how useful they are for analysing social phenomena, rather than being judged as true or false.

If our ambitions are to develop theoretical generalisations based on case studies, a design using analytical narratives or grounded theory can be relevant.

A narrative is a story about an event or events that take place over time. Stories about what happened and why are a significant form of social life; we narrate in order to make the world understandable to ourselves and others. Thus, the narrative has two roles: one is to establish knowledge, the other a way of communicating. Using analytical narratives is a method to uncover and systematise the implicit knowledge and explanatory strategies inherent in our everyday stories, or what emerges from interviews and texts (Czarniawska, 2004). Thus, analytical narratives are a form of interpretative reconstruction in that we uncover the underlying structure in the stories. Seen from a theory of science perspective, the method is anchored in discourse theory.

Grounded theory (Glaser & Strauss, 1967) is a classic method of case-based theory building. The founders of grounded theory were ambiguous concerning the status of the method (Kelle, 2007). They partly claimed that it built on an inductive research logic, partly that scientific concepts were the basis of the analysis. Understood as an inductive methodology, the core of grounded theory is that we code, synthesise, and abstract data in order to develop contextualised scientific concepts, hypotheses, and theories. Today most scientists will think that this self-understanding does not hold water. When analysing case data, we are never independent of a scientific pre-understanding. The approach in case-based theory development should be understood as an alternation between data and theory, where we step-by-step switch between formulating general statements on connections and checking the statements against data from the actual case or cases. Thus, interpretative reconstruction entails an alternation between the development of concepts and theories and the testing of concepts and hypotheses that have already been developed; we do not build theory from zero. This book does not further discuss the methodical principles of grounded theory; they are described in method books dealing with this tradition (Corbin & Strauss, 2008). Nevertheless, Chap. 9 introduces an example of developing a theoretical typology by use of grounded theory.

Interpretative reconstruction and case-based theory development require flexible or open designs and frames of analysis. We should be open to the unexpected when interpreting data. Even so, there are some requirements for systematic when using an interpretative approach: The theoretical frames of interpretation must be made visible, and we must clarify what methods we use for collecting and analysing data. It is also important to create a good research question, even if it has to be considered as provisional and open to revision during the research process (Schwartz-Shea & Yanow, 2012). The guidelines for the design process presented in Chap. 11 also apply to projects aiming at interpretative reconstruction.

References

Alvesson, M., & Sköldberg, K. (2000). *Reflexive methodology. New vistas for qualitative research.* London: Sage.

Andersen, S. S. (2013). *Casestudier: forskningsstrategi, generalisering og forklaring.* Bergen, Norway: Fagbokforl.

Beach, D. (2016). It's all about mechanisms – What process-tracing case studies should be tracing. *New Political Economy*, 1–10. https://doi.org/10.1080/1 3563467.2015.1134466

Beach, D., & Pedersen, R. B. (2014). *Process-tracing methods: Foundations and guidelines.* Ann Arbor, MI: University of Michigan Press.

Bennett, A., & Checkel, J. T. (2015). *Process tracing: From metaphor to analytic tool.* Cambridge: Cambridge University Press.

Blumer, H. (1954). What is wrong with social theory. *American Sociological Review, 18*(1), 3–10.

Bukve, O. (1997). *Kommunal forvaltning og planlegging* (3. utg. ed.). Oslo: Samlaget.

Corbin, J. M., & Strauss, A. L. (2008). *Basics of qualitative research.* Thousand Oaks, CA: Sage.

Czarniawska, B. (2004). *Narratives in social science research.* London: Sage.

Eckstein, H. (1975). Case study and theory in political science. In F. Greenstein & N. Polsby (Eds.), *Handbook of political science.* Reading, MA: Addison-Wesley.

George, A. L., & Bennett, A. (2005). *Case studies and theory development in the social sciences.* Cambridge, MA: MIT Press.

Gerring, J. (2004). What is a case study and what is it good for? *The American Political Science Review, 98*(2), 341–354. https://doi.org/10.2307/4145316

Gerring, J. (2006). *Case study research: Principles and practices.* Cambridge: Cambridge University Press.

Gerring, J. (2007). Is there a (viable) crucial-case method? *Comparative Political Studies, 40*(3), 231–253.

Glaser, B. G., & Strauss, A. L. (1967). *The discovery of grounded theory.* Chicago: Aldine.

Gobo, G. (2008). *Doing ethnography.* Los Angeles, CA: Sage.

Goertz, G. (2006). *Social science concepts: A user's guide.* Princeton, NJ: Princeton University Press.

Habermas, J. (1990). Reconstruction and interpretation in the social sciences. In *Moral consciousness and communicative action* (pp. 21–42). Cambridge: Polity Press.

Kelle, U. (2007). "Emergence" vs. "Forcing" of empirical data? A crucial problem of "grounded theory" reconsidered. Historical Social Research/Historische Sozialforschung. Supplement, 133–156.

Kingdon, J. W. (1984). *Agendas, alternatives, and public policies.* Boston: Little, Brown and Co.

Levy, J. (2008). Case studies: Types, designs, and logics of inference. *Conflict Management and Peace Science, 25*(1), 1–18. https://doi.org/10.1080/07388940701860318

Mahoney, J. (2008). Toward a unified theory of causality. (Author abstract) (Report). *Comparative Political Studies, 41*(4–5), 412.

Morgan, G. (1998). *Organisasjonsbilder: innføring i organisasjonsteori* ([Ny utg.]. ed.). Oslo: Universitetsforl.

Neset, O. (2012). *Interkommunale samarbeid – kven er drivkreftene.* (Master i organisasjon og leiing), Sogndal.

Pettigrew, A. M. (1990). Longitudinal field research on change: Theory and practice. *Organization Science, 1*(3), 267–292.

Pettigrew, A. M. (1997). What is a processual analysis? *Scandinavian Journal of Management, 13*(4), 337–348.

Ragin, C. C., & Amoroso, L. M. (2011). *Constructing social research.* Thousand Oaks, CA: Pine Forge Press.

Rohlfing, I. (2013). Varieties of process tracing and ways to answer why-questions. *European Political Science, 12*(1), 31–39.

Schwartz-Shea, P., & Yanow, D. (2012). *Interpretive research design: Concepts and processes.* New York: Routledge.

Yin, R. K. (1984). *Case study research. Design and methods.* Beverly Hills, CA: Sage.

Zahariadis, N. (2007). The multiple streams framework. In P. A. Sabatier (Ed.), *Theories of the policy process* (pp. 65–92). Boulder, CO: Westview Press.

CHAPTER 8

Integrated Designs

Integrated designs use different strategies for data construction in the same project. It is a complex field, and a number of different designs and methods are proposed and used. "Mixed methods", "nested analysis", "multimethod approach", "comparative method", and "qualitative comparative analysis" (QCA) are terms for variants of integrated designs that are quite different yet have in common that they use more than one strategy for data construction. It is a field that is developing fast and where many questions are still unsettled. Neither has the choice of name been decided; the concepts mixed methods, nested analysis, and multimethod approach are used without clear distinctions. I have tried to define and use the concepts in an unambiguous way in the present chapter, but there will also be other uses of the concepts in the literature.

Below, I discuss various forms of integrated designs based on their view of the purpose of using different methods or strategies for data construction. I begin with a discussion of triangulation, a concept that paved the way for integrated designs by proposing the use of different data sets and analytical strategies to make analyses more robust (Denzin, 1970). In other words, triangulation focuses on arriving at the same result using different methods (Seawright, 2016a).

Another purpose that gives reasons for the choice of an integrated design is the ambition of integrating theory development and theory testing in the same project. Nested analysis is the most thorough example of a strategy that explicitly mentions this purpose (Lieberman, 2005). The

© The Author(s) 2019
O. Bukve, *Designing Social Science Research*,
https://doi.org/10.1007/978-3-030-03979-0_8

141

term "mixed methods" is used in more eclectic ways. Sometimes the combination of methods as such is emphasised as a tool for making the analyses more robust. With this, mixed methods are close to triangulation, while at the same time making a distinction between concurrent and sequential use of different methods (Creswell, 2009). Sometimes the focus is on the combination of research purposes. Thus, nested analysis is often regarded as a form of mixed method.

A third purpose of integrated designs deals with the development of strategies to uncover and test theories about social mechanisms. A focus on social mechanisms is typical of the literature on the multimethod approach (Goertz, 2017; Seawright, 2016c). A main point in this literature is that the uncovering of social mechanisms requires detailed studies of one or more cases, whereas testing can be made by statistical methods, by experiments, or by structured comparisons across cases.

Comparative designs are a type of integrated designs that focus on variation in and comparisons between social phenomena. The study of variation also entails gathering and analysing data within the individual cases and across cases (George & Bennett, 2005; Ragin, 1987). Thus, from a methodical perspective, we can regard comparative designs as a kind of multimethod approach. It is from the specific purpose—the study of variation—that comparative designs can be distinguished as a separate genre. Therefore, I have chosen to discuss comparative designs in a separate chapter.

Comparative and international politics is the academic field where a combination of methods within the same project is the most common approach. The fact that political scientists have often chosen integrated designs may have to do with the properties of the units that make up their field of research. There are a limited number of states in the world, at the most 200 if we count them all. Finding comparable data for all these states is difficult in practice; an even more important question is whether it is meaningful to compare China and Andorra as units of the same kind. Quantitative studies of countries therefore encounter problems of "too many variables and too few cases" (Goggin, 1986). Generalising about connections will be difficult from statistical studies. On the other hand, it is just as difficult to generalise to the entire population of states from the studies of individual countries, since the variation between countries is so big. For many political scientists, the practical solution has been performing studies in which one combines the use of statistical data with case studies of individual countries. With this a need has arisen for reflections around design and the use of method in integrated studies. Hence, a large part of the recent literature on integrated strategies has been written by researchers who have their background in comparative and international politics. The discussions of case studies and generalising in the former chapter are based on writers from this tradition, which is also the case with the introduction of nested analyses and the multimethod approach in the present chapter. Much of the research interest in this group of scientists has dealt with the use of types and typologies as tools to study variation systematically, thus establishing delimited generalisations. I will return to the use of types and typologies in comparative designs in the next chapter.

Political scientists are not alone in being interested in integrated designs. Quite a few researchers in sociology and psychology have also taken an interest in how to make better research designs by applying various strategies for data construction. This literature is often motivated by a wish to get behind the patterns that can be identified by help of variable-centred designs, however, without giving up the ambition of doing research that is more than interpreting unique cases. They have started discussing the generalisation potential of case studies with the psychology-educated Robert Yin as an essential writer. Others, both sociologists such as Denzin (1970) and psychologists (Creswell & Plano Clark, 2011), have investigated the potential by the use of quantitative as well as qualitative data and methods in the same project.

In the following sections I first discuss triangulation in order to show the roots of integrated designs. Then I present mixed methods, nested designs, and the multimethod approach. There is no use in this chapter to write in detail about the basic strategies for data construction, since this has already been dealt with in the preceding chapters. Therefore, the presentation is fairly short and focuses on the strength of each of the design types in relation to certain purposes of a project.

TRIANGULATION

The term "triangulation" denotes the analysis of social phenomena using different data and methods in the same project. The book on triangulation by Norman Denzin (1970) is the classic formulation of how to use several types of data, methods, and theories to make analyses of social phenomena more robust. Triangulation by analysing data with different methods simultaneously means enhancing internal and external validity, drawing more reliable conclusions about connections in the material, and generalising in a justified way.

For quite some time, the use of several approaches in the same project has been termed strategies for multiple triangulation (Denzin, 1970).[1] Denzin's main point in the book *The Research Act* was that research methods are not neutral. The units observed must be understood as social objects in the researcher's environment (Denzin, 1970, p. 278). The researcher's observations are never able to capture all aspects of such an object, but by observing from different angles the researcher may get access to more aspects of the observed units. Thus, the concept triangulation refers to the use of several observation points and tools directed at the same phenomenon.

Denzin is an early exponent of the view that is the basis of this book: Social scientists do not develop and test theories and models through direct confrontation with objective facts; they compare generalising theories and models with empirical models. Data are social constructions, too. The task of social research is to establish a coherence between different forms of social constructions.

Denzin (1970) distinguishes between four different forms of triangulation: data triangulation, researcher triangulation, theory triangulation, and method triangulation. Data triangulation and method triangulation are connected in that data triangulation may enable the use of different methodological strategies in a project. If we compare these triangulation strategies we will see that they give answers to the various requirements of good research designs discussed in Chap. 4.

Data triangulation involves collecting data about a theoretical concept from as many different sources as possible. Denzin makes a difference between collecting data at different points of time, at different places, from different persons, and at different levels. As an example of this he uses a project where the purpose is to explore the social meaning of death. If we do field studies in a hospital, we can focus on persons who have different roles: the dying themselves, the hospital personnel, the next of kin. We can approach other contexts by studying other societies or by focusing on death caused, for instance, by accidents or in the workplace.

---

[1] In the triangulation literature it is common to point to Campbell and Fiske's article on "the multi-trait, multi-method matrix" as the first discussion on triangulation, although they do not use that term (Campbell & Fiske, 1959). They are credited for the term in a later book for which Campbell was co-author (Webb, Campbell, Schwartz, & Sechrest, 1966).

Data triangulation could mean collecting different forms of data within the categories of variable-centred or case-centred data. It can also mean combining quantitative and qualitative data to describe a phenomenon or a connection.

Data triangulation means increasing external validity. We can either view a particular interpretation of the concept as valid across a number of cases and contexts or differentiate the concept into several types and regard each as valid in its context.

As regards method triangulation, Denzin differentiates between what he calls triangulation within a method and triangulation between methods. Triangulation within a method can be useful first and foremost to judge how the use of a particular method, such as a given measurement scale, can influence the results. Thus, triangulation within a method can give potentially more robust results.

Triangulation between methods means combining case-oriented and variable-centred strategies in the same project, studying the same object by collecting data in different ways, and analysing the data using different methods. Using different strategies to assess a concept or theory can be seen as an approach to enhance the construction validity of a design. Different types of data and methods of analysis can make us see different aspects of a phenomenon and consequently investigate the relation between the theoretical concept and the observed phenomenon in a more reliable way.

Bukve's analysis of politicians' roles in municipalities is an example of method triangulation (Bukve, 1991). In this project he launches a theory-based typology with four politician roles. Then he uses personal interviews as well as a survey to refine and test the typology. Qualitative interview data are used to understand the way politicians think as compared with the theory-based roles. Survey data are used in a quantitative factor analysis of roles. The results from both analyses are largely in tune with the theoretical model; however, one of the original roles is divided into two different variants through the factor analysis. Here, a nuance emerges that was not discovered in the more limited interview material. In the next round, this leads to a need for a new analysis of the interview data in order to understand the mechanisms that create different roles, combined with an interpretation of the indicators in the factor model. At this stage, the project is also an example of data triangulation. The outcome is a refined theory supported by the use of different methods and data types.

In addition to data and method triangulation, Denzin discusses two other forms of triangulation that are relevant for research design: researcher triangulation and theory triangulation. I include a brief introduction to these as well, to show how they may help meet the requirements of a good design.

Researcher triangulation can be used as a strategy to enhance the reliability of a project, that is, to make the data more reliable. If a number of researchers research the same kind of data using the same methods and arrive at the same result, we can regard the research as more reliable than if the inquiry had been performed only once. This, of course, requires the approach and the results to be well documented to make it possible to compare the investigations.

Theory triangulation entails testing alternative theories and hypotheses on the same set of data. It means taking seriously other research logics than the hypothetical-deductive. We interpret and explain events and phenomena in the world in different ways, and in most cases, there is more than one opinion or explanation on the market. By using different theories, as either complementary or competitive theories, we may arrive at more precise and detailed interpretations and explanations of a phenomenon. Designs for a structured interpretation of a social phenomenon as well as designs for testing theories will often entail theory triangulation the way Denzin describes it.

Mixed Method Designs

The main interest of the literature on mixed methods is about just that: method; in other words, about how we use different types of data and analytical strategies to answer the questions in a project. An important overview article in the field (Johnson, Onwuegbuzie, & Turner, 2007) shows that 15 out of 19 quoted definitions of "mixed methods" tell us that mixed methods are such methods that combine the use of quantitative and qualitative methods. The authors of the overview article, however, believe that this mix is more than a mere mixture; it is a new research paradigm in addition to the qualitative and quantitative paradigms. Thus, in this article the method combination has received paradigm status. Still, the article is not very precise in defining what constitutes the new paradigm. The article remains in the tradition of viewing mixed methods as a synthesis of qualitative and quantitative approaches. There are also other overview articles that emphasise the method combination when describing what is the core of mixed methods (Östlund, Kidd, Wengström, & Rowa-Dewar, 2011). A characterisation of the explicit or implicit purpose of this literature would be that the purpose is mainly the same as for triangulation: making the analyses more robust by using different types of data and methods.

The author of the most used method books on mixed methods is John Creswell (Creswell, 2009; Creswell & Plano Clark, 2011). Creswell represents the conventional way of discussing design by seeing the choice of design as identical to the choice of method. In this aspect he is one of those who put the cart before the horse, to put it with Gobo (2008). True, he mentions the purpose when discussing the different forms of mixed methods, but his categorisation of purposes builds on a division between explorative and explanatory purposes. He also distinguishes between simultaneous and sequential use of different methods in a research design, simultaneous designs corresponding to triangulation. As main types of sequential designs Creswell puts qualitative inquiries first, then quantitative inquiries, or the other way around. A quantitative inquiry followed by a qualitative one he calls an explanatory inquiry. A qualitative inquiry followed by a quantitative one is explorative. Furthermore, he mentions a form he calls transformative strategy, which is an inquiry guided by theory.

Creswell's discussion of the division between explanatory and exploratory inquiries makes the most sense if we assume that the last method used has its main purpose in supplementing and supporting the findings of the first method. Such an explanation makes mixed methods a form of triangulation. Yet it is not evident that similar findings with different methods answer the same purpose or knowledge goal, the dilemma being that qualitative and quantitative methods basically answer different questions, thus making the answers not readily comparable (Seawright, 2016b). Where statistical analyses ask for the probability of a certain result under a set of initial conditions, the questions in qualitative, case-centred analyses ask what mechanisms and processes create an observed outcome.

As I see it, it would be more useful to test hypotheses developed through a preceding qualitative inquiry by a follow-up quantitative analysis. The other way around it would make sense to believe that a closer qualitative investigation of patterns in a quantitative material could have as its purpose the development of more precise theories on connections and mechanisms. That would make mixed methods a strategy for linking together different research purposes in the same design. The idea about a

148   O. BUKVE

sequential use of different methods can be useful. I have chosen to adopt the concept of sequential design but use it in relation to the discussion of types of purposes that is the foundation of this book, namely, theory-testing and theory-developing purposes.

A situation where a sequential design can be useful is when we are faced with observed regularities and patterns that need an explanation but where we still do not possess theoretical concepts and models that would enable us to explain how they are connected. In such a situation a sequential design with a variable-centred analysis would be a useful first step, followed by an analysis of selected cases.

A typical situation could be that we are studying connections between empirical variables, finding a covariation for which we can find no good explanation. We conclude that there are interesting patterns in the material but do not understand how this could provide a basis for generalising to a causal-effect hypothesis. What we lack are data on the actual mechanisms and causal chains that are the links between cause and effect. We can make up for this by following up with a case study that explores the stipulated connections in more detail.

This can be illustrated by an example. Let us imagine having access to register data on the results of standardised tests for pupils from the whole country. Such register data can tell us how the various schools, municipalities, and regions perform in terms of grade level. We can analyse these records and find patterns that put the grade levels into a context. Some regions are better than others, some types of municipalities are better than others, and performances would possibly vary according to the size of the school. Still, so far these patterns do not provide us with an explanation. At most, we can generate possible hypotheses about what processes and actual mechanisms are the reason for the observed patterns.

One observation from several of such data sets is that the most central and urban regions tend to score well on the grade scale. And there are large variations between the different rural regions. These are, of course, interesting findings but we cannot rest without searching for the underlying mechanisms. We would like to know more about why the central regions score well and why one rural region scores better than another similar one. In a variable-centred study we could have approached the matter by involving the question of the parents' level of education as a variable. This could give us a covariation between a high level of education in a region and good grades for lower secondary school children. Still, we would not have clarified what actual mechanisms are at work. Is it so that highly educated parents spend more time helping their children with the homework? Does the access to books, computers, and other learning resources in the homes differ? Is there a difference in teachers' qualifications? Or does the school treat different groups of pupils in different ways? In this way we can ask a lot of questions about the mechanisms and these can profitably be researched by the use of a case-centred design. When the purpose is to discover good explanations for observed covariation, a sequential design of the mentioned type can be beneficial. We can start with a variable-centred study of covariation between empirical variables, then follow up with a case study focusing on tracing processes and mechanisms.

The other way around we could perform a case study first, either exploratively or to develop theoretical ideas and hypotheses. The case strategy is not necessarily the best way to test these theories, so an alternative would be to follow up the hypothesis testing by a variable-centred inquiry. In a case study like the one I outlined above we would only be able to get hold of data on a limited number of pupils and families. Yet if in such a study we discovered interesting mechanisms that we could conceptualise, we would have a better foundation for constructing a theoretical model for connections, which we could operationalise and study in the next round with a new set of quantitative data. Here, the main purpose of a mixed design would be to test hypotheses that had been developed in the first sequence of the project.

Through deliberately planned sequential design we can utilise the potentials of the two main strategies for data construction. We should possibly utilise sequential designs more systematically than what we usually do. Two variants of integrated designs that have this ambition are introduced in the next sections. I will first discuss nested designs, then multimethod research.

Nested Design

A systematic account of nested analysis was first launched by Evan Lieberman (2005). It was his ambition to develop a more systematic strategy for the use of mixed methods than what had been the case until then. His strategy involves combining statistical analysis of a large number of cases with an in-depth analysis of one or more cases within this material. His rule of thumb is that nested design starts with a statistical analysis of a large number of units. Such an analysis can be used to guide the selection of cases for further investigation but also to give the direction for how to carry out more focused case studies and comparison of cases. As a last step in the process, statistical material can be used to test hypotheses generated from case studies. Lieberman prefers to use the term "small-N analyses" (i.e. studies with a few cases) rather than "case studies", because he believes there should as a rule be more than one case study in a nested design. Studies with small-N can be used to judge the theoretical plausibility of connections one discovers through the use of statistical methods. They can also be used to generate new theoretical understanding through the analysis of cases that cannot be well explained by the statistical model. Furthermore, Lieberman argues that case analyses can be used to develop better measurement strategies in the statistical analysis.

The initial statistical analysis should, according to Lieberman, at best be grounded in a theoretical model taken from literature. In this way we can secure that our data for analysis are as relevant as possible compared with the present knowledge status. If no established theories exist to be used as a basis, the statistical analysis can also build on a modelling of relationships between empirical variables. An important point of such an analysis is to analyse the robustness of the initial model. Lieberman recommends trying a goodness of fit analysis[2] for the model we already have. Dependent on the results of this analysis we can chose different approaches for the case analysis.

If the statistical model is robust and gives satisfactory results we may use case studies for further testing of the model. We should then choose typical cases, that is, cases that are on the regression line in the statistical analysis. It is not decisive whether the cases have been chosen randomly or not; the important thing is that the cases represent typical results as well as a variation on the independent variables. The next question is whether the selected cases are in line with the explanatory model developed in the first round. If a detailed study of the cases gives findings in line with the statistical model, the results are robust. If on the other hand one or more cases show deviant traits we need to decide the cause of the variances. Is the case atypical, or are there weaknesses in the theory that indicate the need of a new round of theory development and testing?

If we have no robust quantitative model as a starting point Lieberman recommends another approach. In such a situation he would use the case

---

[2] The goodness of fit of a statistical model describes how it fits a set of observations. Measures of goodness of fit summarise the discrepancy between observed values and the values expected according to the model.

studies to build a more fitting theory. In this case, too, he believes that the quantitative model should be used to guide the selection of cases. When using the case studies to develop the theory, on the other hand, we should select cases in a different way. Lieberman recommends the use of typical cases—those on the regression line—as well as cases outside this line. With such a selection of cases we could be surer to notice the variation between the cases and thus be able to develop a more accurate and complex theory. The most important cases are those outside the regression line. There, we can have the best hope of finding traces that may lead us in the direction of theory development. Still, the cases outside the regression line should not be selected among the most deviant ones; there could be specific conditions that cannot be utilised to generate ideas that cover a broader class of cases. Another point when selecting cases for model-building studies is that they must have different effects on the dependent variable. The task of the case studies will then consist in tracing and comparing the processes that have created different results.

Nested analysis represents a systematic strategy of combining variable-centred and case-oriented designs and methods. It has quickly become popular in the method literature. However, this is a resource-demanding strategy that requires a larger project stretching over time and preferably a cooperation between researchers who are specialists in different methods. The strategy is easier to implement if we have access to existing register data to be used as a basis in the initial quantitative analysis, a strategy that Lieberman himself recommends.

While many researchers have accepted the outlines of Lieberman's approach, it has also been criticised and further developed. In particular, criticism has been directed at Lieberman's advice for a selection of cases for further analysis when the initial statistical model gives no robust findings. Rohlfing (2008) points out that there can be different reasons for a model to have little explanatory power. It could be underfitted, meaning that it leaves out a variable that is important for a general explanation. Or it could be overfitted, which means that it includes a variable that is relevant in one or a few instances but has little importance beyond these special instances. If we do not know the cause of the model's lack of explanatory power, the statistical model will not give good criteria for selecting cases for the case analysis (Rohlfing, 2008). Consequently, it is not as easy to perform a nested analysis as Lieberman assumes.

Rohlfing (2008) recommends various strategies to overcome the problems of over- and underfitting. Among other things he recommends that not only should we test the quality of the quantitative analysis by performing a qualitative analysis and vice versa; we should also perform within-method tests to test how good the quantitative and qualitative analyses are. A second point is that we should run several different regression models to find if they give the same results before going on to select cases, and we should investigate the results of the model based on visualisations in which it is possible to see how well-known cases are placed (Rohlfing & Starke, 2013). Alternatively, we could start the analysis with case studies and build a model inductively by carrying out several case studies as the first part of a nested analysis (Rohlfing, 2008). This corresponds to the second type of sequential strategy that I discussed in the former section. We should also judge what we could achieve by using a resource-demanding nested design compared with performing either a variable-centred analysis or a case-based study.

Designs for Multimethod Research

In a new book, Gary Goertz defines multimethod research as a combination of case studies and statistics, experiments, comparative analyses, or game-theoretical models (Goertz, 2017). The purpose of performing case studies is, according to Goertz, the exploration of the causal mechanisms that make up the core of social science theories. Statistical analyses alone cannot explain the patterns found because they provide very little understanding of the actual mechanisms that enable us to find a regular connection between a causal factor x and a result y. Goertz states that finding a general connection between a cause and an effect is just half the job. The researcher's job is complete only after having explored through detailed case studies the mechanisms that connect cause and effect. Goertz's science theoretical point of departure is thus identical to the one I have accounted for in the first part of this book.

According to Goertz, multimethod research should hold a balance between three elements: theoretical statements about what mechanisms are present in a class of instances, case-based explorations of the mechanisms that operate in the case, and research across cases to establish generalisations and clarify the extent of the connections that the case studies show. These three elements—one theoretical model and two forms of empirical models—make up what Goertz calls the research triad (Fig. 8.1).

One corner of the research triad is made up of detailed case studies aiming at uncovering how social mechanisms function. There are two main types of such studies. One is process tracing, which I discussed in Chap. 6. The other is counterfactual analyses in which we analyse how properties of

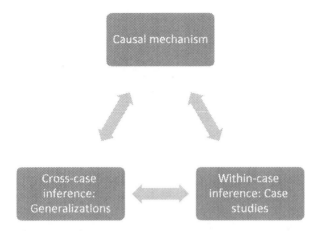

Fig. 8.1 The research triad: causal mechanism, cross-case inference, and within-case causal inference. (Adapted from Goertz, 2017)

a case change if one or more elements in a mechanism are no longer present.

The second corner of the research triad consists of studies that use data across cases and analyse the cases aimed at generalisation. This can be done in a number of ways. In Chap. 5 about variable-oriented designs I discussed statistical analyses and experiments. In Chap. 9 we will take a closer look at strategies for comparison through comparative case studies and QCA.

The third corner of the triad comprises theoretical formulations about social mechanisms and the way they work. Goertz emphasises three different types of such mechanisms. One type has to do with contextual conditions that would make a phenomenon with certain properties happen or not. The other type deals with cooperating mechanisms that together produce a specific type of effect. The third type of mechanisms is based on formal modelling, in particular through game-theoretical models of various types of social interaction.

Here, I will briefly discuss the role case studies play in the analysis of social mechanisms. How to choose good cases to uncover social mechanisms? Goertz's primary advice is to take a broad view of the possibilities and make a list of possible cases within the class of phenomena we wish to investigate. Let us say that we want to explore the relationship between an athlete training environment and the development of top athletes. It is of no decisive importance whether we get the idea of such a relationship through an initial statistical study or via theoretical reasoning contained in the relevant literature. A first step would be making a list of possible cases by searching for athletic disciplines that have created many top athletes, and environments within these athletic disciplines that have excelled in good athletes. The next step would be choosing some excellent athletes from these environments for qualitative studies. These athletes together with the environment around them will then constitute single instances of a specific class of phenomena, namely top athletes. The research interest is oriented towards finding out how this phenomenon comes to be. Thus, we choose the first cases with the aim of finding typical examples of the mechanism we intend to study. By interviewing a few of these athletes the researcher can make a detailed description of what environmental factors have been present around those who have developed into very good athletes. The most important piece of advice when choosing cases for the study of social mechanisms is, then, to choose cases in which we can observe the mechanisms in practice.

This choice of cases can be illustrated by a simple table that schematically illustrates four configurations of the social mechanism (x) and the effect (y). Goertz's advice is to start the case analysis in the cell where x = 1 and y = 1, in other words the cell that contains the hypothetical mechanism that we want to explore as well as the expected effects. This cell is labelled a (1.1) in Table 8.1.

Yet in multimethod research we should not stop there. The next step could be adding new cases with athletes from the same type of environment who have not developed into such good athletes, cell b (1.0). These could very well be athletes with personal capacities corresponding to those of the successful athletes. By comparing the two typical instances we can probably specify even better those environmental factors that create successful athletes at top level. It is for instance possible to believe that a high pressure of expectations at an early age could be a problem for promising athletes, or that too much specialised practice from an early age could be

Table 8.1 Case study selection: X-Y configurations

	X = 1	X = 0
Y = 1	a (1.1)	c (0.1)
Y = 0	b (1.0)	d (0.0)

Adapted from Goertz, 2017

so boring that the athlete does not want to continue. Such findings can be used to make more detailed descriptions of the social mechanisms in work.

The way we draw conclusions around this type of cases is an important distinction between variable-centred analyses and case studies. In variable-centred analyses we would perceive the occurrence of athletes who did not succeed as a source of falsification of the theory of a connection between practice environment and performance. At least, such cases would reduce the relevance of the theory. Goertz says the following about such cases: "Obviously these cases pose potential threats to the proposed causal mechanism. These potential disconfirming cases can be either explained away (e.g. measurement error) or can be dealt with via scope conditions" (Goertz 2017 p. 71). Here we are touching on an important discussion in the literature on multimethod research, a discussion where the last word will not yet have been said: When will cases where the expected causal mechanism does not appear falsify the theory, and when should we use these cases to refine the theory or to specify the conditions for the mechanism to work?

This question has to do with the role counterfactual thinking should play in the analysis of social mechanisms. Variable-centred analyses of causal connections take their starting points in counterfactual thinking. "If the temperature falls under zero degree centigrade the water freezes" is a statement of the type "if x, then y". It has its parallel in the statement "if not x, then not y". If the temperature does not fall below zero degree centigrade, the water will not freeze. If on the other hand we can observe x, not-y, such an observation would falsify the hypothesis in accordance with counterfactual thinking. Yet can we always think in the same way about social mechanisms? Not always, Goertz says, because the reasoning about falsification builds on the assumption that one and the same causal mechanism is present when x = 1 and x = 0. But this is not always the case. There could be different mechanisms in the two instances. A well-known example from the literature is the discussion on the mechanisms behind the democratic peace. By help of quantitative data political scientists have shown that two democratic states never wage war on each other. The mechanisms behind this connection are discussed in a number of scholarly works. That is, however, not the point here. The point is that we cannot draw the counterfactual inference "if not-democracy, then not-peace". There are many cases where authoritarian states do not wage war on each other. Different social mechanisms create war than those that create peace, and they must be analysed on their own premises.

For this reason, Beach and Brun Pedersen have criticised Goertz and others who find the use of counterfactual reasoning important in case studies (Beach & Brun Pedersen, 2016). They find that process tracing is the best strategy for clarifying what social mechanisms it is that produce a specific effect or phenomenon. They propose to use Goertz's formulation to analyse cases of the type (1.1) and go back in time until the case was (0.0). The analysis then has to clarify how the mechanism x developed and how it produced the effect y.

An important point for Beach and Brun Pedersen is that the analysis of social mechanisms should be limited to studying one of the poles in a continuous concept. We should for instance not try to say something about authoritarian regimes in an analysis that deals with the mechanisms that make democratic regimes not wage war on each other. We must limit the analysis to deal with the democratic type of regime.

I am unsure whether one should be as critical as Beach and Brun Pedersen when criticising counterfactual reasoning in multiple case studies. Yet their objection is without doubt relevant. We should not use counterfactual reasoning if it is possible that several different mechanisms may be operating in a situation. Goertz treats this as an exception but we cannot simply take that as a fact. Counterfactual analyses would be most suitable when our goal is to generalise or to delimit the field where a defined social mechanism is present.

Another cell that needs comments is the cell c (0.1), or not x, then y. Returning to the case of the athletes we will see that an example of cases in this cell will be athletes that have developed into becoming good in spite of not having had a facilitating training environment around them from young age on. We should then seek other roads that lead to Rome. We would be hunting for equifinality, meaning that different factors and mechanisms can produce the same result (George & Bennett, 2005). Some sound advice in multimethod research is not to treat the search for alternative explanations of an observed phenomenon too lightly. One of the ways to do it is to search for cases of the type c (0.1).

Neither Goertz nor Beach and Brun Pedersen see the cell d (0.0) as relevant for uncovering mechanisms, but for different reasons. Goertz says that it contains too many different instances and is therefore mostly suited for creating confusion, whereas Beach and Brun Pedersen take as their starting point that the uncovering and testing of social mechanisms should be concentrated around the one pole of the concept.

I will not here deal with the approaches for performing theory-testing analyses across cases, which make up the second corner of the research triad. Multimethod researchers tend to have an open approach to it, believing that it can be done in several ways. Experiments, statistical analyses, and comparative case analyses are all relevant methods. Chapters 6 and 9 discuss these strategies. The important thing is that different approaches can be suitable dependent on the mechanisms under study.

Goertz distinguishes between three types of mechanism-based theories, calling them constraint mechanisms, interactive mechanisms, and mechanisms derived from formal models. Constraint mechanisms are characterised by being necessary conditions for some effect. If a condition x is necessary for the effect y, the lack of x will make the effect y not happen no matter what combinations or other variables and conditions are present. An important point for Goertz is that in the analysis of necessary conditions, cases in the cell d (0.0) are interesting for the identification of the mechanisms. We could for instance imagine that the access to suitable installations and training facilities is such a necessary condition for producing top athletes. Necessary conditions function as a constraint where they are not present, which is a reason for studying cases of the type d (0.0).

Interactive causal mechanisms are characterised by two or more factors acting together to produce a result. Returning to the athlete case, we can for instance imagine that an interaction between training environment, training methods, and talent is what it takes to produce top athletes. The analysis of interactive mechanisms focuses on what conditions are sufficient to produce an effect.

Searching for necessary and sufficient conditions are basic strategies for the study of social mechanisms. It is especially through the use of set theory that the analysis of necessary and sufficient conditions is developed to also comprise more sophisticated types of conditions. Set theory is a branch of mathematical logic in which we study sets, defined as a collection of objects. Set theory analyses the relations between different collections of objects with specified properties. I do not discuss this any further here but return to the use of set-theoretical reasoning in Chap. 9. The interested reader can also turn to the literature on QCA (Ragin, 1987). Statistical models and typologies can be used in such analyses too.

Research design and use of methods in multimethod research is a new field. It is rapidly developing, and is in many respects becoming a hot issue for discussions of design and methods in the social sciences. On the other

158 O. BUKVE

hand, there are still unresolved questions, and many of the scholarly contributions so far have been written by specialists for other specialists. Altogether, my opinion is that the multimethod approach shows a promising avenue for those who want to use an integrative design in their research.

SUMMING UP

Table 8.2 gives an overview of the forms of integrated designs discussed in this chapter. The designs are organised according to what purpose they are oriented towards. A number of variants of integrated designs can be useful

Table 8.2 Variants of integrated designs

Types of integrated designs	Main questions	Purpose
Triangulation Data triangulation Method triangulation Researcher triangulation Theory triangulation	Coherence between data from different sources? Consistency in interpretation of data with different methods? Do different researchers get the same result when carrying out the same study? Are findings compatible with the theories?	More robust analyses Increasing external validity Increasing construction validity Increasing reliability More precise interpretations and explanations
Sequential mixed methods Quantitative data first, then case study Case study first, then variable-centred	Can the case study give a consistent explanation of discovered patterns in the quantitative material? Can we generalise theory that is developed by help of the case study?	Theory development Theory development and testing
Nested designs Model-testing case analysis Model-developing case analysis	Is there coherence between the case analysis and the initial model? What could be the reason for poor coherence? Can the case analysis point to a new and coherent model?	Theory testing and possible new theory development if needed Theory development and if possible subsequent testing on population
Multimethod design	Can we establish coherence between theories of the mechanism type, findings in case studies, and findings across case studies?	Developing and testing of theories on causal mechanisms

INTEGRATED DESIGNS **159**

in a research project. If I were to emphasise one of these design strategies, I am inclined to regard Gary Goertz's book (2017) on multimethod research as the most thorough and ambitious contribution so far. He places the study of causal mechanisms in the centre of social sciences, arguing that we need case studies as well as methods for comparisons across cases if we want to both uncover social mechanisms and clarify under what conditions they are valid. This is a view I can share.

REFERENCES

Beach, D., & Brun Pedersen, R. (2016). *Causal case study methods: Foundations and guidelines for comparing, matching and tracing.* Ann Arbor, MI: University of Michigan Press.

Bukve, O. (1991). Ingen kommer undan politiken…. In O. Bukve & T. P. Hagen (Eds.), *Nye styringsmodellar i kommunane* (pp. 55–66). Oslo, Norway: Kommuneforl.

Campbell, D. T., & Fiske, D. W. (1959). Convergent and discriminant validation by the multitrait-multimethod matrix. *Psychological Bulletin, 56*(2), 81–105. https://doi.org/10.1037/h0046016

Creswell, J. W. (2009). *Research design. Qualitative, quantitative and mixed methods approaches.* Los Angeles: SAGE.

Creswell, J. W., & Plano Clark, V. L. (2011). *Designing and conducting mixed methods research.* Thousand Oaks, CA: Sage.

Denzin, N. K. (1970). *The research act: A theoretical introduction to sociological methods.* Chicago: Aldine Publishing.

George, A. L., & Bennett, A. (2005). *Case studies and theory development in the social sciences.* Cambridge, MA: MIT Press.

Gobo, G. (2008). *Doing ethnography.* Los Angeles, CA: Sage.

Goertz, G. (2017). *Multimethod research, causal mechanisms, and case studies: An integrated approach.* Princeton, NJ: Princeton University Press.

Goggin, M. L. (1986). The "too few cases/too many variables" problem in implementation research. *The Western Political Quarterly, 39*, 328–347.

Johnson, R. B., Onwuegbuzie, A. J., & Turner, L. A. (2007). Toward a definition of mixed methods research. *Journal of Mixed Methods Research, 1*(2), 112–133. https://doi.org/10.1177/1558689806298224

Lieberman, E. S. (2005). Nested analysis as a mixed-method strategy for comparative research. *American Political Science Review, 99*(3), 435–452. https://doi.org/10.1017/S0003055405051762

Östlund, U., Kidd, L., Wengström, Y., & Rowa-Dewar, N. (2011). Combining qualitative and quantitative research within mixed method research designs: A methodological review. *International Journal of Nursing Studies*, *48*(3), 369–383. https://doi.org/10.1016/j.ijnurstu.2010.10.005

Ragin, C. C. (1987). *The comparative method*. Berkeley, CA: University of California Press.

Rohlfing, I. (2008). What you see and what you get: Pitfalls and principles of nested analysis in comparative research. *Comparative Political Studies*, *41*(11), 1492–1514. https://doi.org/10.1177/0010414007308019

Rohlfing, I., & Starke, P. (2013). Building on solid ground: Robust case selection in multi-method research. *Swiss Political Science Review*, *19*(4), 492–512. https://doi.org/10.1111/spsr.12052

Seawright, J. (2016a). Better multimethod design: The promise of integrative multimethod research. *Security Studies*, *25*(1), 42–49. https://doi.org/10.10 80/09636412.2016.1134187

Seawright, J. (2016b). The case for selecting cases that are deviant or extreme on the independent variable. *Sociological Methods & Research*, *45*(3), 493–525. https://doi.org/10.1177/0049124116643556

Seawright, J. (2016c). *Multi-method social science. Combining qualitative and quantitative tools*. Cambridge, UK: Cambridge University Press.

Webb, E., Campbell, D., Schwartz, R., & Sechrest, L. (1966). *Unobtrusive measures*. Chicago: RandMcNally.

CHAPTER 9

Comparative Designs

A comparative design involves studying variation by comparing a limited number of cases without using statistical probability analyses. Such designs are particularly useful for knowledge development when we lack the conditions for control through variable-centred, quasi-experimental designs. Comparative designs often combine different research strategies by using one strategy to analyse properties of a single case and another strategy for comparing cases. A common combination is the use of a type of case design to analyse within the cases, and a variable-centred design to compare cases. Case-oriented approaches can also be used for analysis both within and between cases. Typologies and typological theories play an important role in such a design. In this chapter I discuss the two types separately. But let us first take a look at what differentiates comparative designs from other types of design.

What Is a Comparative Study?

The most common definition of a comparative study is that it focuses on a limited number of cases. Thus, the comparative study is a category between the case study, which focuses on one case, and variable-centred studies that require many cases. This is illustrated in Fig. 9.1.

A drawback with the definition above is that it does not distinguish between comparative studies and multicase studies. In multicase studies there are several cases too, but the purpose is to find common traits, not

© The Author(s) 2019

O. Bukve, *Designing Social Science Research,*

https://doi.org/10.1007/978-3-030-03979-0_9

161

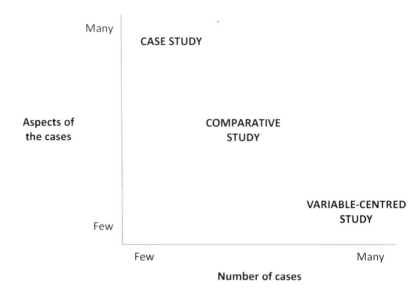

Fig. 9.1 Cases and design

how and why the cases vary. An alternative definition of comparative studies could start with the purpose of such studies, which is to compare cases to study variation (Ragin & Amoroso, 2011). Still, such a purpose-oriented definition may also be too broad because it does not differentiate comparative studies from a purely variable-centred design. We can also use a variable-centred design to study variation but with a basis in multiple units and statistical methods. George and Bennett made this delimitation by defining a comparative study as the none-statistical comparison of a few cases (George & Bennett, 2005, p. 151).

From the discussion above is to understand that we can best delimit comparative designs by including the purpose as well as the strategy for data construction. We can define a comparative study as a *comparative study of a limited number of cases with the purpose of studying variation by use of non-statistical designs and methods.*

What constitutes a limited number of cases cannot be defined exactly. It depends on the complexity of the cases. In the well-known book on comparative methods by Todd Landman (2008), he defines few cases as less than 20 and many cases to be more than 50. In practice it may be challenging to study the aspects of each case if the number of cases is close to

COMPARATIVE DESIGNS   163

20. Most of the time we have to be satisfied with fewer. If we use a variable-centred comparison of the cases and place more emphasis on that than on a thorough analysis of each case, a comparative analysis may probably handle a data set of 20–50 cases (Ragin, 1987).

The definition above delimits comparative designs from designs with one or many cases. That does not mean that it is not possible to compare even if we have only one case or multiple cases. We can make implicit comparisons even with only one case by comparing the case with a theoretical model or hypothesis to find if and to what degree the case complies with the theory. In this case we can use a congruence design, described in Chap. 7 about case designs. We do not combine analytical strategies.

If it is possible to collect data from a large number of units we can also make comparisons by use of a purely variable-centred design. We can compare the way cases are distributed on different variables, and also perform statistical analyses to find out if the difference between two or more groups of cases is statistically significant, and what factors produce the differences. The statistical approach to systematic comparison of groups can be termed controlled comparison, where we compare units that are similar except for the variable we want to study. This is a quasi-experimental strategy; still, units that are suitable for controlled comparison may be hard to find. For instance, in studies of comparative politics there are a limited number of countries to compare. The same is true for ethnological studies of societies. It is often difficult to perform a controlled comparison (George & Bennett, 2005). Said otherwise, there will be too many variables and too few units or cases to draw reliable conclusions about systematic variation between the cases (Goggin, 1986) Thus, a reason for performing comparisons using other methods than statistical ones is that many research fields raise questions for which it is difficult to perform reliable comparisons by use of statistical methods.

If the focus in this book had been on comparative methods it could have made sense to characterise both strategies mentioned above as comparative. However, my focus is on research design generally, which makes a narrower definition more expedient. Designs of the type of studies mentioned above have already been discussed in the chapters on variable-centred designs and case designs.

The main strategy for knowledge development in comparative studies is the combination of a structured comparison of cases with a case-oriented analysis within each case (George & Bennett, 2005). A reason for structured comparisons is that comparing only on the basis of detailed narrative

164   O. BUKVE

case studies tends to make the complexity in the material too big and generalisations too random (Lange, 2013). We therefore need to combine studies of the cases from within with structured methods for comparison.

Two main strategies for structured comparison of cases should be mentioned. One strategy is case centred, building on comparison of types (George & Bennett, 2005). The other is variable centred, in which we compare variable properties of the cases to find one or more decisive properties that produce given results (Ragin, 1987).

The relevant design for analysing cases from within will be known from Chap. 7 on case designs. We may trace processes to uncover conditions and interacting mechanisms that are necessary to produce specific effects. We may also perform a congruence analysis to assess a case against types that the case may comply with to some degree. We can also perform an interpretative reconstruction of the case in a narrative form.

In the present chapter I will not repeat what has already been said about case analysis but rather place the emphasis on how we compare the cases in comparative studies. With each strategy for comparison I will account for the way the strategy can be combined with an analysis of each case for different purposes. First, I discuss the main characteristics of case-centred comparisons, then variable-centred comparisons. Table 9.1 shows an overview of the five types of comparison of cases that are discussed in the present chapter. Case-centred comparisons are based on types and typological theories. Variable-centred comparisons build on most similar systems, most different systems, or on the double congruence method. These strategies must be combined with structured analyses within the cases. For this purpose, we usually use process tracing and congruence design.

Typologies and Typological Theories in Comparative Designs

When using a case-oriented approach to study variation between cases, types and typologies are our most important tools. Types describe variation by characterising variants of a complex phenomenon. The type is a simplified image we can use as a starting point for analysing the actual instances of the phenomenon. We perceive democracy and dictatorship as two types of government systems within states, or hierarchy and networks as two types of organisation. When assessing countries or organisations by the dimensions that are part of the types we can find a number of variants

COMPARATIVE DESIGNS   **165**

Table 9.1   Variants of comparative designs

Type of design	Main questions	Purpose
Typologisation	How does a social phenomenon vary? What types can we construct on the basis of this variation?	Conceptualise variation
Theoretical typologisation	What are conditions for and effects of different types? Do case observations vary in agreement with the type theory?	Concept and theory development Theory testing
Most similar systems	What are necessary conditions for a specific outcome? Do case observations vary in accordance with theory-based expectations and statements?	Theory development Theory testing
Most different systems Similar outcomes, different systems	What is the stable explanatory factor across variation between cases? Can non-validating cases direct us towards new, relevant variables and mechanisms?	Theory development Theory testing
The double congruence method	Do cases with identical outcomes have a common causal variable? Do cases with a different outcome lack this causal variable?	Theory development Theory testing

and mixed forms, yet the pure types are useful for describing and finding patterns in a complex material.

Max Weber developed the use of types as analytical tools for comparison, calling them ideal types (Weber, 1971). The term may easily be misunderstood since ideal type may be understood as the best type. Weber, however, used the name to emphasise that he was talking about a simplified or stylised type, thus an equivalent to what I call type here.

The type may be understood as one of several cells in a typology. In the examples mentioned above we can talk about a typology of government systems with two types—or a typology of organisation forms with two types. Fully developed typologies will also outline the various dimensions or aspects that characterise these types. The types of a typology give us a basis for grouping cases, enabling us to compare a limited number of types instead of performing a statistical analysis of several units. Typologies are models. They must be judged by their possible use in analysing a phenomenon and not as being true or false.

According to George and Bennett (2005), a main purpose of comparative studies is to proceed from typologies to typological theories. A typological theory is a theory that places types into a context. Typological theories attempt to identify causal mechanisms and conditions that produce a certain type, or they attempt to explain how a type produces specific processes and effects. Since typological theories are open to variants and different types they make the study of equifinality possible. We can use the types to explain why different paths lead to the same place.

Typological theories exist at a level of abstraction that distinguishes them from historical explanations. When using typological theories, we study revolutions as a general phenomenon with different variants, not the Russian Revolution specifically. For practitioners, typological theories are interesting because they can be used for a diagnostic purpose. They tell us something about what we can expect when encountering an event or a phenomenon of a specific type.

A classic reference for the development of types and typological theories is Max Weber's theory about the three types of authority (Weber, 1971). Based on historical-comparative studies of different societies he distinguishes between traditional, legal, and charismatic authority. The conditions for the first type are found in pre-modern societies, in which family and social class were the essential institutional structures. In such societies, authority is derived from tradition, heritage, and habits. Legal authority prevails in modern societies with a fully developed legal system and specific administrative institutions. In modern societies, laws give authority its legitimacy. Charismatic authority is a personal type of authority where the ruler claims legitimacy based on his personal qualities. Religious and revolutionary leaders are examples of this type. Charismatic authority tends to be less stable than the other two types from the very reason that it depends on the person in power.

This example shows that Weber develops a theoretical typologisation around the types of authority. He analyses what properties it is that vary between the types, what the conditions are for types to come into existence, and what consequences they have for the exercise of authority. Behind the development of types are thorough studies of a great number of historical cases. By uncovering processes and mechanisms that are present in the individual cases and comparing these, Weber generalises to types that can be further refined and compared.

Another example of a theoretical typology is Richard Matland's synthesising typology of forms of implementation of public policy (Matland,

1995). By studying the literature on implementation, Matland concludes that two main explanatory variables appear constantly. One is the degree of conflict in the implementation situation. When conflicts arise around the measures or the policy that are to be initiated, the result will often be an implementation that is incomplete or biased. The other variable he deducts from the literature is the degree of ambiguity about effects and the use of measures. When there is considerable ambiguity, implementation may vary and be changed during the process. On the basis of these two dimensions Matland developed a theory-based typology with four types characterising different implementation situations (Fig. 9.2).

The first type, which Matland labels administrative implementation, is routine driven and characterised by rational decision processes, the assumptions being that there is low ambiguity and little conflict. Differences in outcomes are most often due to differences in resources. The second type of implementation is also characterised by low ambiguity but with more conflict. Such a situation leads to what Matland calls a political form

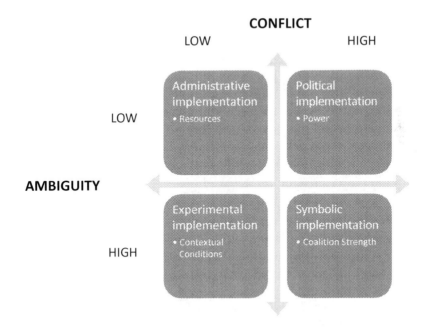

Fig. 9.2 Implementation of public policy—a typology. (Adapted from Matland, 1995)

of implementation. Conflicts arise because different groups have different interests and are influenced in different ways. Power relations between policy levels and groups will then decide how policies are implemented. Moreover, different issues tend to influence each other.

The third type is when there is a low degree of conflict but high ambiguity. Then the implementers tend to experiment, which creates the type Matland calls experimental implementation. The local context will play a role for the implementation of the policy; thus, we can expect implementations that vary with the local conditions. Where there is ambiguity as well as conflict, implementation tends to become symbolic with the focus on showing that something is being done rather than on actual results. What is being done will also depend on local coalitions formed around different perceptions of the situation.

The Use of Typologies

Matland's typology is an example of a common approach in the use of typologies for theory development. Theoretically oriented empirical studies are the basis for theory development in this type of study and it often entails a secondary analysis of existing studies. Matland does not perform pure induction; he has a theoretical view on the material and proposes a typologisation of it by use of two dimensions known from the literature on processes in organisations. With a starting point in these dimensions, Matland develops types and hypotheses on conditions for and results from the various types of processes. He also illustrates the types through selected cases.

When a typology of this kind has been established it can form the starting point of new types of studies. It can be tested on new cases using a congruence design and refined if we find deviant cases. It can also be used for theory-informed analysis of cases to find what kind of conditions characterise them. Such theory-informed analyses need no theoretical ambition from the beginning, but if a case shows deviant results from what is expected it could provide a stimulus for searching for factors that can refine it, or a stimulus for launching alternative theories.

Theory development can also take place with a starting point in typologies that do not build on theoretical concepts but rather on groups of data. Such typologies often have the purpose of reducing variation in a data set to make it handier for analysis. Let us say we are wondering if it is access to professional competence, or financial resources, that have the greater influence on the standard of availability of mental health care in a municipality. We could then set up a municipality typology, dividing municipalities into categories with either good or poor access to competence, and either good or poor economy. Next, we can select cases and study the organisation of mental health care in different types of municipalities. The benefit of making this type of analysis rather than a purely variable-centred analysis is that it is possible to capture interacting mechanisms and factors that we did not include in the model from the beginning.

An example of such an approach that resulted in a new theoretical typology is Bukve's study of local development networks (Bukve, 2001). The starting point for the selection of cases was an empirical typology where the dimensions were the degree of municipal efforts for industry development and the industry structure in the municipality. This empirical typology is illustrated in Fig. 9.3.

The ambition of this project was to study to what degree high municipal efforts in local economic development could counteract the effects of having many people employed in declining industries. Was it possible for a municipality to overcome structural problems? In the study, the detailed process analysis of eight case municipalities instead pointed at other mechanisms as the cause of good results in local economic development. Strong networks between public and private actors seemed to be an essential

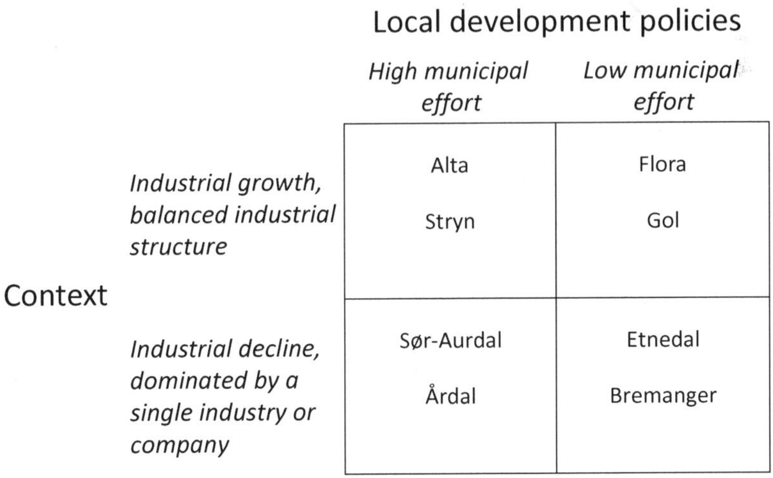

Local development policies

	High municipal effort	Low municipal effort
Industrial growth, balanced industrial structure	Alta Stryn	Flora Gol
Industrial decline, dominated by a single industry or company	Sør-Aurdal Årdal	Etnedal Bremanger

Context

Fig. 9.3 Example of empirical typology with selected cases for analysis

factor, as did also the question whether the networks were broad enough to include different groups of industry actors. The comparison of the cases used a structured coding based on grounded theory.

From the results of the analysis, Bukve developed a theoretical typology based on network theory, using the dimensions' degree of integration in the network and the degree of heterogeneity between the actors. The overall hypothesis introduced on the basis of the data analysis was that municipalities with heterogeneous and inclusive networks would have more success in their industry development. In the next round, the cases were regrouped based on the new typology, as shown in Fig. 9.4. The hypothesis was tested against some simple measurements of result, and the findings in the testing matched expectations (Bukve, 2001).

Theory testing using a comparative case design assumes the construction of theoretical types from the onset, built on the literature and knowledge of the field (George & Bennett, 2005). We could also start with a familiar typology and specify expectations to the material based on the typology. In both instances we need to specify expectations about outcomes as a basis for the data analysis.

The selection of cases is important in comparative designs of this kind. Cases must be selected strategically to ensure that they have properties that match the type they are to represent in the data set. It is also important that

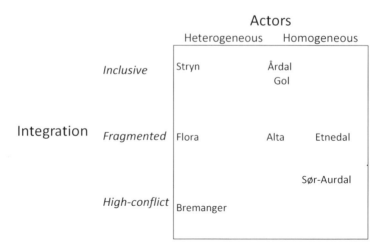

Fig. 9.4 Example of theoretical typology with the placing of cases through congruence analysis

the typology is not too complicated, that we are not testing several variables at the same time. If we study variation along one dimension we need at least two cases. When studying variation along two dimensions, as Matland's model is an example of, we get four types and a need of four cases. Bukve used eight cases in a corresponding model, two in each cell, to reduce the chance of random conditions having an influence. The number of cells in the typology increases exponentially with the number of independent variables. If we create a typology that includes four dimensions we get 16 types and a corresponding number of cases.

To avoid a too large complexity in case-based comparisons we should be able to reduce the complexity in the data set. This can be achieved when we work with types and typologies. With the use of typologies, several properties of a phenomenon can be reduced to one type to be used in the comparison. The type could describe a complex mechanism or a system, not just a single variable.

The case methods that are most suitable to combine in type-centred comparisons are the tracing of processes and the congruence design. We use congruence design to compare cases, to match data about a single case against the pure type, and to compare types. To analyse processes and patterns within each case we usually use process tracing.

There are examples in the literature of comparative studies based on detailed descriptions of each case and inductive generalisations around common traits and variation. Performing detailed analyses of single cases increases internal validity; however, if data are not structured for comparisons generalisations may turn out to be random.

VARIABLE-CENTRED COMPARISONS

Within a variable-centred framework there are various strategies for comparison of cases. The classic discussion is found in *A System of Logic* by John Stuart Mill, first published in 1843. Mill distinguished between two main variants of design, calling them "the method of agreement" and "the method of difference".

When using the method of agreement, also called the positive method, our goal is to identify the independent variable that results in a common outcome in two cases. The same independent variable is obviously present in both cases. We try to find this variable through elimination. Elimination logic is used to exclude possible candidates from being the cause (the independent variable) when they do not appear in both cases.

With the method of difference, also called the negative method, the goal is to identify independent variables that lead to different outcomes. Elimination logic is then used to exclude the independent variables that are similar in both cases (with different results).

Mill himself was sceptical to the question whether social sciences could benefit from his methods. He found societies too complex to be analysed in this way. In spite of these reservations much of the literature on comparative methods uses Mill as the point of departure. There is a comprehensive literature dealing with his methods, pointing out a number of conditions for so-called Millian logic to be reliable. One condition is deterministic regularity where one single condition is necessary or sufficient for an outcome. Another condition is that all causally relevant variables must be identified prior to comparison; a third that there must be available cases for the study.

Further, Mill's methods cannot be used where there are complex and multiple determinants rather than decisive single factors. If the condition for an outcome is an interacting mechanism and not a single factor, the methods will get into trouble. Also, his logic cannot be used with equifinality, that is, when there are alternative determinants for a result (George & Bennett, 2005).

A number of writers have tried to improve Mill's methods based on the same variable-centred logic. This literature is partly rather technical and the use of different terminology can be confusing. Here I will not go into detail but instead use Todd Landman's terminology in his much-used book *Issues and Methods in Comparative Politics* (2008). Based on Przeworski and Teune he distinguishes between "most similar system designs" and "most different system designs" (Przeworski & Teune, 1970). Here, concentration is called for as most similar system designs build on Mill's method of difference while most different systems build on the Millian method of agreement.

In designs used to study most similar systems we try to find cases that are as similar as possible except for the variable that we want to study the effect of. On this variable we need cases with different values. That makes it possible to study if outcomes are different when the main explanatory factor varies. This can be illustrated by an example (Wickham-Crowley, 1992), also used by Todd Landman (2008). The purpose of the study he quotes was to study the causes of guerrilla activities in a country. The study comprises a group of relatively similar Latin American countries. The hypothesis is that the farmers' situation would influence the way they view the guerrilla. Since guerrilla groups depend on support from the population around them for supplies and hiding places, support from farmers is an important factor behind extensive guerrilla activity. The studies of countries showed that in five countries where farmers were tenant farmers, serfs, or land occupants the guerrilla had support from the farmers. Despite different ways of operating farms, the common trait for these countries was that farmers were not freeholders. In Bolivia, on the other hand, farmers were freeholders and here the guerrilla had no support from the farmers. Thus, the hypothesis was supported.

An alternative set-up for most similar system designs could be the selection of cases that had shown different outcomes on the dependent variable but were otherwise similar on several relevant factors. It would then be possible to trace backwards from the outcome to find the factors that produce different results. Selecting cases based on the dependent variable is not advisable in all situations but could be in this instance. The condition is that we focus on finding necessary causes rather than sufficient causes (Dion, 1998). An example of such a design could be a study of the causal factors behind a voluntary merger of municipalities. We could choose cases that have different outcomes but where the municipalities are as similar as possible on structural factors such as size, geography, and economy. Such a design is suitable for finding contextualised explanatory factors. For instance, leadership, citizen involvement, and experiences with previous cooperation are factors that could have an impact in this instance. Yet we need to supplement the variable-centred comparison of cases with process tracing within each case in order to uncover the complete mechanisms producing a given result.

In designs with most different systems we choose cases that are as different as possible on all other variables than the variable we want to study the effect of. A relevant example is a study of how different class alliances will produce different regimes in a country (Luebbert, 1991). The starting point is a listing of three possible forms of class alliances. One is an alliance between the working class and the farmers. This form was common in Scandinavia and could also be found in countries such as Czechoslovakia. The second form is an alliance between the middle class and the farmers (opposed to the workers). This form was represented in the study by very different countries such as Germany, Italy, and Spain. The third form was represented in countries with a dominating class conflict between working and middle class. Great Britain, France, and several smaller countries on the continent make up the cases. The interesting findings in this study are

174   O. BUKVE

Table 9.2   Most similar system designs and most different system designs

	Most similar system designs (Method of difference)			Most different system designs (Method of agreement)		
	Case 1	Case 2	Case n	Case 1	Case 2	Case n
Properties	A	A	A	a	d	G
	B	B	B	b	e	H
	C	C	C	c	f	L
Main explanatory factor(s)	X	X	Not x	x	x	X
Results to be explained	Y	Y	Not y	y	y	Y

Source: Landman (2008, p. 71)

that different alliance and conflict patterns systematically result in a specific type of regime. The first form gave social democrat regimes, the second fascist ones, and the third liberal regimes.

As the examples show, good studies using these designs will rarely build on mechanical modifications of the analytical model; model-based reasoning must be combined with sound knowledge of the field. Knowledge of the individual cases is decisive for generating good hypotheses and choosing relevant variables and cases. The logic behind most similar systems design and most different systems design is illustrated in Table 9.2. The readers may insert the above examples into the table.

Another well-known development of Millian theory is the indirect method of difference that Ragin (1987) calls the double method of congruence. It builds on analyses of cases with similar outcomes with the purpose of finding whether they have a causal variable in common, as well as on cases with different outcomes in order to see if the causal variable is missing. To perform such analyses, Charles Ragin has developed an approach he calls qualitative comparative analysis (QCA). The method builds on a deterministic causality where the values of a variable are either true or false, usually denoted 1 and 0. QCA shows that we can use numbers as the essential data basis and starting point of the analysis also in qualitative projects. The approach is described in *The Comparative Method* from 1987.[1] I will not here discuss the method in detail but instead illustrate the design by using an example from his book.

---

[1] Later Ragin has developed the method to make it possible to use continuous variables and a probability logic, so-called fuzzy-set logic (Ragin, 2000).

COMPARATIVE DESIGNS   175

Table 9.3 Hypothetic truth table with three causes of strike success

Conditions			Success	Frequency
A	B	C	S	
1	0	1	1	6
0	1	0	1	5
1	1	0	1	2
1	1	1	1	3
1	0	0	0	9
0	0	1	0	6
0	1	1	0	3
0	0	0	0	4

Source: Ragin (1987, p. 96)

The example is a hypothetical study of the conditions for a strike to be successful. The study has three independent variables: growth in the market for the company's products (A), threats of a sympathy strike (B), and ample strike reserves (C). The analysis comprises 38 cases. The result of the case analyses is summarised in a so-called truth table (Table 9.3). In the table, the 38 cases are reduced to eight different configurations or types. Four of the configurations lead to successful strikes. These four configurations may in their turn, using Boolean algebra,[2] be reduced to two different types of conditions for strikes to succeed. One condition is growth in the product market combined with large strike reserves (AC). Under this condition, found in two of the configurations, the strikes are successful—independent of whether there is a threat of a sympathy strike or not. The other condition is the threat of a sympathy strike combined with low strike reserves (Bc). This is not as easy to explain. Ragin suggests that the threat of a sympathy strike will perhaps be taken seriously only when the strike reserves are low.

QCA is the most sophisticated analytical form of comparison of cases but has its drawbacks. One disadvantage is that the analysis requires very many cases to become reliable; thus, it is a time-consuming design. Neither can the analysis be used mechanically. We need to be aware of possible causal factors not present in the initial analysis; also, the analysis is not

---

[2] Boolean algebra describes logical relations in a similar way that ordinary algebra describes numeric relations.

adapted to processes with interacting factors. If we were to establish as probable Ragin's hypothesis in this example, stating that threats of a sympathy strike are not always taken seriously, we would have to make a new round of analysis within the individual cases. Yet the important progress as compared with Mill's methods is that the double congruence method makes it possible to include interacting causes. Thus, combined with process studies of the cases we can analyse mechanism-based explanations.

Such properties of variable-centred comparisons make many of the writers on comparative designs argue that the best strategy in comparative analyses is to combine structured comparisons of cases with the tracing of processes within each case. Strong arguments for this are set forth by writers such as Alexander George and Andrew Bennett (2005). Also, Matthew Lange shares their viewpoint in his book on comparative-historical methods (Lange, 2013), where he accounts for some of the most recognised works in comparative politics and argues that what writers such as Theda Skocpol (1979) and Jeffrey Paige (1975) do, in practice, is to combine these two strategies. Among the first writers to explicitly state that they combine process tracing and structured comparison of cases are Ruth and David Collier in their book on politics in Latin America (Collier & Collier, 1991). A view advocated by George, Bennett, and Lange is that much of the academic discussion on comparative methods is lagging behind compared with best practice in the field. They believe we need an understanding of comparative designs that is updated to be in touch with best practice, and their books have been written with this purpose in view.

References

Bukve, O. (2001). *Lokale utviklingsnettverk ein komparativ analyse av næringsutvikling i åtte kommunar.* Høgskulen i Sogn og Fjordane, Sogndal.

Collier, R. B., & Collier, D. (1991). *Shaping the political arena: Critical junctures, the labor movement, and regime dynamics in Latin America.* Princeton, NJ: Princeton University Press.

Dion, D. (1998). Evidence and inference in the comparative case study. (Case studies in politics). *Comparative Politics, 30,* 127.

George, A. L., & Bennett, A. (2005). *Case studies and theory development in the social sciences.* Cambridge, MA: MIT Press.

Goggin, M. L. (1986). The "too few cases/too many variables" problem in implementation research. *The Western Political Quarterly, 39,* 328–347.

Landman, T. (2008). *Issues and methods in comparative politics: An introduction* (3rd ed.). Milton Park, Abingdon, Oxon: Routledge.

COMPARATIVE DESIGNS 177

Lange, M. (2013). *Comparative-historical methods*. Los Angeles: Sage.

Luebbert, G. M. (1991). *Liberalism, fascism, or social democracy: Social classes and the political origins of regimes in interwar Europe*. New York: Oxford University Press.

Matland, R. E. (1995). Synthesizing the implementation literature: The ambiguity-conflict model of policy implementation. *Journal of Public Administration Research and Theory: J-PART, 5*(2), 145–174.

Paige, J. (1975). *Agrarian revolution: Social movements and export agriculture in the underdeveloped world*. New York: Free Press.

Przeworski, A., & Teune, H. (1970). *The logic of comparative social inquiry*. New York: Wiley.

Ragin, C. C. (1987). *The comparative method*. Berkeley, CA: University of California Press.

Ragin, C. C. (2000). *Fuzzy-set social science*. Chicago, IL: University of Chicago Press.

Ragin, C. C., & Amoroso, L. M. (2011). *Constructing social research*. Thousand Oaks, CA: Pine Forge Press.

Skocpol, T. (1979). *States and social revolutions: A comparative analysis of France, Russia, and China*. Cambridge: Cambridge University Press.

Weber, M. (1971). *Makt og byråkrati: essays om politikk og klasse, samfunnsforskning og verdier*. Oslo, Norway: Gyldendal.

Wickham-Crowley, T. P. (1992). *Guerrillas and revolution in Latin America: A comparative study of insurgents and regimes since 1956*. Princeton, NJ: Princeton University Press.

CHAPTER 10

Intervention-Oriented Designs

In the present chapter I discuss two types of intervention-oriented designs by looking at purpose and strategies in evaluation research and action research. I limit the discussion of evaluation and action research to dealing with the question of how such projects may be designed to develop testable knowledge, in other words scientific knowledge. Less emphasis is placed on issues related to the role of the researcher as participant and adviser in such projects. My main argument is that comprehensive evaluations of interventions and measures must combine studies of process and effect. Measures, interventions, and reforms in society build on a more or less explicit theory of action about the effects of the measure. To evaluate the measures, we need to know something about the effects, and this can best be done through a variable-centred effect study with a control group. However, in order to develop knowledge about why the action succeeded or failed in producing the expected effects, we also need to analyse the underlying theories of action and implementation processes. Therefore, it is possible to talk about intervention-oriented designs as combinations of process and effect designs.

WHAT IS AN EVALUATION DESIGN?

When we use the term "evaluation research" for a research project, it is because of two traits characterising the research object and the purpose of the project. One is that evaluation is about mapping and evaluating a

© The Author(s) 2019
O. Bukve, *Designing Social Science Research*,
https://doi.org/10.1007/978-3-030-03979-0_10

179

180   O. BUKVE

measure, a reform, or an intervention of some (Vedung, 2009). The object of the evaluation is an intervention that somebody carries out. The evaluation may focus on various aspects of the object: outcomes, implementation, or the way the intervention was designed. The other trait is concerned with the fact that the knowledge goal of evaluation research is to direct action (Foss, 2000). The research should give information that can be used in future interventions. Thus, we may talk about evaluation designs as intervention-oriented designs.

The object of the research together with the knowledge goal makes up the characteristic traits of evaluation research, leading our interest towards specific types of questions. I will return to the discussion of how different foci of the research questions lead to different evaluation designs. Here, the point is that evaluation research is not based on a separate set of methods; the same requirements of a systematic approach pertain to evaluation research as to the types of designs mentioned earlier in this book. The same strategies, variable-centred designs, as well as case studies may be used in evaluation research. The same basic rule prevails that we must choose our methods based on the knowledge goal and the research questions. I therefore base the following discussion of evaluation designs on specific research purposes for evaluations, placing each design in relation to the general design variants and choices of method introduced above.

The fact that evaluations are concerned with defined interventions delimits them from general studies of change processes. Another delimitation concerns the distinction between evaluation and action research, where the researcher is participant in the team that carries out the intervention. I will return to action research.

Yet another common delimitation of evaluation research is the delimitation against consequence analyses that involve evaluations of a measure prior to a decision or implementation. Evaluations build on research-based data; they are in principle ex post analyses. Consequence analyses, on the other hand, are performed ex ante, that is, before the event. Not all definitions of evaluation make this delimitation; in this context it is, however, useful. That evaluations build on ex post analyses does not mean that the evaluation has to take place subsequent to the project; the researcher may very well collect data during the project, especially data on the implementation processes. This is common in so-called formative evaluations where the researcher's data may be used to make relevant changes in the project. With formative evaluations as well, the evaluation researcher will have to give advice based on the results of a systematic data collection; thus, the analysis is ex post.

Evaluation research can be oriented towards a variety of objects. Policy measures and reforms constitute the classic field for evaluations. Today, most large public reforms are followed by evaluations. Even more limited measures are often evaluated. And evaluation is not necessarily limited to public interventions; many organisations implement evaluations after large change projects such as an introduction of new forms of organisation or information systems. In combination with the considerable growth in evaluations of public projects it has raised the topic of living in an evaluation society.

The role of the evaluation researcher will vary when it comes to advice and intervention. The division between summative and formative evaluations is a main one in this context (Scriven, 1991). With summative evaluations the researcher concludes after the intervention has been carried out and results begin to appear. Findings and possible recommendations from summative evaluations may be used when new interventions in the same field are to be designed and implemented. The advisory role of the researcher in such projects is therefore indirect and delimited.

In formative evaluations, however, the researcher acts as adviser for the actual intervention. Data collected during the project should be fed back to those who are responsible for the intervention and form the basis of possible changes and adaptations of the course of the intervention. In such research processes, the researcher to a higher degree becomes a player in the intervention project that is to be evaluated.

Evaluation research may be initiated by the organisation responsible for an intervention project as well as by the researchers. When the project owner initiates, it is usually because decision makers want knowledge about outcomes and implementation of the project. Typically, a project owner hires an external research institution to perform the evaluation. With such contract-based evaluations, it can be a challenge to the researcher to handle the relation to the contractor and at the same time create a justifiable design. A typical situation that may arise is that the contractor has a relatively detailed opinion of what should be studied, often in connection with the goals of the intervention, whereas the evaluation researcher believes that other aspects are relevant for research as well. Another challenge is in what ways the researcher is expected to act as an adviser to the contractor. When the researcher trails the measure all through the implementation process the contractor will often want the researcher to give feedback during the process, to be used as a basis for adjusting the implementation of the intervention. Research based on such a researcher role is usually called trailing research. The role of the trailing researcher is to give seen as one where the researcher gives feedback on the basis of collected data on the process, whereas it is the role of the contractor to make decisions about changes and carry out adjustments to the process. In this way, trailing research is different from action research in which the researcher is part of the team that carries out an intervention.

Another challenge is connected with designs where those who are to implement the intervention also have the responsibility of collecting data. This may raise the question of how impartial and valid the data are. Taking care of the integrity and anonymity of those who answer the researcher's questions can also be a challenge since they are at the same time informants for the researcher and responsible for implementation on behalf of the contractor. Handbooks of evaluation research discuss such topics in detail and can be important to a trailing researcher.

When the researcher is the one to initiate the project, this type of dilemma will usually not be as acute. Yet in such instances the researcher will have to secure sufficient trust from the owner of the intervention in order to get access to relevant data. Then the question of usefulness to the owner of the intervention can be raised and we are close to a contractor-researcher relation. The consideration concerning the integrity and autonomy of the respondents applies no matter the type of evaluation. One of the ethical demands of evaluation research is that we bring this consideration into the design and clarify with the owner of the measure and the respondents how the evaluations are to be carried out and used.

The sections below discuss variants of evaluation designs, introducing the main questions and knowledge goals of each evaluation design. Table 10.1 sums up the variants that are discussed. The designs are discussed only briefly here as the literature on evaluation methods gives a good overview (Hansen, 2005; Rossi, Freeman, & Lipsey, 2004; Tornes, 2012).

GOAL EVALUATION

Evaluations of goal attainment are the variety of descriptive design found in evaluation research. Designs for goal attainment compare the status in a field after the measure has been carried out, with the goals that have been set prior to implementation. They build on the comparison of a desired and a real situation. Thus, two descriptions are compared. For instance, in the evaluation of the Norwegian Welfare (NAV) Reform three

INTERVENTION-ORIENTED DESIGNS   **183**

Table 10.1   Variants of evaluation designs

Evaluation designs	Main questions	Purposes
Goal attainment designs	What is status in the field after the intervention? How has status changed in the process period? To what degree have the goals of the intervention been reached?	Descriptive
Effect evaluation	What effects has the intervention led to? How are the effects compared with the goals? What are the effects for different interest groups?	Testing hypotheses Contextual, value-based evaluation
Process evaluation	How was the intervention carried out? Was the use of resources as planned? Was the implementation as planned? How has the implementation influenced the results?	Tracing of processes and actual causal mechanisms
Action theory evaluation	Was the intervention based on the right action theory?	Theory testing Reconstruction of the action theory and evaluation against data
Programme evaluation	Comprehensive evaluation of the connection between structural/contextual conditions, programme design, effort, execution, and effects	Combined process and effect study Process tracing Theory and hypothesis testing

sets of goals were compared with the results after the reform. Were more people employed and fewer people dependent on social welfare? Was it easier for the users of the welfare services, and were the services better adapted to the users' needs? Was the administration more complete and efficient? The picture of goal attainment shown by the evaluation is a mixed one (Andreassen & Aars, 2015).

A common problem with this type of evaluation is that the goals of an intervention can be so vague or contradictory that they make it difficult to conclude whether the goals have in fact been reached. Often, political interventions build on such goal compromises, making evaluation difficult.

The aspect of time also plays a role; goals may change over time, and we cannot be sure that the most relevant goals for evaluation of a measure afterwards are actually identical to the goals set up when the measure was planned and designed. Context as well as societal values may have changed in ways that make the original goals less relevant.

EFFECT EVALUATION

Effect evaluation goes a step further by not only registering the status afterwards but also analysing to what degree the status is an effect of the intervention evaluated. If we include quantitative effect goals, an evaluation of effects requires us to control for effects of other factors that may have had an impact on the status after the measure. Consequently, an effect evaluation must comply with the requirements of experimental designs. Since the conditions for real experiments are rarely present, we have to use quasi-experiments or natural experiments, discussed in Chap. 6. This involves the use of control groups or statistical control methods. The design is like a classic hypothesis testing. We can compare the status in a group that has participated in an intervention with a control group that has not participated. We can for instance evaluate the effects of physical activity on pupils' school performance by giving selected groups of pupils an offer of daily physical activity, then comparing their school performances before and after with corresponding groups that have not received this offer (Resaland et al., 2015).

One question is often raised with such designs, and that is how we can discover and control for unintended effects. A control problem in evaluations—as in other experiments—is that test persons may act strategically in order to influence the results. This is the case with measurements of results in Oslo schools. A strategy that some schools seem to have used is to excuse a number of poorly performing pupils from taking the tests. An indicator of this is that there is a positive connection between the percentage of excused pupils and the test results in a selection of schools in Oslo, which could be an example of a negative unintentional effect. The main question for a good design is how to be aware of unintended effects as well.

Effect evaluations with control groups are best suited where the measure is expected to have effects in a number of cases. If it is not possible to establish adequate control groups we could alternatively use a design of tracing the processes that lead from initiation of the measure to the effects on users and others. The evaluation of the NAV reform is an example of an effect evaluation in accordance with this strategy. The evaluators first accounted for the results of the reform. Next, they accounted for the measures and processes that were meant to realise the goals, emphasising four main organisational changes that were to contribute to desired effects, then evaluating the effect each of these organisational changes had in practice (Andreassen & Aars, 2015). In this way it is possible to focus on the conditions for change effects as well as the mechanisms that produce them.

An essential question to be asked with effect evaluation is who is to define what good or less good effects are. Early effect evaluations mostly evaluated the effects compared with the goals. This was perceived as a value-free design, but the concept was criticised for regarding the interests of those who designed the measure as universal interests. More recent forms of effect evaluation therefore have emphasised the importance of evaluating the effects as seen from the point of view of a variety of stakeholders. For instance, in research on measures in the health sector patients, the professions of the sector, and the administration as well as the political leadership may be relevant stakeholders (Donabedian, 1988; Øvretveit, 1990). What stakeholders to include is a question that in some cases may have ethical and value implications.

PROCESS EVALUATION AND ACTION THEORY EVALUATION

An intervention that has not given the desired result may have failed for two principally different reasons. One reason is that the intervention may not have been implemented the way we expected; another that the measure rested on an inadequate or wrong theory about what kind of factors and measures could influence the result. The other way around, even if the goals of a measure have been realised we cannot be sure that it is the intervention that have been decisive in realising the goals. Other factors may have created the result, which means that the coherence between goal and result is an effect of a third variable that is not present in the evaluation model.

To clarify such questions, we must look at the processes leading from design of the intervention to effects and trace the chains from implementation to result. Was the use of resources and other measures as planned? Did the actors responsible for implementation of the measures influence what was actually done and how? Did this distort the implementation? If so, what were the consequences? How have the implemented measures influenced the result? A process evaluation like this can be performed by use of the methods of process tracing that were discussed in the chapter on case studies. Process evaluation is about tracing the actual chains of action and causes during the realisation of an intervention; thus, the goal of the evaluation is to build an empirical model of the connections in the evaluated intervention.

Evaluation of the action theory, on the contrary, deals with identification of the theoretical model that is the basis of the intervention. How does the action theory connect goals and measures? Is this done in a justifiable way? How does the action theory view the connection from implemented measures to effects? Is the causal model the right one?

The evaluation of the NAV reform mentions an example of inadequate action theory (Andreassen & Aars, 2015). The reformers wanted access to the NAV services to be easier for the users. They believed this could be done by making all services accessible in one place. To achieve this, a decision was made that first-line services were to be organised according to a generalist model. Executive officers were to have knowledge of and provide all services related to NAV's activities. This turned out not to work in practice. NAV was responsible for so many services and administered such a number of laws and regulations that first-line officers were not able to handle it. The generalist model had to be abandoned.

Process evaluation and evaluation of the action theory may, when seen in connection, say something about the reasons why an intervention succeeds or fails. Was the problem to be found in the implementation or in the underlying action theory? And if the intervention succeeded, was it because of a good design, because the process was adjusted during the implementation, or was it pure luck?

Process evaluation and action theory evaluation are usually part of trailing evaluations where the researcher gives feedback in the course of the project. In this way, those responsible for the intervention get the opportunity to change the implementation of the measure based on data about the process.

Comprehensive Programme Evaluation

A comprehensive evaluation of an intervention is often called programme evaluation. In an evaluation like that, the aspects mentioned above are included in an integrated evaluation. What role did structural and contextual conditions have for the result of an intervention? How much of the result is due to the intervention and what could be due to other factors? Did the action theory make realistic judgments of how the intervention could be implemented? Did the implementation proceed as planned? Did deviations make problems for the intervention or can they be viewed as adjustments in the right direction? Was the action theory built on the right analysis of causal conditions? Did the projects attain their goals? What were the effects on stakeholder groups and values? These questions are relevant in a comprehensive programme evaluation. Such a programme evaluation should therefore be carried out as a process-effect study, where a process-oriented study of the way the intervention was implemented is combined with a variable-centred study of the effects of the intervention.

Underlying programme evaluations is a practical interest in the use of the evaluations. Results from evaluations may be used to improve the design and realisation of new interventions. Evaluations may also be used selectively as a legitimation of desired measures or to reject unwanted measures. Evaluations are never independent of the social context they are part of. Evaluation researchers cannot fully protect themselves from being used in other ways and for other purposes than what they think is right. But what they can do is take responsibility for performing the evaluation design and the implementation of the evaluation project as solidly as possible.

ACTION RESEARCH

As the term indicates, action research denotes a strategy for intervention-oriented research. In this type of research, the researcher participates in planning, implementing, and evaluating an intervention in some field. Thus, the researcher has a participatory role. Another characteristic of action research is that it aims to reduce or do away with the distinction between researchers and other participants in interventions. Researchers do not hold a unique position in terms of knowledge development; they, too, need to understand and learn from a situation and a set of experiences in the same way as the other participants (Greenwood & Levin, 2007).

I will not in this context discuss the issues that concern the role of the action researcher in relation to the practitioners, or questions about how to best get relevant data and carry out an action research project. I will limit my discussion to saying something about the conditions for action research to actually be research, that is to say the conditions that are necessary for developing statement knowledge that can be tested.

Action research is especially important in three different social fields: organisation development, working life research, and in the professions (Duus, Husted, Kildedal, Laursen, & Tofteng, 2012). The organisation psychologist Kurt Lewin is seen as the originator of action research (Nielsen, 2012). With a starting point in research showing that performance and contentment in organisations increased when workers were involved in the processes rather than being led through authoritarian structures, he developed strategies for worker involvement in organisational change, creating the field of study that was later to be termed organisation development. In working life research, action research has been used as a tool to improve the interaction between the technical and social systems of a company. By utilising workers' resources and ideas, the enterprise could become more productive as well as more democratic. The Norwegian cooperation projects between the working life parties from the 1960s onwards, carrying out a number of action research experiments of industrial democracy and autonomous work groups, were essential in this context (Thorsrud & Emery, 1970). In the professions, action research has been given a lot of attention in the last decade as a strategy for quality development in professional practice. In particular in education, but also in welfare services and health care, action research has become a widespread working method.

Much of today's action research links up with theories of learning when accounting for how action research contributes to developing new frames of understanding and a better practice in organisations and groups. The classic point of departure is Argyris and Schön's theory of single and double loop learning in organisations (Argyris & Schön, 1978). Single loop learning is instrumental in the sense of having to do with finding the best means to reach a given goal. Double loop learning, on the other hand, is transformative, involving a questioning of the organisation's goals and fundamental frames of understanding. Reflection on our own practice and experiences is seen as the main tool in this type of learning (Schön, 1983). Alternation between reflection and practice is essential for the understanding of knowledge development and change processes in action research. By alternating between practical interventions and reflection on the experiences, we will probably find better ways of performing the job. Much of the method development in action research deals with developing arenas for reflection and dialogue between the actors in a development project. In working life research, dialogue conferences and search conferences have been developed as main reflection arenas. Another field of interest is arenas for citizen participation in public planning and activity. In the professions, methods such as learning circles and action experiments have become common, just to mention a few (Duus et al., 2012).

As a field of research, action research is heterogeneous. A large number of methods are used and action researchers link up to various frames of understanding in their views of science and knowledge. We could probably say that the normative is a common characteristic. Action researchers tend to emphasise democracy and equality as the normative basis of this way of organising research. Another element is the emphasis on the value of the practitioners' knowledge. Beyond this, we cannot say that action researchers represent a specific philosophy of knowledge. As for Kurt Lewin, he understood organisational interventions more or less as experiments. With such an approach, we can apply a logic where we compare the outcome of the experiment with theory-based expectations, or we can study interventions as comparative cases and thus a basis for theoretical analysis. From this philosophy, much of what has been discussed above about evaluation design will also be relevant for the design of action research. Clarifying goals, underlying action theories, and the difference between evaluations of process and result is important in the design of an action research project too.

At the other extreme point, we find action researchers who make a division between theoretical and practical knowledge and regard theoretical knowledge as less valuable than the type of practical knowledge developed through familiarity with a particular situation. Theoretical knowledge is often seen as synonymous with abstract generalisations; thus, they tend to discard such knowledge as of little use to practical development work. Practice and the reflection on practice are emphasised as the best strategy for learning and development.

Already Aristotle believed that acting in the right way in a given situation does not only require knowledge, there is also an ethical and normative element. Aristotle distinguished between the virtues of episteme, statement-oriented knowledge or expertise, and phronesis, practical wisdom. To this he added the virtue of skills or craftsmanship: techne. Statement-oriented knowledge alone cannot set the direction for practical wisdom. Practical wisdom is necessarily local and situational. Neither can phronesis ignore episteme—understood as statement knowledge about phenomena and rule-bound connections in society. The Norwegian philosopher and action researcher Olav Eikeland has shown that Aristotle uses two different concepts about theory, about abstract generalising theory (theoresis) and contextualised theory (theoria) (Eikeland, 1997). Eikeland believes that reflection in action research must involve a dialectical confrontation between practice and theoria (Eikeland & Nicolini, 2011). Action research cannot reject theory; action researchers, too, must be confronted by the demand of clarifying their action theories and theoretical frames of reference before using these to confront experience and data. Neither can practical reason, phronesis, an intrinsic element in interventional projects, be a substitute for theory. It should rather be understood as critical reason, questioning abstractions (Ricoeur, 1988 [1986]).

From this argumentation, the elements of evaluation designs, which also include the study of interventions, are in my opinion relevant also for the design of action research projects. In an action research project there will be an underlying theory of action, explicit or not. An evaluation of coherence between the underlying theoretical frames of the project and data on actual processes and effects will then be a necessary element. If we, for instance, are testing new teaching forms in an action research project, it will be relevant to have reliable data on how the project influences the pupils' learning, what the main conditions for this influence are, and how different groups judge the results. Such knowledge needs to be thematised so that it can be assessed critically. It is a well-known fact that test situations can lead to so-called placebo effects so that we get results that match the expectations even if the action theory behind the testing is not the right one. Such results are, however, short term; they will hardly last beyond the test situation. The Hawthorne experiments are a well-known example. There, the researchers changed the physical working environment in a factory to find out how environmental factors influenced the performance of the workers. To their surprise, the researchers found that performances improved no matter whether the physical environment was changed for the better or for the worse. Thus, they discovered a case of the placebo or test effect.

In action research, too, we need systematised knowledge about effects and what processes actually create the effects. The main difference between action research and evaluation lies in how we organise the research process and who is involved, not what counts as valid knowledge and how to proceed to establish knowledge of scientific type.

References

Andreassen, T. A., & Aars, J. (2015). *Den store reformen: da NAV ble til.* Oslo, Norway: Universitetsforlaget.

INTERVENTION-ORIENTED DESIGNS 191

Argyris, C., & Schön, D. A. (1978). *Organizational learning: A theory of action perspective*. Reading, MA: Addison-Wesley.

Donabedian, A. (1988). The quality of care. How can it be assessed? *JAMA*, *260*(12), 1743–1748.

Duus, G., Husted, M., Kildedal, K., Laursen, E., & Tofteng, D. (2012). *Aktionsforskning*. Frederiksberg, Denmark: Samfundslitteratur.

Eikeland, O. (1997). Erfaring, dialogikk og politikk: den antikke dialogfilosofiens betydning for rekonstruksjonen av moderne empirisk samfunnsvitenskap: et begrepshistorisk og filosofisk bidrag. In ([3. utg]. ed., Vol. 11). Oslo: Det historisk-filosofiske fakultet, Universitetet i Oslo Universitetsforlaget.

Eikeland, O., & Nicolini, D. (2011). Turning practically: Broadening the horizon. *Journal of Organizational Change Management, 24*(2), 164–174. https://doi. org/10.1108/09534811111119744

Foss, O. (2000). Evaluering – samfunnsforskning i politikkens tjeneste. In O. Foss & J. Mønnesland (Eds.), *Evaluering av offentlig virksomhet. Metoder og vurderinger*. Oslo, Norway: NIBR.

Greenwood, D. J., & Levin, M. (2007). *Introduction to action research*. Thousand Oaks, CA: Sage Publications.

Hansen, H. F. (2005). Choosing evaluation models: A discussion on evaluation design. *Evaluation, 11*(4), 447–462. https://doi.org/10.1177/135638900 5060265

Nielsen, K. A. (2012). Aktionsforskningens historie – på vej til et refleksivt akademisk selskap. In G. Duus, M. Husted, K. Kildedal, E. Laursen, & D. Tofteng (Eds.), *Aktionsforskning* (pp. 19–36). Fredriksberg, Denmark: Samfundslitteratur.

Øvretveit, J. (1990). *Quality health services*. London: Brunel Institute of Organisation and Social Studies, Brunel University.

Resaland, G. K., Moe, V. F., Aadland, E., Steene-Johannessen, J., Glosvik, Ø., Andersen, J. R., et al. (2015). Active Smarter Kids (ASK): Rationale and design of a cluster-randomized controlled trial investigating the effects of daily physical activity on children's academic performance and risk factors for non-communicable diseases. *BMC Public Health, 15*(1), 709. https://doi.org/10.1186/s12889-015-2049-y

Ricoeur, P. (1988 (1986)). Det praktiske förnuftet. In *Från text till handling: en antologi om hermeneutik (Orig.: Du texte à l'action, Essais d'hermenutiques)* (Vol. 1, pp. 167–205). Stockholm: Brutus Östlings bokförlag Symposion.

Rossi, P. H., Freeman, H. E., & Lipsey, M. W. (2004). *Evaluation: A systematic approach* (7th ed.). Thousand Oaks, CA: Sage.

Schön, D. A. (1983). *The reflective practitioner: How professionals think in action*. New York: Basic Books.

Scriven, M. (1991). *Evaluation thesaurus* (4th ed.). Newbury Park, CA: Sage.

Thorsrud, E., & Emery, F. E. (1970). *Mot en ny bedriftsorganisasjon: eksperimenter i industrielt demokrati* (Ny utg. ed. Vol. 2). Oslo: Tanum.

Tornes, K. (2012). *Evaluering i teori og praksis.* Trondheim, Norway: Akademika.

Vedung, E. (2009). *Utvärdering i politik och förvaltning* (3. uppl. ed.). Lund, Sweden: Studentlitteratur.

CHAPTER 11

The Design Process

THE DESIGN PROCESS: AN OVERVIEW

A research design is a plan for carrying out a research project. As has already been stated in this book, in a design process we must find a way to link our research interest and questions with, on the one hand, general ideas and theories, on the other, a strategy for data construction. Doing this in practice is a process; nothing comes cut-and-dried. We usually start with a phenomenon we are wondering about, a societal problem we know or have heard about. But we can also start with a doubt about the explanations and stories we hear about some connection or phenomenon, the doubt making us want to put these explanations to a test. There can be a number of reasons why we choose a particular research topic. A decisive test of whether the topic is worth researching is that we are able to show its importance or relevance to others and not alone to ourselves. In other words, we must state the reasons for the choice of that particular topic—already in the first phase of the design process.

Another important step in the design process is to clarify the purpose of the project. The purpose is what we want to learn or achieve with our research. Thus, formulating purpose and problem statement is related to the interest behind the choice of project topic. The purpose largely guides the questions we ask to our material, in other words the formulation of our problem statement. We need to know what we want to find in order to be able to ask good questions.

© The Author(s) 2019
O. Bukve, *Designing Social Science Research*,
https://doi.org/10.1007/978-3-030-03979-0_11

Still, the purpose and the problem statement cannot be formulated independent of our prior knowledge about the research topic and the way we plan to use that knowledge in that particular project. As researchers we must be aware of where we place ourselves in the knowledge field. Consequently, going through the relevant research literature and making a summing-up evaluation of knowledge status are main elements in a design process. Research can be seen as a systematic approach to producing arguments in an ongoing debate on how society can be understood and changed. If research is to develop new knowledge, we have to become familiar with the topic and enter into a dialogue with the knowledge that has been established through previous research.

In this phase we also need to seek information about general ideas and theories that are relevant to our own approach to the topic. This has to be limited to the extent that we only select concepts and theories that will be useful to us further on in our project. This selection and clarification of concepts and theories is part of the effort to establish an analytical framework for the project. This framework can take different forms. If we have a clearly defined theory or hypothesis that we want to put to test, or there are alternative competing theories, a structured frame is called for. If we start with a phenomenon or problem that is not sufficiently explained in the literature, we may need a flexible frame that enables us to steer the project in the most relevant direction. If the topic is a new one or little explored, we may need an open frame and take into consideration that the empirical data may lead us in different directions. In such cases, the design process may become a pendulum process in which in the course of the project we return to the problem statement and analytical frames in light of new data about the topic. What the analytical frame will look like and how delimiting it will be in our work will depend both on what we want to learn from the project—the knowledge goals—and on what we already know about the research object. The frame may vary from a detailed theoretical model with operationalisations to a few guiding concepts—so-called sensitising concepts.

When formulating the analytical frame, we usually return to the problem statement we formulated at the outset and will then be able to define it precisely in light of the analytical frame. We do that by supplementing the overall problem statement by a set of research questions. In this way, we can ensure that the analytical frame and the questions match.

Thus, the first part of the design process deals with clarifying and narrowing the purpose—together with a problem statement and possibly also

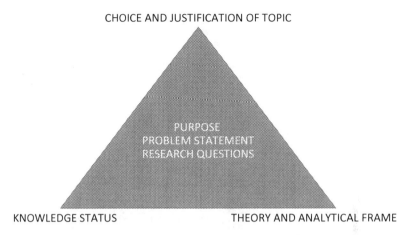

Fig. 11.1 The first phase of the design process

detailed research questions. To do this clarification and pinpointing we must first delimit and justify the topic for research. Then we have to get familiar with established research knowledge about the topic in order to be able to show where our project stands in relation to this knowledge. Finally, we must introduce the theories and concepts that guide our own inquiry and clarify a frame for analysis. The first part of the design process is visualised in Fig. 11.1.

The second part of the design process has to do with clarifying and concretising a strategy for data construction. With purpose and problem statement as the point of departure we have to decide on a suitable strategy for data construction. Are the purpose and the field of research such that a holistic perspective would be most suitable, meaning that we construct data as cases? Or should we use the reductionist perspective and construct data as units with variable properties? As mentioned above, the purpose may also make it relevant to choose combinations of these strategies.

When we have chosen a strategy for data construction, we are ready to deal with the questions concerning research method. These questions have to do with how we select, collect, and analyse the data needed for answering our research questions. We should evaluate our choice of method critically, considering whether it will give the desired validity and reliability. The choice of strategy for data construction and method can be illustrated as in Fig. 11.2.

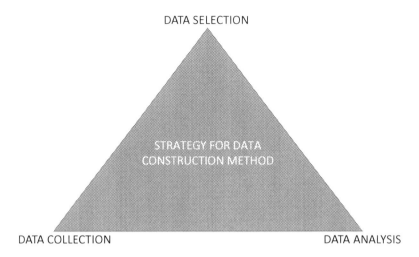

Fig. 11.2 Choice of strategy and methods for data construction

The design process can vary in many ways. The individual elements can rarely be completed in sequence. We will usually go back and forth between the various tasks that belong to the design process. Nevertheless, with the intention of making the approach and the underlying logic in each partial task clear I will discuss the design elements successively. But we must remember that the work with the design is not a linear process; we work with several partial tasks simultaneously, and it is important to consider to what degree a choice at one point will influence the work with the other tasks.

Still, at the end we will join the various elements we are working with into a project draft, and the pieces must be placed in a fairly logical sequence. In the last part of this chapter I propose a standard structure for a project draft. Such a structure can be useful to a novice researcher. The more experienced researcher can, of course, vary and improvise. Still, it is in research as in music: Improvisations on a theme is possible only if we are familiar with the theme we are making variations on.

Choice and Justification of a Topic

Only our imagination is the limit for what could be the topic of a project that investigates society. Still, some types of topic are more common than others. Quite a few research projects and postgraduate degree theses deal with a societal issue. It may be problems or issues that are important to one or another social group; it may have to do with development patterns or events in working life or society; it may deal with public policy and administration or with the production of public services. The reasons why we take an interest in a topic may also vary, spanning from wondering about the unknown via a general interest in a topic, to our own experiences. Our own experiences with a problem field will often be the starting point for a wish to find out how things are tied together. Or we may be attracted by what is unknown and exotic and have a wish to understand it better.

What is new, either completely new social phenomena or new developments in well-known areas, is also a common topic for research. Or our starting point could be that we question, or wish to explore further, established or rivalling theories and ways of understanding by testing them on new data or problematise them through a theoretical critique.

If you are a student about to carry out your first research project and are at a loss to find ideas, a piece of good advice is to take a look at previous theses and the topics chosen. It can give you an idea about suitable topics and how extensive the inquiry should be.

Another piece of advice is to take your time with the choice of topic, learning as much as possible about the field you wish to study. A good idea is to read quite a bit about the topic, for instance in relevant research literature, in public reports, or in media coverages. The library and the internet can give good help in this phase when you are searching for relevant material.

There are two questions we should ask ourselves in the process of choosing and formulating a topic for our research project. The first question is about our own interest. Am I interested in and enthusiastic about this topic so that the work with the thesis can be beneficial and pleasurable? The other question is about relevance. To whom can the research topic be important or useful? New knowledge needs a field where it can be used, either by providing new data about a research topic, a new perspective on a social phenomenon, or by saying something about how a social problem can be solved. The research topic therefore has to have relevance also to others, not only to the researcher.

The question about relevance can also be formulated as a question about the background or context of the research topic. Why has this phenomenon, this problem, or this way of understanding emerged, and why has it become important to provide more knowledge about it?

198   O. BUKVE

Yet another piece of good advice is to start writing already during the work with finding, formulating, and justifying the research topic. Often, thoughts become clearer during the writing process. Make notes while writing. Do not limit the writing to reporting; also write ideas and questions to the material. Another useful way of writing is so-called thought writing or idea writing, writing down thoughts and ideas without bothering with structure.

When you have worked your way through the topic and the choice seems fairly clear, time has come to write about the choice of topic and the justification in a more structured way. Try to find a short, precise, and interesting formulation of the topic. Give an outline of background and context, for the sake of your own understanding as well as for the readers to understand what you are interested in. After that, you should try to say something about why your topic is relevant. When you have completed this you will have an outline for the introduction in your project draft. This will, however, not be the final introduction. You will probably return to it and revise it after you have finished step two in the design process. That step is about establishing the knowledge status in the field and about placing your own project in the field.

LITERATURE REVIEW AND KNOWLEDGE STATUS

The general goal of all research is that it should contribute to enhancing knowledge about the topic or field that the research is oriented towards. But if we want to participate in developing new knowledge, we must be familiar with existing knowledge. A literature review is the most important tool for placing our own project in a research field and an academic context. The goal of all research is to provide new knowledge. Yet what constitutes new knowledge can be decided only by getting to know the research field and the knowledge that has already been established. By reading up on existing research we will avoid studying phenomena that have already been explored and using the same approach that other researchers have used before. With such a starting point, we would not be able to say anything of interest to other researchers or to the users of the research.

Therefore, it is important to read available research literature and use what we find to describe and evaluate the present situation regarding knowledge about the topic. Creating a status about knowledge, termed literature review, is a task in three different steps: the search for relevant literature; description of the content; and an evaluating summary of the knowledge that exists and what new questions could be asked.

The search for new literature always involves a balance between two considerations. On the one hand, we must search widely enough to get at the important research and knowledge. On the other hand, we should not search so widely that we drown in literature, not managing to proceed. Striking a happy medium is usually done by searching systematically. It is also a good idea to start with a relatively narrow set of search words and extend the search when needed.

The number of sources we can search in is large. Literature search via internet databases has become the standard method, but we can also visit the library and search on the shelves under relevant subject headings. Regarding internet search, most research and educational institutions have libraries offering good help in finding the best databases. A course in literature search is often part of the offer given to students who are to write a thesis.

Good search words are decisive for what we will find. It is important to formulate the search word as precisely as possible, preferably using alternative search words for the same topic. The following search words were used in a master's degree thesis about implementation of standardised care pathways in the health services: *critical pathway, clinical pathway, care pathway, integrated care pathway, implementation* (Hatlen, 2016). We should read up quite a bit in the literature before formulating search words, as it is essential that they correspond to the terminology used in the relevant literature. If the result is meagre, we must widen the search. If the search gives us too many titles, we need to use more limited search words or delimit the search by using combinations of search words. In the example above, a search word such as *implementation* would give very many hits, which shows that it would be an advantage to delimit the search by combining search words. A search for *implementation* combined with *care pathway* is an example. If this is too limited, we could for instance combine *implementation* and *health care*.

The best approach is to use several databases in order to compare the findings. Searching in literature databases is a field that is rapidly developing. New databases are appearing that search across in various primary bases. Internationally, Google Scholar is a very wide database. A probable result is that you will get too many and not very relevant hits by searching in these databases. It would therefore be a good idea to combine them with more specialised databases. What bases are most relevant depends on your field of study. Ask librarians or experienced colleagues if you are new to the field.

As you search, you should make a log of what you find by using various search words and what you find in the databases (Vom Brocke et al., 2009). Use the most relevant hits as search criterion and compare what you find by using different databases. Scan the abstract to find the most relevant articles and to isolate those that are not relevant. Remember that the literature lists in the most important articles are also sources of relevant literature.

An alternative to the systematic literature search is using the so-called snowball method for searching. You begin with the literature lists of the newest or most important articles and books in your field of study. Then use these to find out what previous research this literature is based on. By proceeding in this way, you can get a picture of how the knowledge status of a topic has come to be.

A recurring question is how extensive you should make the literature study (Boote & Beile, 2005; Denney & Tewksbury, 2013; Maxwell, 2006). My view is that concerning the presentation of the literature, relevance should trump volume. There can be good reasons for making the search as complete as possible. But when the literature is to be presented, the relevance for your own research is decisive (Maxwell, 2006).

Already when reading the articles, you must look for main content and relevance. Make notes and ask questions to the text while reading. When you write the outline for the section on knowledge status, you should not use the space to repeat the content of each article. Instead, you should sum up the knowledge status across the articles, judging what of this knowledge is already existing knowledge and pointing to possible new questions and research topics. By doing this, you can also develop your own project by delimiting the topic and building a foundation for formulating purposes and research questions in a good way. Applying two well-used metaphors, we can say that it is the literature review that anchors the project in a research field (Krathwohl & Smith, 2005, p. 49), and that the completion of this review creates the bridge from the field to the project that is to be performed (Denney & Tewksbury, 2013, p. 232).

Existing literature can be viewed from different angles. It is useful to distinguish between gap-spotting and problematisation (Alvesson & Sandberg, 2011; Sandberg & Alvesson, 2011). Focus can be on empirical findings, theory, or method use in the existing literature (Maxwell, 2006). Gap-spotting is the most common strategy for developing new research ideas. We usually start by focusing on findings obtained in empirical inquiries. Focusing on the findings means that our research interest will be oriented towards finding knowledge gaps that can be filled. Sandberg and Alvesson (2011) identify a number of ways of identifying knowledge gaps. One common way is to identify topics or research areas that have been neglected in earlier research. Possible research topics may have been overlooked or not sufficiently investigated. We can then perform new analyses in a research field or repeat the research in a new field.

Another problem is that there could be insufficient empirical support for conclusions drawn in previous research. In order to find knowledge holes of this kind we must direct our attention to the methods that were used in the literature. The findings in the literature may also be unclear because there are competing explanations that have not been tested against each other. Our research purpose could then deal with comparing these explanations through new investigations. Another variety of knowledge gaps may be caused by the use of theoretical perspectives that are insufficient, which may in our case lead to ambitions to develop the knowledge by applying new perspectives.

Identifying knowledge gaps is not the only strategy we can use in a literature review. Alvesson and Sandberg (2011) argue that it is possible to develop interesting research questions by a more confronting problematisation of the literature. Such problematisation can constitute new thinking with regard to a theoretical tradition or critique of applied concepts, or new thinking through constructing a new field for empirical research. Problematising approaches to literature challenge conventional wisdom in a field whether they deal with ideological blinkers or with underlying ontological, epistemological, or methodological assumptions. A problematising literature review can be particularly relevant when the purpose is to develop new theory or interpret a phenomenon from a theoretical perspective. Alvesson and Sandberg (2011) also give relevant advice about how to perform a problematising literature review.

PURPOSE DESCRIPTION

The beginning of a research project is quite often that we are wondering about a problem, a phenomenon, or a connection. That which we are wondering about or are curious about can be said to be the topic of the project. After having delimited the topic and got to know it, there are two new tasks we need to take in hand.

Now is the time to develop a precisely formulated purpose with the project and concretise it in a set of research questions. The point of formulating a purpose is to delimit the project as well as saying what we wish to know, in other words the knowledge goal. The purpose of a research project can be defined as a formulation of *what knowledge we wish to arrive at through the project*. A good definition of the purpose is essential for the rest of the design work. That is why it is important that you start working on the purpose formulation early in the research process. You will perhaps have to change it and polish it in the course of the process but you need it to be able to relate to in the subsequent phases of the project. In this phase it is also important that you decide what type of purpose is adequate for your project. Is the goal of the project to test an established theory? Is the ambition to develop new theory about phenomena and connections you do not fully understand? Do you intend to use established theory to analyse and interpret a phenomenon or to explain connections? Is your goal to strengthen the basis for practical interventions or improvement work? You should use these types of goals, discussed in Chap. 5, to find out how you can categorise your purpose.

A good description of purpose will in a few words communicate what the main knowledge goal of the project is. What do you want to learn, and about what? To ensure that the purpose description is effective you should use words such as *purpose*, *intention*, or *goals* in the introductory part of the description: The goal of this project is … The intention of this project is … (Creswell, 2009).

The purpose description also has to say something about what it is you seek knowledge about. Does the project focus on a single phenomenon, a concept, or a theoretical idea, or does it focus on connections between phenomena? The foundation for what to say about this has already been laid by the choice of topic and the literature review.

In the course of the project outline it can be useful to return to the purpose description as a recurrent theme. Already in the introduction you should identify the general knowledge goal of the project. After having introduced the literature review, you can then delimit and define the knowledge goal. A good delimitation of the knowledge goal is possible only after you have secured an overview of what is already established knowledge and what you intend to contribute with in the form of new knowledge. A suitable completion of the literature review would be to formulate the main problem statement of the project. Are there knowledge gaps that should be filled, or established knowledge to be problematised and challenged? At this point the problem statement could be formulated as a question. Yet you are still not completely through with the problem statement. It is usually relevant to break it down into more detailed research questions, which can at best be done after you have introduced the theory and the analytical framework to be used in the project.

THEORY AND ANALYTICAL FRAMEWORK

Completing the first phase of the design work, you present the theoretical ideas and perspectives that were your starting point and show how these are used to design an analytical framework for the project, and further, how this framework leads to a set of research questions.

How to present theoretical perspectives and ideas is closely linked to the general knowledge goal of the project. If the knowledge goal is about testing established theories or carrying out a theory-informed analysis of a social phenomenon, you will have to present the theory sufficiently detailed and clear to make it possible to see what expectations and hypotheses about empirical findings the theory will lead to. If the purpose is theory development, the presentation of existing theory may take another direction. You could account for the reasons for being critical to the explanatory strength of the theories that are dominant in the field and, consequently, conclude that new and better theories are needed. Or it could be sufficient to present some guiding concepts that give the investigation a direction or, as it were, show what theoretical terrain you will have to orient yourself in. Whichever of these approaches suits your project, the point of the theory presentation is to show if, and possibly how, established theory and familiar concepts can shed light on your topic. Most importantly, you should make clear what you can use as a starting point and how you can use it; you should not write long and detailed descriptions of the theory.

The concept of analytical framework has to do with how we use theory in a project. Depending on our use of theory, we can have different types of framework: fixed, multiple, flexible, or open frames.

If the project aims to test a particular theory or carry out a structured interpretation of a phenomenon based on a theory, we can say that the project has *fixed frames*. The theory used in the project will lead to a definition of specific expectations, statements, or hypotheses. You will then have to account for the theories and how they lead to specific ideas about phenomena or connections that you intend to study in the project. The processes or connections you want to study can be visualised in a concept model. The product of a project with fixed frames is usually either a weakening or a strengthening of the initial statements.

If a number of rivalling or complementary theories are the starting point of the analysis, the project can be said to have *multiple frames*. In this case, too, you will have to define hypotheses and test them against data. But in this case the analysis must also compare the theories. Can different theories explain the same phenomenon, can they be complementary so that a more detailed explanation can be developed, or are they opposed to each other?

If the project aims to explore an empirical phenomenon or a set of empirical connections in order to, if possible, develop generalisations and thus new theory, the framework can be made more flexible. By using *flexible frames*, we can explore several possible connections. The goal is to arrive at a more specific framework as a result of the project. The product of a project with flexible frames is usually a new model with better defined connections.

A project can also have *open frames*. This is common in explorative and interpretative projects where the data collection is not based on specific models. The product of a project with open frames is that we characterise the researched phenomenon by one or more generalising concepts, or that we develop a frame of interpretation that shows how the phenomenon has been formed, has changed, or has produced particular effects.

The analytical framework of a project can be visualised by use of a model. Such models define what kind of connections we plan to explore in the project. By defining connections as clearly as possible, our thoughts will also become clearer and the internal validity in the project design increases.

The final step in designing an analytical framework is about operationalising it, which means saying how we intend to observe and measure the phenomena and connections we plan to study. It has to do with connecting the concept model and the empirical model of the project. The operationalisation decides the construction validity of the design. A well-founded operationalisation is very important prior to the collection of data and it is a good idea to use several types of data if this enhances the validity of the construction.

The Research Questions

The final formulation of the research questions can be done in connection with the concretisation of an analytical framework for the project. At this point in the project we will probably have been struggling with proposals for questions for some time. The research questions may also be placed further to the front in the finished project draft. But only when we have finished with the general purpose and are formulating the analytical frame is it possible to see clearly what questions will be useful.

Often, a research project will include more than one research question. The presentation of the questions will then be organised around one or, at most, two main questions and, additionally, a detailing of the main questions by a few subsidiary questions. There should not be too many questions, and they should be organised in such a way that they are logically connected. Which is to say that the first question should lead to the next. A shopping list of pell-mell questions is no good strategy for the job ahead.

A few sentences about terminology are called for. Often, the terms "problem statement" and "research questions" are used synonymously. Not too bad, really. Still, I have chosen to differentiate the terms, using the term "problem statement" only when I am talking about the overall problem formulation that guides the project, whereas the term "research questions" denotes the individual partial questions to be studied. Said differently, the problem statement can be divided up and concretised by the formulation of a set of research questions. The important thing is that the research questions constitute a concretisation of the problem statement, not an addition.

Descriptive research questions tend to start with *what, how, how much, how many, how often, how far, how long*. When we start a question with *what*, the purpose is usually to describe or investigate an event, an opinion, or a property of someone or something. What-questions can therefore be called descriptive questions. What happened with the interaction between health care providers and municipalities after the parliamentary resolution about a cooperation reform had been passed? What do professionals think about the cooperation after the reform? What characterises the adaptation of the health services undertaken by the municipalities? We can also formulate descriptive questions to deal with the placing, extent, or expansion of events, opinions, or properties in time and space. In this case, the interrogatives are *when, where, how many, how much, how often, how far, how long*. How many of the professionals employed at the health care providers think that cooperation with the municipalities has improved after the reform? How often do surgical patients have to be re-hospitalised? Descriptive questions often belong to the formulation of a detailed set of research questions in connection with a problem statement. We will often need a description of the case or the set of data as a starting point for the explanation-establishing analysis. We will usually start the research questions with what-questions, going on to questions about why and how.

In theory-testing projects, the main questions usually start with *why*. With *why* as an interrogative, we direct the interest towards the causes for something to have happened. We can also say that we are searching for an explanation. A research question starting with *why* directs our attention primarily to the decisive causal factor. Why do patients have to be re-hospitalised after having been discharged? Why does information exchange fail across organisations in the health sector? Thus, why-questions are the questions we ask when the purpose of the research is to explain an event or a phenomenon.

Important to note is that the way I use the term *why-questions* actually denotes questions with such a structure that they might have begun with a why. It is the structure of the question that is important, not the choice of words. We may reformulate a why-question to make it a what-question. The first question above could also have been formulated as: What is the reason for patients being re-hospitalised after they have been discharged? We should not be fooled by the choice of words but ask what the real structure of the question is.

When an explanatory question begins with *why*, it is formulated in an open way. It does not consider what explanations could be relevant. Yet the researcher will often have a prior understanding of what causal factors are the most probable on the basis of established theory or previous experience. Thus, explanatory questions will often be formulated in a *closed form*, as a statement or hypothesis about a specific connection between two phenomena. *The hypothesis* is a *statement or an expectation about a specific answer to the why-question*. We can say that a hypothesis introduces a potential answer to the question of why a phenomenon appears under certain conditions. Thus, good hypotheses are connected to established theories about phenomena of the same kind as those we intend to investigate in the planned project, or to specific experiences that can point to the connection expressed by the hypothesis.

In the project about re-hospitalisation used as an example above, we could have formulated alternative hypotheses and tested them against collected data. One hypothesis could be that there is an unusually high degree of re-hospitalisations in municipalities where home care service offers for rehabilitation and assistance are scarce. Another hypothesis could be that there is an unusually high degree of re-hospitalisations in hospitals that have introduced severe cost-cutting procedures. These hypotheses point to different explanatory and improvement factors as causes. Other hypotheses can also be feasible for this project.

Questions aimed at explaining events and phenomena or uncovering processes usually begin with *how*. How could this incident happen? How can we best understand this phenomenon? How did a set of conditions lead to a particular outcome? Thus, how-questions are an essential part of theory-developing and theoretical-interpretative projects.

A set of questions can also include normative questions characterised by the use of the modal verb *should*. How should we proceed to solve this problem? This use is especially common in intervention-oriented projects. The important thing to remember is that we need to clarify questions concerned with describing and explaining connections first in order to have a sufficient knowledge basis to answer the normative questions. Why this is important was discussed in Chap. 1.

A precise formulation of the research questions should have a main question or problem statement linking on to the primary purpose of the project. Then we should formulate a set of subsidiary questions, or research questions adapted to the planned progression in the project.

DATA CONSTRUCTION AND CHOICE OF METHOD

The first step in this phase is the choice of a strategy for data construction. This entails concretising what perspective should guide the construction and production of data. Is the perspective a holistic or a reductionist one, or a combination of the two in an integrated design? When we have answered this in addition to having settled the purpose, we will have placed our project within one of the design types introduced in Chap. 5.

Now is the time to decide what kind of data to select and collect. This depends on the kind of project and on what kind of data are available and convenient to collect. We must also decide if the data are to be analysed using qualitative methods, quantitative methods, or a combination of both. The answer to this partly follows from the kind of data we collect. Finally, we must consider that our set of data must be able to meet the requirements for validity and reliability. This has to do with construction

208   O. BUKVE

validity—internal and external validity. Furthermore, it has to do with collecting reliable data. You are advised to use the discussion of these questions in Chap. 5 and in the literature on method.

Questions related to the choice and use of method are dealt with in the literature on method; thus, I will not give detailed advice on the procedure for selecting, collecting, and analysing data but instead refer to method books. Here, I limit the discussion to two main elements that should be discussed in a project design, namely what requirements are essential in the selection of data, and what types of data are relevant.

Selection of Data and Requirements for Representativeness

When collecting data to illuminate a social phenomenon it is essential to collect data that are relevant to the phenomenon we are focusing on. The procedure for securing that data are relevant, thereby securing external validity, differs in case designs and variable-centred designs. When collecting quantitative data in the frame of a variable-centred design we try to achieve statistical representativeness. For this we must use a randomised selection that is sufficiently large. The units we collect data about are to make up a representative sample of the whole population or universe of similar units. Using statistical methods, we can judge the probability that the selection possesses properties that correspond to the population. Statistical knowledge about selection and analysis of data is an essential aspect of a quantitative research method.

When collecting qualitative data about one or a few cases, we are not able to secure that the cases are statistically representative of the population. Instead, we must base our collection on strategic selections of cases and informants. By selecting strategically, we try to secure that the selection of cases is theoretically representative of the phenomenon or the connections we are studying.

The procedure for achieving theoretical representativeness depends on what kind of study we are carrying out. If from the onset we have a theoretical model or hypothesis about relations and variation connected to the phenomenon we are studying, we can make a *strategic selection*. The model or the hypotheses then guide the selection of cases. This book has several examples of design using strategic selections. The chapter on comparative designs discusses most similar and most different designs, as well as designs that use empirical or theoretical typologies. In such contexts, strategic selection has to do with selecting cases in such a way that we can study the conditions for different outcomes. Critical case designs are another example of designs where strategic selection must be used.

In an interpretative or theory-developing study we do not have the same possibility of selecting cases based on specific theories or hypotheses. Yet we should remember that a good case study presupposes that we regard the case as an instance of a class of phenomena. The first step to ensure the relevance of a case is, therefore, choosing a case that clearly belongs to the class of phenomena we want to study. This requires a bit of prior study of the relevant case. With only one case, we cannot be sure that the case is representative of the class, but we can increase representativeness by studying several similar cases. One approach could be adding new cases or informants until we no longer get relevant supplementary information by adding yet another. When new information does not add anything new we can say that there is *theoretical saturation*. In Table 11.1, in order to make the division clear, I have chosen to differentiate between strategic selections and adding new cases to achieve theoretical saturation. I could just as well have treated these types as different variants of strategic selection.

In the case of intervention-oriented projects, the question of representativeness is different. The case is already given. The question is whether it is possible to find relevant control cases to establish a quasi-experiment. No matter what research project we are implementing, it is important to use recognised methods to ensure that we are collecting representative and reliable data about the phenomena and connections we are studying.

Table 11.1 Strategies for data selection

	Form of representativeness	*Procedure for selection*	*Criterion for data evaluation*
Variable-centred designs	Statistical representativeness	Randomised selection	Non-response analysis and selection control
Case designs	Theoretical representativeness	Strategic selection	Selection from theoretical model or hypotheses about empirical connections
	Theoretical saturation	Adding new cases	Relevant supplementary information in new cases is nearing zero
	Uncertain	The relevant or interesting case	?
Intervention-oriented designs	The case is given prior to selection of data	Can control cases be established?	Congruence between case and control case

210   O. BUKVE

Various Types of Data

When selecting data types, there is often room for more creative solutions than the usual ones. Many projects collect qualitative data through interviews with informants. The scale of possible data sources is, however, much wider. We can use observation data of various kinds; fieldwork, participatory observation, and shadowing are some strategies for collecting observation data. We can also use texts and documents of various kinds. Media texts, public documents, logs and diaries, stories and memoires are some of the most common types. We can also use symbols and artefacts as data for qualitative analysis. The most common types of quantitative data

Table 11.2 Types of data

Fieldwork	Participate in a community, a group, or an organisation over time to observe and understand what is going on.
Observation/ participatory observation	Used about more limited observation of activities in the community/group/organisation. With participatory observation, the researcher is at the same time a participant in the community/group/organisation.
Shadowing	Accompanying a person closely over a period of time to register what kind of activities the person is involved in and how the person communicates. Often used in leadership research.
Interview	The researcher interviews/has conversations with persons who are involved in or know the case. Interviews can be more or less structured.
Logs and diaries	The actors' notes about what happened in a case. Could have been produced for research purposes but also originally meant for other uses.
Stories and memoires	The actors' notes about what happened—written afterwards (thus, possibly edited).
Texts, documents	Can be used to understand what happened and also to uncover what is not being said—the critical perspective.
Artefacts and symbols	Non-verbal objects that nonetheless give a message—a symbolic function.
Survey data	Use of questionnaires with informants.
Register data	Use of registers and databases that have been collected for other purposes.
Quantitative text data	Counting the frequency of words or attitudes in texts.

are survey data and register data. We can also make quantitative content analyses of texts.

No matter what data we collect, it is important to reflect on and document the procedures for data collection in a satisfactory way. It is decisive for ensuring the collection of reliable data in the project, and for enabling others to assess the reliability. Here, too, you should follow the advice given in the relevant literature on method.

From a practical perspective, we also need to remember that social science projects often collect data that must be reported to the relevant local or national data security authority, or for which you must have authorisation (Table 11.2).

STRUCTURE OF A PROJECT DRAFT

During the design process we go back and forth between the various tasks and elements. Yet at the end we must collect it all in a presentable project draft, where we present our project plan in such a way that it makes sense to others. Here, it is important to be aware of the difference between writing to understand a matter and writing to present it to others. When presenting to others, we should use another logic and another narrative form than what we used when we were writing to understand things ourselves (Nygaard, 2008; Øyen & Solheim, 2013). Below, I propose a suitable structure for a project draft. This is, of course, just one proposal among several usable ones. In any case, a clear structure helps make our thoughts clearer.

A Standard Structure of a Project Draft

- **Introduction**
  - Topic
    - *Identify research topic/issue to be explored*
  - Purpose
    - *What do you want to know?*
- **Background/context**
  - Experiential or social context
    - *What makes the project relevant/interesting?*

- Knowledge status/previous research
  - *What do we already know? Where are possible knowledge gaps? Can existing research be problematised?*
  - *Finish by narrowing/pinpointing purpose and presenting a problem statement (usually at question level)*

- **Theory and analytical framework**
  - Outline of theoretical perspectives or concepts
    - *Emphasise how established theory and concepts throw light on the topic*
    - *What you can use and how you can use it is the important thing, not long discussions of the theory*
  - Analytical framework
    - *Fixed, multiple, flexible, or open frames?*
  - Delimiting problem statement and detailing of research questions

- **Choice of strategy for data construction**
  - Case-centred, variable-centred, integrated?

- **Method**
  - How to select data—with regard to requirements for representativeness
  - What kind of data/data sources?
  - How to collect data?
  - Preliminary thoughts about the data analysis
  - Validity and reliability
    - *Advantages and possible disadvantages with the chosen design*
    - *Evaluate possible problems with getting valid and reliable data—show that you have considered it*

- **Work schedule**
  - Milestones

The introductory chapter of the project draft could contain a kind of appetiser, something to catch the reader's interest. Still, the main thing in this chapter is formulating the topic and purpose of the project. Many researchers like to include all the research questions as early as possible in the draft. I do not think that is necessary; a general problem statement should be sufficient. And it is important not to mix up the placing of elements in the draft with the placing in your thought process. You will definitely have to polish your purpose formulation, overall problem statement, and research questions several times in the course of the project.

The next chapter of the draft has to make clear why the project is relevant. It has to do with placing the project in a societal and academic context. What kinds of social questions, problems, or experience is the project related to? The problem that constitutes the starting point may also be a theoretical problem. The literature review should be placed in this chapter together with a discussion of the knowledge gap around the topic and a specification of what new knowledge is called for. In light of this you should define and delimit the problem statement because you now know more precisely what new knowledge would be needed.

Following this, it is time to establish the theoretical framework of the project. What this chapter should look like depends on the framework. When presenting the theory, it is important to emphasise how established theory and familiar concepts throw light on the topic. The important thing is stating what you can use and how, not writing longish descriptions of the theory.

For variable-centred designs you must present the expectations or hypotheses that the theory leads to. Moreover, you should include a concept model and show how it can be operationalised. For case designs you should as a minimum identify concepts and theories you will be using in your interpretation. However, some case designs use a fixed framework that involves presenting theory-based expectations and explain how the concepts are to be operationalised in the testing. Many projects would be well served with a visualisation of the essential model in the project and asking detailed research questions in connection with it.

In the last part of the draft you will have to say something about strategies for data construction and the use of relevant methods for selection, collection, and analysis of data. It is also important to account for how the research design can ensure validity and reliability. A work plan or schedule is also important, securing a few milestones as you proceed through the project. With this, the design work has come to its conclusion and you can start the job of selecting, collecting, and analysing data.

References

Alvesson, M., & Sandberg, J. (2011). Generating research questions through problematization. *Academy of Management Review, 36*(2), 247–271.

Boote, D. N., & Beile, P. (2005). Scholars before researchers: On the centrality of the dissertation literature review in research preparation. *Educational Researcher, 34*(6), 3–15. https://doi.org/10.3102/0013189x034006003

Creswell, J. W. (2009). *Research design. Qualitative, quantitative and mixed methods approaches.* Los Angeles: SAGE.

Denney, A. S., & Tewksbury, R. (2013). How to write a literature review. *Journal of Criminal Justice Education, 24*(2), 218–234. https://doi.org/10.1080/10511253.2012.730617

Hatlen, E. M. (2016). *Utfordringer ved implementering av standardiserte pasientforløp.* (Master i organisasjon og leiing), Sogndal.

Krathwohl, D. R., & Smith, N. L. (2005). *How to prepare a dissertation proposal: Suggestions for students in education and the social and behavioral sciences.* Syracuse, NY: Syracuse University Press.

Maxwell, J. A. (2006). Literature reviews of, and for, educational research: A commentary on Boote and Beile's "scholars before researchers". *Educational Researcher, 35*(9), 28–31. https://doi.org/10.3102/0013189x035009028

Nygaard, L. P. (2008). *Writing for scholars: A practical guide to making sense and being heard.* Oslo, Norway: Universitetsforl.

Øyen, S. A., & Solheim, B. (2013). *Akademisk skriving: en skriveveiledning.* Oslo, Norway: Cappelen Damm akademisk.

Sandberg, J., & Alvesson, M. (2011). Ways of constructing research questions: Gap-spotting or problematization? *Organization, 18*(1), 23–44.

Vom Brocke, J., Simons, A., Niehaves, B., Riemer, K., Plattfaut, R., & Cleven, A. (2009). *Reconstructing the giant: On the importance of rigour in documenting the literature search process.* Paper presented at the ECIS.

Index[1]

A
Abduction, 8, 58, 59, 133
Action research, 79, 82, 95, 179, 180, 182, 187–190
Amoroso, Lisa, 36, 90, 91, 124, 162
Analytical frame
  flexible, 85, 194, 203, 204, 212
  multiple, 84, 203, 212
  open, 85, 194, 203, 204, 212
  structured, 48, 84, 120, 194, 203
Analytical narrative, 125, 137
Argyris, Chris, 188
Aristotle, 189

B
Backgrounds, 21, 22, 33, 34, 36, 38, 39, 46, 50, 62, 99, 103, 104, 143, 197, 198, 211
Beach, Derek, 34, 57, 78, 123, 125, 131, 133, 156

Bennett, Andrew, 78, 80, 90, 91, 118, 119, 123, 128, 130, 131, 142, 156, 162–164, 166, 170, 172, 176
Bourdieu, Pierre, 32
Bukve, Oddbjørn, 31, 137, 145, 169–171

C
Cartwright, Nancy, 34, 54, 57
Case study
  comparative, 78, 117, 118, 152, 153, 161
  multiple, 89, 90, 116–119, 128, 156, 161
  single, 88, 116–119
  theoretical interpretive, 135–138
  theory informed, 128–130
  theory testing, 121, 122, 127, 128
Categorical statement, 15–18, 21, 22, 38, 43, 54, 55

---

[1] Note: Page numbers followed by 'n' refer to notes.

© The Author(s) 2019
O. Bukve, *Designing Social Science Research*,
https://doi.org/10.1007/978-3-030-03979-0

216 INDEX

Cognitive frames, 7, 11, 19, 20, 26, 39, 49, 55, 85
Collier, David, 41, 78, 107, 176
Collier, Ruth, 176
Concept
    dimensions, 42, 136, 137
    levels, 41, 42
Constructivism, 7, 20, 24, 26, 29, 49, 64
Creswell, John, 142, 143, 147, 202

D
Data
    construction, 1, 2, 49, 50, 73–76, 74n1, 85–87, 89–91, 94, 100, 141, 143, 149, 162, 193, 195, 196, 207–208, 212, 213
    types, 116, 143, 145–147, 204, 208, 210–211
Deduction, 55, 58
Denzin, Norman, 141, 143–146
Design
    case, 8, 73, 84, 91–94, 115–138, 161, 163, 164, 170, 208, 209, 213
    comparative, 8, 73, 89, 90, 94, 95, 137, 142, 143, 161–176, 208
    congruence, 37, 115, 123, 128–130, 135, 163, 164, 168, 171
    critical case, 115, 126–127, 209
    cross-sectional, 97, 108, 111–112, 121
    evaluation, 79, 83, 95, 179–185, 187, 189, 190
    experimental, 83, 94, 97, 108–111, 161, 184
    integrated, 8, 89, 94, 141–159, 207
    intervention oriented, 8, 73, 79, 84, 89, 91, 95, 179–190
    longitudinal, 108, 111–112, 121
    mixed, 141–143, 146–149

    most different systems, 164, 172–174
    most similar systems, 164, 172–174
    multimethod, 152–158
    nested, 89, 141, 143, 149–152
    process, 8, 9, 48, 74–76, 138, 193–213
    process tracing, 76, 94, 115, 123, 125, 130, 131, 164, 171, 173, 186
    sequential, 142, 147–149
    theoretical interpretive, 135–138
    triangulation, 89, 143, 144, 146, 147
    variable-centred, 8, 73, 75–77, 84, 88, 90, 92–94, 97–112, 125, 131, 143, 148, 149, 151, 152, 161–163, 176, 179, 180, 208, 213
Dilthey, Wilhelm, 59, 60
Discourse analysis, 8, 61, 64–68, 70
Downs, Anthony, 47

E
Eikeland, Olav, 189, 190
Evaluation, 17, 22, 79, 82, 83, 91, 95, 179–187, 189, 190, 194
Experiment
    natural, 109, 110, 184
    quasi, 109, 110, 161, 163, 184, 209
Explanation
    causal, 31–35, 56, 76, 105
    external, 29, 31, 32, 49, 53, 56, 77
    functional, 32, 35
    intentional, 32, 56
    internal, 32, 33, 49, 53, 56, 77
    mechanistic, 78

F
Fairclough, Norman, 65
Foucault, Michel, 68

G

Gadamer, Hans Georg, 60
George, Alexander, 80, 90, 91, 118, 119, 128, 130, 131, 142, 156, 162–164, 166, 170, 172, 176
Gerring, John, 77, 118, 126, 127, 131
Gobo, Gianpetro, 4, 74n1, 85, 86, 86n2, 126, 147
Goertz, Gary, 41, 42, 136, 142, 152–157, 159
Grounded theory, 125, 137, 138, 170

H

Habermas, Jürgen, 24, 31, 60, 123
Hermeneutics, 8, 59–64, 70
Hypothesis, 3, 43, 45, 46, 55, 58, 80, 109, 110, 118, 122, 123, 126, 127, 148, 149, 155, 163, 170, 172, 173, 176, 184, 194, 206–208
   testing, 3, 55, 58, 77, 78, 80, 126, 127, 138, 146, 149, 184

I

Induction, 54, 168
Interpretive reconstruction, 82, 94, 115, 123–125, 135–138, 164

K

Keohane, Robert, 77
Khan, Deeyah, 34
King, Gary, 77
Kingdon, John, 133–135
Knowledge
   goal, 1, 2, 6, 74–76, 79, 89, 94, 117, 147, 180, 182, 194, 202, 203
   types, 12–14, 74, 124, 189, 190

L

Landman, Todd, 90, 162, 172
Lange, Matthew, 78, 90, 164, 176
Lewin, Kurt, 188, 189
Lieberman, Evan, 141, 149–151
Literature
   review, 84, 198–202, 213
   search, 199, 200
Logical positivism, 55

M

Matland, Richard, 166–168, 171
Mill, John Stuart, 171, 172, 176
Model
   analytical, 102, 120, 174
   empirical, 45–47, 99, 101–103, 105, 106, 144, 152, 186, 204
   theoretical, 43, 45–49, 84, 87, 88, 92, 99–102, 105, 130, 145, 149, 150, 152, 153, 163, 186, 194, 208
Morgan, Gareth, 136

N

Neset, Oddvin, 135
Neumann, Iver, 64–66

O

Observational statement, 7, 15, 17, 18, 20, 21, 23, 39, 54

P

Paige, Jeffrey, 176
Paradigm, 21, 39, 146
Peirce, Charles Saunders, 58
Popper, Karl, 13, 15, 18, 25
Pre-understanding, 20–22, 55, 68, 124, 136, 138

218 INDEX

Problem statement, 5–6, 193–195, 202, 203, 205–207, 212, 213
Process tracing, 76, 94, 115, 123, 125, 130–133, 152, 156, 164, 171, 176, 186
Project draft, 196, 198, 205, 211–213
Przeworski, Adam, 172
Purpose description, 201–203

R

Ragin, Charles, 36, 90, 91, 124, 142, 157, 162–164, 174–176, 174n1
Reconstruction, 7, 8, 19, 29–50, 53–70, 85, 105, 123, 132, 135, 136
Reliability, 59, 93, 99, 146, 195, 207, 211–213
Representativity, 34, 41, 77, 92, 93, 98, 107, 208, 209
Research design, 1–3, 6–8, 13, 38, 70, 73–95, 143, 144, 146, 147, 157, 163, 182, 189, 190, 193, 213
Research logic
  abductive, 56–59, 136
  discourse analytical, 64–68, 124, 136
  hermeneutic, 8, 56, 59–63, 77, 123, 136
  hypothetical-deductive, 8, 54–57, 65, 68, 70, 77, 78, 146
Research purpose
  intervention, 8, 73, 76, 79, 82, 94, 95, 180–182, 187, 188, 190
  theoretical interpretation, 8, 73, 76, 79, 94, 125, 207
  theory development, 8, 73, 76, 78–80, 89, 94, 124, 129, 130
  theory testing, 8, 59, 69, 73, 76, 78–80, 89, 94, 130, 157
Research question, 4–6, 8, 79, 85, 89, 108, 117, 122, 138, 180, 194,
195, 200–203, 205–207, 212, 213
Ricoeur, Paul, 60, 61, 64, 190
Rohlfing, Ingo, 78, 131, 132, 151, 152

S

Schön, Donald, 188
Scientific knowledge, 7, 11–26, 54, 77, 78, 179
Searle, John, 20, 22, 29, 30n1, 39
Skirbekk, Gunnar, 24
Skocpol, Theda, 176
Social facts, 7, 29–33, 30n1, 35, 50, 70
Social mechanism, 34, 35, 57–59, 76, 78, 89, 90, 142, 152–157, 159

T

Teune, Henry, 172
Theoretical
  interpretation, 76, 79, 84, 94, 115, 123, 125, 131, 135–138, 207
  typologisation, 166
Theory
  action, 82–84, 179, 185–187, 189, 190
  critical, 8, 63–65, 124, 126–127
  development, 8, 69, 73, 78–80, 84, 88, 89, 94, 97, 106–107, 123–125, 129–133, 138, 141, 150, 151, 168, 203
  knowledge, 20, 23
  scientific, 3, 7, 11, 15, 29, 81, 119
  testing, 8, 59, 68, 69, 73, 76, 78–80, 87–89, 94, 97, 101–105, 121–123, 126–128, 130, 131, 141, 146, 148, 157, 170, 206

Topic
  choice of, 193, 197, 198, 202
Tranøy, Knut Erik, 14
Triangulation, 89, 141–147, 144n1
Typology, 94, 135, 137, 143, 145,
    157, 161, 164–171, 208

V

Validity
  construction, 92, 99–102, 106, 145,
    204, 207
  external, 92, 93, 99, 105, 106, 109,
    110, 143, 145, 208
  internal, 92, 100, 109, 110, 143,
    171, 204, 208

Variable, 2, 8, 46, 49, 50, 57, 73,
  75, 76, 84–91, 93, 97–99,
  101–109, 111, 112, 127, 131,
  133, 142, 148–151, 157, 163,
  164, 167, 171–175, 174n1,
  185, 195
Verba, Sidney, 77

W

Weber, Max, 65, 165, 166

Y

Yin, Robert, 74, 78, 92, 116, 117,
  119, 120, 123, 128, 143

Printed in the United States
By Bookmasters